TWO SPRINGS, ONE SUMMER

FRANK WOLF

TWO SPRINGS, ONE SUMMER

A YEAR INSIDE THE LIFE OF A CHRONIC ADVENTURER

RMB

First Edition

For information on purchasing bulk quantities of this book, or to obtain media excerpts or invite the author to speak at an event, please visit rmbooks.com and select the "Contact" tab.

RMB | Rocky Mountain Books Ltd.
rmbooks.com
@rmbooks
facebook.com/rmbooks

Cataloguing data available from Library and Archives Canada
ISBN 9781771606844 (softcover)
ISBN 9781771606851 (electronic)

All photographs are by Frank Wolf unless otherwise noted.
Copy editor: Peter Midgley
Proofreader: Peter Enman
Map data from OpenStreetMap openstreetmap.org/copyright.
Cover photos: Author portrait by Noel Hendrickson. Views of icebergs off Baffin Island by istockphoto.com/HeartSurgeon.

Printed and bound in Canada

We acknowledge the financial support of the Government of Canada through the Canada Book Fund and the Canada Council for the Arts, and of the province of British Columbia through the British Columbia Arts Council and the Book Publishing Tax Credit.

Canadä | Canada Council for the Arts | Conseil des arts du Canada | British Columbia | British Columbia Arts Council An agency of the Province of British Columbia

Disclaimer

The views expressed in this book are those of the author and do not necessarily reflect those of the publishing company, its staff, or its affiliates.

To Pea and Mor

CONTENTS

TWO SPRINGS, ONE SUMMER

I wake early on day 18, after another restless sleep in temperatures south of -30°C. My right foot's been throbbing all night. I'm encased by clumps of frozen down – a poor version of a sleeping bag ill-suited for an Arctic journey of this nature. It never closes properly as the zipper broke three days into the expedition, so I've stuffed all my clothing around me, including my down jacket and pants, in order to insulate my body. I sleep coolly all night, waking frequently to dreams that exist for a minute in my memory but disappear into the ether quickly thereafter.

This morning I look at my feet. There's a big ugly blood blister on my right foot, and one developing on my left. Both of my feet are swollen and the nails are black. My toes have no feeling; I suspect nerve damage. For the past few mornings, I stuff the barking dogs into my boots, and then can't feel them for the first few hours, making me concerned about frostbite and other permanent damage. When I pry my boots off in the evening, I hobble uselessly around camp, slow and feeble in helping with the chores. I tried to manage this the past two weeks, literally chopping big holes in the boots to let the swollen feet spread out. I was hoping they'd stabilize to a base level of damage and let me get to the end, but to no avail.

We've come 350 km, dragging two sleds each – over 200 pounds – behind us. We're now within 30 kilometres of the Inuit hamlet of Kugaaruk. It will be the easiest point along the way to step out, minimize the damage, and not burden the journey. David and Richard can carry on to the goal, still over 200 km away. I have to decide: my body or the mission?

PREFACE

I mark the seasons by adventure. My life cycle rotates around canoe, kayak, ski, cycling, and packrafting trips through wild places. A paddle across Canada by canoe in the summer of 1995 got its hooks into me and I haven't been the same since. The typical pattern of a job, house, and kids never appealed to me; in fact was never even on my radar as a way to live, for better or worse. For me, nothing that exists within human societal structure compares to the immediate and immersive experience of being on a journey through a wilderness landscape completely new to my eyes. Seeing a polar bear up close and personal, running a remote whitewater river, hacking a campsite out of the bush with a machete. These and most every other moment of an expedition are viscerally vibrant.

And so, as my life creeps on at the middling age of 53, I adventure more than ever. I try to do two major expeditions per year, mostly in the Canadian wilderness as it's the most remote, least populated, and most pristine landscape on the planet. Virtually every other place on Earth is tangled with an overabundance of people. Don't get me wrong, I'm not a misanthrope, as I seek and require human companionship like anyone else. But living within society is a constraint on pure, authentic freedom. It's the nature of our species to tell others like us what to do, where to go, how to live. Democratic, communist, Amish, it doesn't matter – all ideologies ultimately come down to control. To escape these oppressive inclinations, I regularly strike out for the great beyond, accountable only to the journey and the people I'm travelling with.

For this book, I chose the year 2018/2019 as an example of this life to shine a light on my motivations by immersing the reader in the experience of carrying out three consecutive journeys through some of the most remote terrain on Earth. I've continued to do a couple of big wilderness pilgrimages annually since that year (completing another ten major expeditions), but that season stands out in my mind as a seminal example of the outdoor-tripping life. As time moves on I'll continue to seek out these experiences, laying down lines through the wilds until my very last breath. It's rarely easy, but nothing worthwhile ever is.

INTRODUCTION

Movement. It's what we're hardwired to do. Ever since humans first evolved into some facsimile of our current genesis in Africa, staggering around on two legs for the first time like a newborn zebra, we have wanted to move. Sure, some folks wanted to stay in familiar surroundings, to call a place home, to never set foot beyond the visible horizon. But then there were always the curious, restless wanderers, those who wanted to see past that mental wall, to experience the new, the different – the crackling possibility of what lies beyond.

We spread out from our African origins for thousands of years, horizon to horizon, expanding across once-nameless tracts of land we now call Europe and Asia, over the Bering land bridge across North America, South America, by boat to Australia. We fanned out over the whole globe until we'd seen and mapped it all.

The endless unknown is now the limited familiar, connected by technology and eight billion others like us. The mysterious horizons disappeared, but that internal, eternal lust for wandering never did.

There is, however, still respite for the wanderer. Vast, lightly tracked pockets of land that have been largely left alone, do indeed exist. They are rugged, ice-locked, bug-infested places protected by their inhospitable nature. This is where the wanderers find solace, can still move through the mysterious horizons, and quell that infernal wanderlust.

This book is about three remote, northern adventures I undertook in the course of a year: a 230-km ski traverse of Baffin Island was followed by a 1750-km canoe trip across Nunavut, then capped with an attempt to retrace the 550 km overland ski route of famed explorer John Rae to the Northwest Passage. Not only do I delve deeply into these journeys, but I also reveal the displaced time between these life-giving, primordial wanderings. Remote explorations are physically challenging and uncomfortable but are often far easier for the wanderer than the fallow times.

Thoreau once said, "The mass of men lead lives of quiet desperation." It's not the adventure that will kill the adventurer, it's the quiet desperation of the everyday. Caught somehow in the paradoxical comfort of modern society – a place where most everything is easy and catered – the skin of the wanderer crawls, beads of sweat run down the back, the mind twists between hysteria and numbness. There is seemingly no peace in peace.

In these times we cling with our fingernails to our sanity until we can flood our minds and bodies with the sweet opiate of adventure once more. One, however, cannot exist without the other. The highest high of adventure must be countered by the lowest of comfortable lows. Light cannot exist without darkness. Once the wanderer accepts this balance – this rhythm – they can passionately follow a lifelong path of adventure.

PART ONE
A SEASON BEGINS

CHAPTER 1

I'm a bit drunk. My wife Shannon and I have just stumbled into our Airbnb in Bellingham after a boozy dinner at a bar in town. We nipped down here for a little weekend getaway from our home in North Vancouver, over the border and a couple hours away. We like eating dinner at restaurant bars, perched on high stools where there's a good view of the mixologist at work, and conversation can be struck with the pourer of drinks. The bartender tonight was creative, we were curious; he crafted great cocktails, we drank them. Sobriety gave way to drunkenness, and here we are.

We have sex – the good, uninhibited kind reserved for somewhere other than our home. An unfamiliar room, a different town, and some bourbon on the brain makes you feel like you're a different person, like you're *with* a different person. It adds some spice to the monotony of monogamy and is probably what the whole song and dance of weekend getaways are all about.

Shannon promptly falls asleep afterwards, but I stay up. Post coitus, a revelatory thought pops into my head about a possible expedition partner for my summer canoe trip. I decide I need to reach out immediately. The expedition is only an idea at this point, but I need someone else to join me on the journey from conception to completion. I'm generally not a soloist, preferring to do my long expeditions with a small team, but it gets harder and harder to find expedition teammates as the years go on.

Amazing trip partners of the past have, as expected, taken different paths in life than I. Taku (two previous trips) is raising three kids, Todd (three trips) has a busy new job, Kevin (four trips) has two jobs and a family, Shawn (two trips) has a new and intense relationship, another Todd (two trips) moved provinces and has a couple of young kids. On and on the list goes. I consider all of them good friends and respect their chosen paths. *C'est la vie*. My journeys typically require at least a month's commitment. This year's big canoe trip will probably be closer to two months. I've been pondering my choices but have been unable to come up with someone I think will be up to the task.

I've been doing this on an annual basis, sometimes one trip, sometimes two, even three. They've been up to six months long in remote wilderness areas of Canada's North, Asia, and Europe. It's been going on for 22 years, ever since I canoed across Canada back in '95. My expedition partner at the time and I became the first people to canoe coast to coast across the country in a single paddling season. That trip hurled me into the vortex of this life and I haven't been released since. The day-to-day simplicity of moving forward through a fresh, wild, and ever-changing landscape remains irresistible to me. Life between these journeys sometimes feels like a handful of sand escaping through my fingers.

And so here I sit on November 19, at 1:13 a.m. in a cramped, "groovy" (as the ad said) little hippie abode beside my naked, passed-out wife, texting a literal shot-in-the-dark note to Ryan Bougie. It's never the best judgment to be drinking and dialling, but sometimes an altered state is required to see through the haze of day-to-day life.

I randomly bumped into Ryan on the local trails on Mount Seymour near my home a couple of weeks ago. I was mountain biking with some friends while Ryan was hiking with a couple and their newborn. We were riding down the trail. They were walking up. I went about ten metres past them before I realized who it was. Ryan is an accomplished backcountry expedition skier and packrafter, having completed many an epic journey, including a gargantuan ski traverse of the Coast Mountain Range from Vancouver to Alaska several years ago. We met each other mountain biking a long time ago and have kept in touch here and there ever since. I don't know him that well but always get a great vibe from him. His adventure resumé is impressive and, in the wee hours of the morning with a good buzz on, I suddenly think he'll be the perfect choice.

I tap out the words, "Bougie – weirdly fantastic to see you in North Vancouver a couple of weeks ago. We both wanted to say many things that were unsaid. You are the man. I'm thinking of a cool 45-day,

1800-km canoe trip this summer in the North (Yukon, NWT, Alaska)… upstream, downstream, over passes, dancing through the mountain valleys, a good time. I think you need to do this with me. We only have one spin on this planet…you in?"

I pause for a moment, before sending off the message. Like every drunk texter out there, I smile and think to myself that this is perhaps the best text I've ever sent. Minutes later, I'm snoring beside my wife.

I wake up late (for me), just after 8:30. Shannon is still sound asleep. Shuffling down the narrow corridor and through the bead door to the kitchen, I find the complimentary coffee and get it brewing in the vintage Mr. Coffee machine. I return to bed and am about to lie down and stare at the ceiling until the brew is done when I notice I have a new text on the phone. Shit, I suddenly remember my blurry text in the wee hours of the morning. What exactly did I say to him again? I check the reply and it is indeed from Ryan. It was sent at 4:44 a.m.

> Hey Frank, it would have been cool to take the time to regale one another with tales from the trails that day but alas we probably needed more time to get to the end of the stories. 45 days should be ample time to come up with some more stories and dare I say come up with a few more. I'm in!

I give a fist pump, letting out a hissing "Yes!"

My wife murmurs, "Whaaat?"

I whisper back, "Shh, go back to sleep."

There is no regret with this late-night text. I have my trip partner. The summer is on.

CHAPTER 2

I meet Ryan a month later at the Deep Cove Brewery, a ten-minute bike ride from our ground floor condo in North Vancouver. He's down from Terrace, BC, where he works as an avalanche forecaster for a mining operation up there. He worked as a ski patroller and in avalanche mitigation for the ski resort at Whistler for a dozen years before striking out on his own in the industry. The main reason he moved permanently up to Terrace is that his girlfriend got a job there, as good an excuse as any not to live in a mining camp. Ryan also works part-time as a paramedic for the town. He's down here for the holidays, visiting his parents who live out in Port Coquitlam, in the Fraser Valley east of Vancouver. I've since switched our summer canoe trip route from the Mackenzie Mountains region to the heart of the barren grounds via a 1750-km crossing of Nunavut, starting in Yellowknife and then going down the Back River. Ryan is still keen.

I lock my bike up outside. It's an old Sekine, a pig iron bike from the '70s that I bought for $100 at a used sporting goods shop after a nice touring bike I rode for six years was stolen recently. I learned my lesson...better to have a beater bike that gets you around than something nice that'll be swiped. This city is infested with bike thieves, as numerous as sewer rats.

Ryan is sitting at a side table in the cozy, golden glow of the brewery. He's staring into his phone and doesn't notice me until I step in front of him. He looks up and grins a bright, beaming smile and we hug in greeting before sitting down to chat. He's curious about what kind of preparation and gear he needs, having only done one canoe trip before (he and some friends paddled the Nahanni River a couple of years ago).

I assure him he's well prepared already and that I'll take care of the food, gear, and logistics. Ski mountaineering is far more technical and dangerous than any canoe trip. It's why over the years my partners have primarily been "mountain people," who have a higher degree of tolerance for discomfort and risk than any other group I know. Dealing with a blizzard in the heartless cold of a peak or skiing a steep avalanche-prone couloir makes for an easy transition to long-distance Arctic canoe journeys.

My wife is used to me going away; it's been like that ever since we met. There is something to the saying, "Distance makes the heart grow fonder." We're both independent people who like our own space, so this arrangement works for us. We've done lots of week-long canoe trips together but she has absolutely no interest in joining me on my long journeys, and really no interest in hearing about them afterwards. This suits me just fine. Our life in the city is her world, primarily directed by her, and easy living for me. On an expedition, I transform from meek city boy into a highly focused person, ravenous for adventure. It's my own little private world, free from the entanglements of a relationship. It's a refresh and reset, and part of the rhythm of our lives.

Some couples do everything together and their interests align completely. You see them out there on the trail: biking together, hiking together, running together, skiing together. That would be suffocating to me. The outdoor space is my own, my freedom. Though I always do my expeditions with at least one other person, on a day-to-day basis I'm a loner. Mountain biking or running through the trails is my meditation. I move steadily and quietly, getting into a flow and rhythm that clears and calms me. Just give me an hour of that per day and I can deal with anything else urban life throws at me.

I ask Ryan about his girlfriend, if she's okay with him going away. He lets out a sigh and his eyes drop a thousand-yard stare into the bubbles of his beer.

"We broke up a couple of weeks ago."

"Oh, what happened?"

"She's been really stressed. We got into an argument. Then she pulled a kitchen knife on me and cornered me. I was lucky to get out of there without getting hurt. I broke up with her immediately."

I could only shake my head in astonishment. Ryan seems like such a sweet, down to earth guy. What would prompt anyone to attack him?

He continues, "Yeah, she wanted to patch things up afterwards, but I said no way. I moved out. I'm trying to figure out what to do next."

I brighten, "Well, I guess you're really free to go on this trip now."

Ryan half smiles, "Yup, I guess so."

We part outside, a quick hug goodbye, both excited about our summer mission. Ryan drives back to Coquitlam and I hop on my bike and begin pedalling along the Dollarton "highway," a small road that runs along the shore of Burrard Inlet – the entrance to the southernmost fjord on the west coast of North America that separates North Vancouver from Vancouver. It's quiet tonight, with no cars on the road. Many have already fled the city for their holiday vacations. I can smell the freshness of the ocean coming through the darkness of the forest by Maplewood Flats, a conservation area known for its great bird watching. Across the water from Maplewood Flats, on the south side of the inlet, I glimpse the sprawling refinery that sits on the shoreline. It belches smoke and its hundreds of white lights twinkle like a gigantic holiday ornament, inadvertently festive at this time of year. Turning off of Dollarton, I climb through a residential area, where actual holiday lights of white, blue, red, and green are strung in front of houses along the way. I'm breathing steadily by the time I top out on Mount Seymour Parkway, which soon leads to our condo building.

When you say "condo," most people imagine towers clustered together in a sea of concrete, but this place is different. Our four-floor building straddles the border between the urban and the wild. At this time of night, everything north of our building is dark and quiet. We back onto Mount Seymour Provincial Park and a swath of recreational green space that extends seemingly forever. If you wanted, you could walk out the back door here and travel through true wilderness all the way to the Arctic Ocean 5000 km away. It's a fabulous playground of known and unknown trails, rugged peaks, and steep gullies. A 20-minute bike ride south puts you in Vancouver where anything that any major city in the world offers is there to be experienced. Go a few minutes north and you can wander endlessly in all directions in a coastal temperate rainforest. Where we live reflects my life. I spend part of it in this city, and the other part immersed in the wild. Both mentally and physically, I seem to have one foot in each at all times. It kind of feels like I have commitment issues, straddling a fence. I should just commit fully to the wilderness, live wild all day everyday. I should be uncompromising. I've been pondering this paradox for almost 30 years, but I'm still here in no man's land, in the DMZ.

CHAPTER 3

May 1992...somewhere in a swamp outside of Longlac, Ontario.

It's two in the afternoon. The sun is high and merciless, beating down on the cracked earth of the clear-cut. My tongue sticks to the roof of my mouth as my shovel breaks dirt and I jam a small spruce sapling into the hole I've made before sealing the roots in place with my brand-new steel-toed boots. Every step I make kicks up a cloud of fine particulate dust. I've run out of water and the temperature hovers near 40°C. It's like being part of Operation Desert Storm, someone would later remark. The televised war between the United States and Iraq is still fresh in the collective consciousness and an easy parallel to draw.

It would have been lovely to at least be wearing shorts and T-shirt, perhaps get a bit of a tan while I labour. But no. This is northern Ontario tree planting in May, not a war against Iraq. No bullets fly about – it's something far more malicious. A thick horde of black flies moves in unison with me, bouncing off the mesh of the bug net over my face and crawling, crawling, crawling over my clothes looking for any rip or other area of exposed flesh where they can dive in 20 at a time and ravage me. I wear gloves, tape over the gaps of my ankle and wrist cuffs, and a bandana around my neck. But they won't relent until they get what they came for. They drive me onward, not allowing me to rest, inadvertently ensuring my productivity. But the thirst, oh the thirst!

Each tree planter is responsible for their own water. Somehow, I've blown my ration for the day with still a couple of hours to go before we can board the rickety, graffiti-strewn planting bus back to our base camp. My head throbs with heat under my yellow construction helmet. As I stumble past a slash pile, an oasis appears. Perhaps three feet long, two feet wide, and one foot deep, a murky pool of water sits there in the dirt. I know about Giardia, and this little puddle looks like the perfect breeding ground for the infamous stomach parasite. My thirst, however, overcomes all logic. I kneel beside the little "beaver-fever" pond, remove my helmet and dip it in. The water is surprisingly clear, although filled with a cluster of underwater bugs that scatter at my intrusion. I tip back the edge of the helmet and drink down the cool water along with a requisite amount of the swimming bugs. At that moment, it's the best thing I've ever tasted. I dip the helmet in again, and this time pour the contents slowly over my head, allowing it to stream through my head net and clothes. Giardia be damned, this is the highlight of my day. The heat, the bugs, the general misery of the job all fall away in that moment, and it still seems like yesterday. Funny thing is, I can't remember anything about the rest of the day. The gulag-like work conditions and general drudgery have long been erased from the memory banks.

Same goes for the rest of that planting season. We had one day off per week, and those still seem like the best times of all. The camaraderie and commiseration over that miserable job culminated in a huge weekly lakeside party. It was like the army, and we were soldiers on leave. That's why you went back year after year. The 99 per cent misery is forgotten. That 1 per cent that made up some of the best times of your life kept you coming back. I never did get sick from that little puddle either. It just ended up being a good story, with no real consequences. Things don't always work out that way.

As humans, we're conditioned to highlight the good times and erase the bad. Ironically, one can't come without the other. You need the low to get the high. A constant stream of mediocre is the worst thing of all. Constant struggle with small victories is our ideal state.

CHAPTER 4

A week into the New Year, plans for another journey firm up. My friend Dave Garrow has managed to book the three of us flights to Qikiqtarjuaq, an Inuit hamlet on the east coast of Baffin Island, with his Aeroplan points. We're planning to do a 230-km ski traverse across southern Baffin Island from "Qik" to the town of Pangnirtung. Our plan includes skiing up and over the 6,000-foot-high Penny Ice Cap and then dropping down into Summit Lake, the high point of well-travelled Akshayuk Pass, before skiing on to "Pang." That means I now have two major journeys this year and have to plan accordingly. The Baffin traverse will end in mid-May while the canoe trip will begin at the end of June, so most of the prep for both will have to be done by April.

Unlike Ryan, Dave is a known entity. He contacted me out of the blue to do a packrafting and hiking trip through northern BC back in November 2014. The email read,

> Hey Frank,
>
> Random e-mail but looking for someone to walk/packraft the Muskwa-Kechika from the Alaska Highway to the Stewart Cassiar. Probably in September one of these years. Looks like the kind of shit you may be into.
>
> Anyway, e-mail me back if that ignited anything in your heart.

I've had complete strangers drop me notes about teaming up over the years; they rarely lead to anything, but something in his straightforward proposal and unique idea did indeed ignite something in me. I emailed Dave back and we got the ball rolling on that trip. That venture eventually never happened, as Dave realized he couldn't get off work with his Parks Canada job during their busy summer season. I did, however, join him for a 100-km ski trip in Banff that March for an annual mammal survey in the park. This involved us skiing from warden hut to warden hut collecting camera trap memory cards en route with images of a winter's worth of mammals. Also along the way, we identified and logged all the species that crossed our route via the tracks they'd left in the snow. The survey is used to determine density and type of species in the park, which helps them with their wildlife management strategies.

I wrote a feature on the experience for *Explore* magazine, which got the collective underwear of the Stephen Harper–era Parks Canada bureaucracy all twisted in knots. The paperwork was all in order so I was fully approved to participate in and write about the experience. Perhaps my mistake was to send a rough copy to Dave, which he shared with his superiors. Dave was fine with it, but his bosses freaked out about a few of my revelations and wanted me to remove most of the interesting anecdotes about our journey. They understandably walked on eggshells around their cost-cutting political bosses of the time and were hyper-sensitive about any perceived negative PR about the park. I could have completely ignored them but did take one anecdote out as I didn't want Dave to risk his job over the article.

It all smoothed out in the end and the article was well received. It was an authentic, entertaining piece that showed off important work being done in the park from an insider's perspective. Leave writing to writers, not bureaucrats. Readers can quickly sniff out the difference between an actual piece of journalism versus a whitewashed advertorial. That's why it's hard to trust anything written by anyone but a freelancer these days.

Most importantly, Dave and I maintained the friendship we formed that week. He's a very meticulous guy, with a dry sense of humour and lots of practical experience doing long journeys in the outdoors. Some of these included multiple three-week ski journeys through various mountain ranges in the north and west of Canada, as well as a 1000-km kayak trip along Australia's Great Barrier Reef.

After the mammal survey, we did a week-long packrafting and hiking trip the next year through a labyrinth of canyons called "The Maze" in Utah's Canyonlands National Park and followed that up in 2017 with a ski trip to Bylot Island. Bylot is a mountainous mass sitting off the north end of Baffin Island, and forms part of Sirmilik National Park. In the course of 12 days there we topped Mount Angilaaq, its highest peak, as well as several other unnamed summits. It gave us a taste of the special, lonely beauty of the Arctic in spring – when the land is still encased in ice and snow, the sun shines around the clock, it isn't too cold, and skiing conditions are favourable.

Dave's mission in life is to visit every one of Canada's National parks, including our remote and rarely explored Arctic outposts. Last year was Sirmilik (meaning Place of Glaciers), and this year we hoped to do a 230-km traverse of Auyuittuq (The Land That Never Melts), where the Baffin journey largely takes place. I've only travelled with Dave as a pair in the past but this year we're adding a third member to the team, John McClelland. Dave and John go way back and have teamed up on several long mountain ski traverses, including an attempt to ski to the summit of Mount Logan, Canada's highest peak. Both of them are far more experienced mountaineers than I am so I was happy to have a third team member along, and since Dave enthusiastically vouched for him, it was a no-brainer.

CHAPTER 5

I haven't really worked any kind of steady job for a couple of years, getting by with writing gigs and doing corporate speaking around my journeys. For 18 years I had a pretty good arrangement with an outdoor retailer called Mountain Equipment Co-op (MEC) in Vancouver. I worked there casually when I was in town, putting in three days a week selling skis, canoes, kayaks, and other outdoor gear. When a planned trip came up, I could disappear for a month or three and then come back and pick up where I left off. It allowed me to follow my passion, and I in return provided experience-based advice to their members (not "customers" as they are a retail co-operative). MEC formed in 1971 for the simple goal of providing people in Canada with quality, affordable equipment that would allow them to enjoy the outdoors. Their reputation grew based largely on the experienced staff of climbers, paddlers, and hikers who gave honest recommendations to the members, and lived their passions outside of work.

I've met most of my expedition partners at MEC. Skiing and paddling with them regularly, I figure out who I can trust to team up with me on a long-distance expedition. It was a great arrangement, and I journeyed far and wide with a cast of amazing characters from this store that I'll always consider friends. Dave Berrisford, Taku Hokoyama, Keith Klapstein, Todd Macfie, Dave Stibbe, Todd McGowan, Shawn Campbell, and Rob Hart joined me on various expeditions from 2000 to 2016. Alas, it seems all good things must come to an end.

Over the years, MEC grew from a small co-operative where everyone had a say to a large, corporate-style entity. Slowly but surely, they transformed from a place sensitive to the individual needs of their employees into a profit-driven organization that instituted a broad swath of policies that painted everyone with the same brush. Time off to follow your passion in the outdoors was discouraged rather than encouraged. Outdoor training sessions for staff to give them more practical experience was slashed. A well-salaried corporate elite jammed their heels onto the throats of the lowly, hourly wage employees of the stores, and a once-unified co-operative became partitioned into a managers-versus-employees situation.

As a result, long-time staff who worked there because it suited their lifestyle began to disappear. They were at the top of the hourly wage scale because of their long service there, so getting rid of them was seen as a cost-cutting measure. To avoid any kind of compensatory payout, they were given the choice to either work a rigid schedule at the stores or follow their passion. Instead of being blended, work and passion became mutually exclusive.

In February 2016 I put in my usual leave of absence to go on an 1800-km canoe trip through Saskatchewan and Nunavut. It took a while to be approved this time around, when usually it was just an easy matter of, "Okay, have a great summer, come back with some awesome stories" type of thing. After the request had lingered unanswered for a month, I re-queried the manager of the ski department where I worked about the delay. It wasn't too hard to see what was going on. One by one the veteran, knowledgeable staff who'd remained with the organization because of the work-life balance there had fallen away. With the decision delay, I was relatively sure I was next.

My manager at the time was Jerry. He reminded me of Ricky Gervais's character from *The Office* – a middle manager who had little actual outdoor experience or useful knowledge of the equipment we sold. He spoke loudly and forcefully when he tried to sell a piece of gear to a customer, but most of it was pure bullshit, and we staff rolled our eyes when he went into a spiel. It was shocking to me that a man who lacked any people skills could be in put in charge of managing anyone, much less hang onto the job. As the two years I was under him wore on, the answer became obvious. He was a yes-man who hid behind company policy and never stuck up for the staff in his department. Jerry blindly implemented changes from higher up with a robotic bluntness and absolute lack of grace and compassion. He didn't give a damn about his staff because he didn't have to. We were irrelevant. Policy, policy, policy. Jerry was a Stalinist at heart – the perfect hatchet man. Many of the old guard were dispatched to the gulag under his reign.

Unsurprisingly, when my time came Jerry gutlessly cut me loose via email rather than face to face. Eighteen years of complaint-free, dedicated work at MEC evaporated into the air with this short paragraph:

> Hi Frank,
>
> Robson, Pam and I have reviewed all of the time off requests for this upcoming summer and weighed them against the staffing needs of the department. Due to conflicts with multiple other requests I am afraid it will not be possible to grant your three month time off request. I would be happy to discuss a possible compromise, but the July 1 to October 1 time span will not be feasible given the constraints on the availability of other staff during this period.
>
> Regards,
> Jerry

Ah yes, cold, impersonal corporate-speak. A thinly veiled "Fuck You." It's the kind of language no one uses in an actual conversation, typically reserved to sanitize the most distasteful parts of business. Phrases like "due to," "not possible," "not feasible," and "constraints" are words I'd never heard come from Jerry's mouth when he actually spoke.

The main reason I stuck with MEC at the very lowest level of employment for all these years was the simplicity of it. I could effectively do my job there while still pursuing my passion for adventure, writing, and filmmaking on the side. It was never anything I'd take home with me, and my co-workers were fabulous. I was classified as casual staff, only worked three days per week and had no benefits. The store I worked in had over 100 staff and there was never any problem covering my absence in the past, particularly in the summer when lots of students were looking for work. It was a simple, bread-and-butter job that kept my head above water. I certainly never saved up any money from it.

A few years earlier I'd heard directly from a higher-up at head office that they were transitioning to a "High turnover, minimum-wage model of retail" in order to maximize the bottom line. Experience-based advice was no longer valued. And so I was thrown on the slagheap with the other veterans. They didn't fire me or let me go, but they forced me to choose between my job and my passion. As a result, I immediately gave my two weeks' notice.

I have to thank Jerry in the end. He forced me into a decision I should have made years before. The convenience and ease of the work at MEC kept me there. One of my former managers called it the "velvet handcuffs," rather than the "Golden Handcuffs." You didn't make any money at it, but MEC used to treat their staff so well and the job had great flexibility. As the velvet turned to iron, I felt more and more dissatisfied with my time there.

I remember one time in particular, I spotted an acquaintance looking at a canoe in the department. I knew him through a good friend from back in the university days. He was wearing a nice suit, and he'd dropped by after work to browse our wares, as many folks do. I also knew he was living the proverbial dream – married, a nice house, a high-paying job, a couple of kids in private school. In the past I would have gone and chatted him up and given him some good advice on the canoe. But no. I felt suddenly self-conscious. I was a 45-year-old man working retail at a shitty company like I was Al Bundy, the shoe salesman from the show *Married with Children* (not far off, as I sold ski boots and paddling footwear). I'd been on a lot of adventures, aired a half-dozen of my films nationally on the CBC, and published countless feature articles but had never been able to make a real living out of my passion. In that moment, I felt like a failure. I stood there like a child, peering through a rack of paddles at him, completely embarrassed to be working at MEC. I slipped out the back door into the loading bay and killed time organizing some rental gear in the back, not reappearing on the floor until he was long gone.

MEC went bankrupt a few years after I left – a once-thriving co-operative scuttled due to hubris and greed. When you cut the roots from a tree, it dies.

CHAPTER 6

It's cold this late-April evening…dead still with the thermometer nearing -30°C. I'm lying zipped up in my sleeping bag beside John, who I met for the first time the other day. We came in earlier on the final leg of a milk-run of flights and are tenting on the sea ice in front of the tiny hamlet of Qikiqtarjuaq (mostly referred to as "Qik" by the locals) on the west coast of Baffin Island. None of us on the team have much money, but there's always a way to make things work if you're set on an adventure. In the months leading up to this trip we ticked the list of needs one by one to get to this point.

When flying to the remote outposts of Canada's North, flights are the biggest financial obstacle. It would cost us each about $5,000 to fly here from Vancouver (John and I) or Calgary (Dave). Considering I pull in about $20,000 in income on an average year, that would be out of my affordability range. Thankfully, Dave has been racking up points on his Air Canada Aeroplan credit card for years, and he's finally cashing in the rewards. Last year he flew the two of us to Pond Inlet, and this year he's flown all three of us on his points plan. Hot tip: with Aeroplan it's the same number of points to fly to Toronto as it is to Qik, though the actual cost would be ten times as much.

Being an adventurer is akin to being a wild scavenger like a hungry wolverine or seagull. You scour the landscape for opportunistic missions and strike with full gusto when they present themselves. There were overnight stopovers in both Iqaluit and Yellowknife on our route here as well as on the way back. With all of our gear packed up for the numerous flight legs, it was impractical to camp along the way. Unfortunately, accommodation is pricey in these remote territorial capitals, running over $200 for a night's stay. You've got to put yourself into the scavenger mindset and seize any opportunity for free room and board en route.

CHAPTER 7

In February, I went to Toronto to give a talk about one of my previous expeditions at a gathering called the Wilderness and Canoeing Symposium. It's an annual event held at the gymnasium of a high school where fringe wilderness travellers from around North America gather to tell tales of their adventures and conspire with other like minds to hatch new plans.

In the past this hasn't been my thing. I've always been an outlier among wilderness outliers, a step beyond this fringe world. I mostly plan my trips by myself and secure the sponsorship I need, then drop in a travel partner when the time comes. It's a simple and efficient way to get things done, though a lot of work. I'm often the clear leader of the trips I plan, and as a result produce all the films and articles that have come out of these journeys. Since I started doing trips with Dave, it's been more divide and conquer, and I've enjoyed that even more. It's a collaborative effort and I still get to shoot and write about our trips to help get sponsors on board, and Dave has a busy work and family life so he's not interested in hustling magazines after the trip. Doing trips with Dave, plus looking for opportunities now that I've ditched MEC, has brought me to more of these events.

I'm not a natural networker. I can fake it for a while, but overall I get a bit antsy and glaze over when there's too much idle banter at these conference-type situations. These events tend to be one big circle jerk – a mutually masturbatory sharing of past accomplishments. Every time I go to one of these things, I pretty quickly regret it. And yet here I am, peacocking about an expedition that happened two summers earlier. This, unfortunately, is the game.

Thankfully, the symposium is a bit of a different conference. Instead of a bunch of slick movers and shakers, it's a collection of oddball misanthropes. People there are more like me, who are most comfortable when alone or with a small group of people as far away from civilized society as possible. It proves that on some level everyone is a social creature when even members of this group of misfits lurch from their hiding places to rendezvous with their tribe. Some of the attendees are even familiar with my under-the-radar work. Usually the only people aware of my film work outside of my mother and wife are people in remote Canadian communities who watch satellite television. Six of my films have been broadcast on something called the CBC Documentary Channel – a channel found in an outpost numbered somewhere in the 600s in the program guide. Only the rare combination of someone interested in wilderness travel, desperately bored enough to scroll down into the hinterland channels, and then see the show description at just the right time, could possibly chance upon my films. I'm perhaps best known in the remote Inuit coastal community of Nain, the northernmost town on the Labrador coast. I began a canoe trip there in 2012 that took me across the Labrador Plateau and into the George River to Ungava Bay. We took an old coastal ferry up there with our canoe and other equipment on board and spent a bit of time in town preparing and doing interviews with some of the locals for a film I was shooting on the journey.

In less than 24 hours, three different people recognized me from an earlier film I'd shot called *Mammalian*, about a canoe trip across the Northwest Territories and Nunavut. I inserted a piece of performance art at certain key points of that film where I wore a leopard-print body suit. Its skin tightly wrapped my upper body and arms, but my legs were bare, and it connected with a thong-strap through the crack of my ass. The locals in Nain were apparently quite amused by it. One man did a double-take when he saw me in the grocery store, then nervously came up to me about 15 minutes later down by the water and asked, point-blank, "Are you the Snow Leopard?" I confirmed I was indeed the feline in question and he asked for my autograph. Two more townspeople also subsequently recognized me. So I'm "famous" in Nain – but nowhere else. Or so I thought.

I was taking my seat to watch one of the talks when a man came up to me. He stared awkwardly for a moment before blurting. "I've seen your film *Kitturiaq* a dozen times. It's my favourite film!" I had no idea anyone had seen that film, which was about that very same trip I started in

Nain. It proved this was definitely an out-there crowd. I began to feel a little more comfortable. These were my people.

After the talk, I wandered into the reception area. I knew the esoterically famous Eric McNair-Landry was attending the Wilderness and Canoeing Symposium, as I'd seen him on the speakers list in the program. I scanned around the milling crowd in the lobby to see if I could pick him out. A gangly, bespectacled fellow, with a wispy beard and wearing leather and canvas mukluks, was talking with a couple of folks. He looked like the last guy you'd expect to be a world-class, hard-man adventurer. Despite this, he stood out. It wasn't just that he wore mukluks in Toronto, perhaps unintentionally setting a trend. Among the assembled mass, he possessed a distinct aura, a person set apart. Slight and smiley, his body language revealed a man with an openness and ease about himself. He glowed.

I walked over and introduced myself and we had a little chat. He was there with his wife Kate to talk about a skiing and hiking trip they'd done across Baffin Island the previous summer with his sister and her partner. Eric and his sister Sarah's adventure resumés are unmatched by anyone in the world as far as I'm concerned. Born and raised in Iqaluit by their outdoor-guide parents, they skied to the South Pole as teenagers with their mother and later kite-skied the entire Northwest Passage. Eric also unintentionally set the record for travel by kite ski in a single day, when he and a Scottish client travelled almost 500 km across the Greenland Ice Sheet. He's an absolute adventure stud but looks and acts as if he just got out of engineering school.

We chatted again the next day at the lunch break between talks. I learned that he now lived in Yellowknife, where he'd moved with his wife for her work as an emergency doctor. Coincidentally, both of the expeditions I was planning for the summer required time in the NWT capital. We were stopping overnight there in both directions on the way to ski across Baffin, and I was also going to start there for my planned 1750-km canoe trip to the Arctic Ocean via the Back River with Ryan.

"Oh, I'm going to be in Yellowknife a couple of times this year," I casually mentioned.

"Well, if you need somewhere to stay when you're in town, you're welcome to stay at my place."

"I'll definitely take you up on that."

With that exchange, I secured key accommodation for both of my upcoming expeditions. That alone made attending the Wilderness and Canoeing Symposium worthwhile.

With flights to Baffin arranged, I met John McClelland for the first time in the Vancouver airport. As I said, he's an old buddy of Dave's and in our pre-trip emails he definitely seemed like a highly organized, switched-on guy. I wasn't even sure what he looked like and figured I'd meet him on the flight.

He was easy to spot – dressed casually in shorts and flip-flops, and wearing a white, flat-brimmed baseball cap with aviator sunglasses. A dude for sure, and he was instantly very friendly and chatty.

We had a few days to get to know each other before the trip as we were on the same flight plan. Our routing had us flying to Yellowknife, staying for two nights there, then flying to Iqaluit for a night and finally flying to Qik the day after that. Dave would meet us on our flight in Edmonton, then do one night in Yellowknife, three nights in Iqaluit, and arrive in Qik the day after us. Like I said, a milk run – but the only way to do it with Aeroplan, as it only reserves two seats per flight for points users.

All three of us would be together the first night of our travels in Yellowknife. Eric McNair-Landry wasn't at his place but proved to be an amazing host despite his absence. I'd been corresponding with him regarding logistics. He said it was no problem for us to stay with them in Old Town, the original part of the city located on a peninsula that juts out into the broad expanse of Great Slave Lake. The one catch was, he wasn't going to be home the night we arrived and his wife Kate had flown out of town that very evening. No problem at all, though. He was just going to leave his car for us. Eric wrote to me a few days before our arrival:

> Kate will leave the car keys in the centre arm rest along with the parking validation ticket. You will need to take this ticket

> back inside the airport to one of two machines by the doors to validate it (there will be a small charge due, that I can repay you for) before leaving the parking lot. From there make your way down to 30 Morrison Street in Old Town, the keys to the house will be on the same key chain, the deadbolt is what will be locked. As the house is undergoing its yearly spring shift the front door will be a bit stiff. Scobie our dog will be inside, he should be happy to see you. He will have been fed, but could use some food in the morning (bag by the chest in the mudroom).

After the three of us had assembled all of our equipment from the plane, I scurried outside to see if I could find Eric's car. He said it was a distinctly beat-up Subaru with a roof rack held together by Ancra straps. I spotted the vehicle, found the keys as he'd described, and pulled in front of the airport.

John, Dave, and I had a mountain of gear with us: Three SkiPulk sleds, bear fence, food, clothing, mountaineering equipment, skis and ski boots for a two-week winter conditions journey. We completely packed the station wagon to the roof and just barely squeezed the three of us in, but it worked. Everything was as Eric said and we found his place and made ourselves at home. Scobie the dog was indeed there, and very happy to see us.

The next morning I drove Dave to the airport so he could catch his flight to Iqaluit, while John and I had another day to go. When I got back, I scanned Eric's backyard, still half-covered in snow in late April. Tucked behind the shed I saw it: my canoe. I'd had my canoe sponsor Esquif ship it out to Yellowknife alongside an annual shipment they send to a local outdoor retailer here in town. Eric had generously picked it up for me and stored it in his backyard for my summer trip. The canoe was still wrapped in its packing material, a larva in a cocoon that would have to wait two more months before it would be freed to fulfill its destiny. I could see Great Slave Lake, only 50 metres away through a veil of trees at the bottom of Eric's street. It too was wrapped up. But instead of plastic, a couple of metres of ice encased it. It was almost unbelievable that this seemingly endless field of white would transform into a crystal clear inland sea by the time I returned eight weeks from now.

John and I crossed paths finally with Eric and his friend John, who were back in town and preparing for a week-long kite-skiing journey to the East Arm of the lake. He and his sister grew up kite skiing in Iqaluit and are world-renowned for their prowess in that sport. Though Yellowknife doesn't compare to the treeless, windswept barrens of Baffin Island, Great Slave Lake is decent for kiting, and Eric takes advantage whenever he can. The four of us drank coffee and swapped trip stories. Despite his accomplishments, Eric is one of the most genuine, humble people I've ever met. That's usually the way it is with truly exceptional and accomplished wilderness travellers. He does what he does because he loves it, and that's good enough. He's great at what he does because it's his passion. He seems completely unaware of any adulation or status he gets from others because it's completely irrelevant to him. The experience of the journey is everything and the only thing.

Eric drops us at the airport the next day and we fly on to Iqaluit where we stay one night with Dave at an Airbnb. We refresh our safety systems by practising some glacier rope work on the slope in front of the accommodation so we're ready to go once we hit the icefields of Baffin Island.

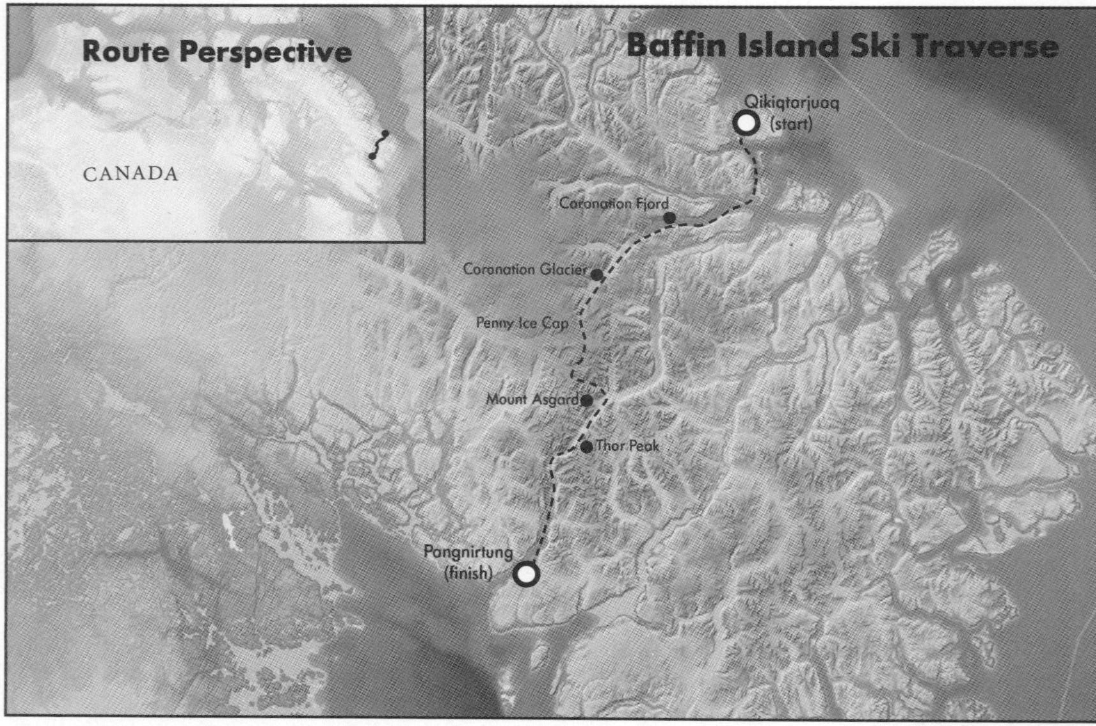
Route Perspective
CANADA
Baffin Island Ski Traverse
Qikiqtarjuaq
(start)
Coronation Fjord
Coronation Glacier
Penny Ice Cap
Mount Asgard
Thor Peak
Pangnirtung
(finish)

CHAPTER 8

On our final leg to Qik from Iqaluit, we do a quick touch down in Pang, where we're planning to finish the 230-km ski traverse. I step out of the plane for some fresh air and walk to the edge of the gravel runway. Across from me, past Pangnirtung Fjord, rises the Baffin Mountain Range. The peaks spring from sea level at the end of the fjord, a seeming wall that we will have to snake our way up and over from the other side. On the flight over to Qik, John and I get a bird's-eye view of our route – interconnected ribbons of snow-covered ice that wind through the range. This is Auyuittuq National Park. In Inuktitut, Auyuittuq means "The Land That Never Melts," and I see on the north edge there seems to be no mountains at all, only an endless field of white that bleeds into the sky. This is the Penny Ice Cap, which covers two-thirds of the surface of the 21,000-square-kilometre park and encases all the mountains in the North inside its 6,000-foot-high cocoon of ice. South of the Penny Ice Cap, the imposing faces of the Norse Mountains flank Akshayuk Pass. Akshayuk is a popular spring and summer hiking area, as well as a destination for world-class alpinists who take on the walls of granite there, which are the biggest vertical faces on the planet.

Our mission is to ski from Qik and then up and over the Penny Ice Cap, before descending down to Akshayuk on our way to the finish at Pang. This rarely completed route, with its many uncertainties, promises adventure in spades.

Upon landing in Qik, John and I haul our gear a few hundred metres from the airport down to the sea ice in front of town. In order to do so, we have to assemble the harnesses of our two sleds and get our skis on so we can glide the gear out through the jumbled ice at land's edge and out to a nice flat spot. We don't have the luxury of an Eric McNair-Landry in town so tonight we are tenting it. In any case, it's a good way to do a little dry run on our camping set-up.

Our main mission that evening is to rendezvous with Jay Moussassi, a local Inuit guide who agreed to receive a food parcel on our behalf. Shipping to these remote communities is exorbitantly expensive, but we ordered all of our freeze-dried dinners and a bunch of energy bars from MEC. If you buy over $50-worth of stuff from them, they'll ship it anywhere in Canada for free – including Qik.

Qik is a typical Nunavut town. Located on Broughton Island, it consists of a collection of low, utilitarian houses that line a small grid of dirt roads hard-packed with snow at this time of year. There are two stores in town – the Northern Store and the Co-op – as well as a motel, the Parks Canada office, a grade school, high school, and Catholic and Anglican churches. There is a working snowmobile in front of every house, alongside a couple of others in various states of disrepair.

Everyone knows everyone in this hamlet of 600 souls, and the first person we ask directs us to Jay's house. The man points in a general direction, "It's a blue house, right on the water."

We ski through the snowy streets of the town, with an empty sled to haul the food back to camp. Free-range children wave and smile at us as we pass, some asking who we are and where we're from. Most of the kids seem to get around town by bicycle, and several posses cruise around on the hard-packed, beige snow. They ride around without hats on, seemingly impervious to the ambient icebox temperature. We walk by one particular house with a fresh polar bear skin stretched out and drying on a rack. A boy of about 10 swings idly on a beam beside the skin, giving us a broad, silent grin as we pass.

Though the site of the hide is distasteful to our southern eyes, polar bears have been harvested by Inuit throughout their history and are still an important part of the economy. They have become a symbol for climate change as depletion of the ice pack in the Arctic makes it harder for them to catch their staple prey, the ringed seal. It's virtually impossible for bears to catch seals in open water, but they are masters of crouching by a crack in the ice, waiting for an unsuspecting seal to come up for a breath and then snatching them with a quick lunge of their huge mouths as they wrap their teeth around the skull of the seal, instantly killing it and then flopping it down on the ice.

Inuit I've spoken with over the years claim the polar bear population is fine. In fact, according to most, they are more numerous than ever. Living side by side with these animals, the Inuit respect them but also harvest them for various purposes. They sustainably harvest the animals as each town has a set quota of approximately 20 to 25 bears. Within the community, bear meat is popular and the furs can be used for clothing, blankets, etc., or sold to bring much-needed money into places that have few economic opportunities. This is important for the survival of the people up here, for though they do receive basic financial support from the government, a head of lettuce at the Northern Store costs 20 bucks, making it hard to make ends meet.

Towns can also choose to let some of their quota be used as tags for sport hunters from the South, who are obligated to hire local guides. It's yet another revenue stream for guides like Jay, who we're on our way to meet.

Trucks constantly go back and forth through the streets. They all seem to have somewhere to go, but you can walk across this town in about ten minutes. I'm always amazed at how many vehicles exist in these remote communities, where there are only a dozen kilometres of road in total. Everyone has a truck, a snowmobile, and an ATV or "Honda" as they call them.

We walk down the street a little further and spot the blue house. Making our way up a small stairway to the door, we give it a knock. Muffled voices are heard, and then footsteps. A man of about 50 opens the door and looks at me.

"Yes?"

"Hi...are you Jay?" I ask.

"Yes, that's me. Are you Dave?"

"No, we're skiing with Dave but he's not flying in until tomorrow. You have a parcel for us?"

"Yeah, I have it outside in the shed. Wait a second, I'll get some boots on and get it for you."

Jay goes back to a pile of boots and begins to pull a pair on.

Dave had promised Jay something special for receiving and holding our parcel of food from MEC. I was leery about the choice of gift, a bottle of Johnny Walker Red, as alcohol has caused lots of problems over the years in these hamlets. Most Inuit who drink, drink hard – they aren't into moderation. It's why many of these communities are dry, and why there are no bars even if alcohol is allowed. You have to bring it in on the plane; you can't buy it. People are shuttered in and isolated, with little to do in terms of employment or activity, so drinking-related violence and suicide is a problem across Nunavut.

The previous year up in Pond Inlet I had an interesting chat with a young guy named Stewart. He was a really nice, genuine fellow and we hit it off. The day after I met him, I saw him walking down the street with a black eye.

"Stewart, where are you coming from?"

"The drunk tank…cops just let me out."

"What happened?"

"My best friend called me over last night, said he had a bottle of vodka…so we mixed it with orange juice and drank the whole thing. We got in a big fight, I tried to kill him."

"What, why?"

"I don't remember."

"Are you still friends?"

"Yup, cause neither of us can remember what we were mad about. I didn't even get this black eye from him. One of the cops who arrested me smashed my face into the dashboard when I was sitting handcuffed in the front seat of his truck."

During the course of a 2000-km canoe journey I did from Yellowknife to Rankin Inlet in 2009, my friend Taku and I were camped about 20 km east of the town of Baker Lake when a motorboat with four Inuk men cruised in and pulled up on the shore in front of us. A couple of hundred metres behind us was a cabin, and they were there to clean up the surroundings, including some wolf skeletons lying not far from our site. The man in charge ran a program where Inuit convicts are put in his charge to reconnect with their land and culture. As part of the program, they also were put to work. The wolf skeletons were left over from one of the programs they had that taught the convicts traditional clothes-making techniques. This involved hunting and skinning wolf and wolverine so they could use their fur to line the cuffs and hoods of traditional caribou skin jackets.

The three convicts were such nice guys it was hard to believe they could commit any crimes whatsoever. All of their offences were alcohol-related. One guy had repeatedly crashed his snowmobile while drunk, the other had beaten his girlfriend, while the third had tried to burn down the local school. I talked to them about their crimes and they were quite open about it. All the incidents had occurred in the course of hard-alcohol benders.

I have a favourite shot that Taku took that night of me with those guys, arms over each other's shoulders, all of us smiling. One guy, Roy from Pangnirtung – where we were now headed on skis – told me a story with wide eyes about a trip he took down to Ottawa for a trial and sentencing. He'd never been away from the treeless barren grounds where he lived. The biggest plants he'd ever seen were the dwarf willows and birches that rarely got even knee-high, and whose branches were only a centimetre thick at most and very flexible. He went for a walk that evening in a park and was amazed at the huge trees everywhere, like he'd stepped onto another planet. He went up to a large maple tree and gave it a push.

He gave me a look of wonder. "The tree didn't budge an inch. It was as solid as a building."

From his experience, all plants and trees bent over easily and this new revelation about trees absolutely blew him away.

So yeah, I obviously was a bit nervous about presenting a bottle of booze to Jay, but Dave thought he'd appreciate it.

John pulls out the bottle of Johnny Walker with a big grin and presents it to Jay. "Here's a little something to thank you for holding onto our food for us."

Jay's whole body freezes up and his eyes go wide as saucers. He glances nervously behind him, through the mud room door that's wide open to the main part of the house. We can see a pair of feet propped on an ottoman in front of a glowing TV. The voice of an excited televangelist pleads for donations.

Jay stammers, "We, uh, don't do that here."

"Oh…oh!" John replies awkwardly, the smile dissolving from his face. He quickly tucks the bottle away.

I brighten at the prospect of Jay's refusal. We misjudged our own whisky supply and only have a 500 ml bottle to sustain the three of us for two weeks. This sudden surplus ensures we'll be able to have a few hearty sips at the end of each day.

We step outside with Jay and are joined by his 4-year-old grandchild Lucas.

In the cooling evening air, Jay visibly relaxes. He steps into a shed and comes out with a large, beat-up box that contains all of our dinners and Clif Bars for the journey. He puts the box down on a table by the shed. Little Lucas tugs at my pants, and points at a snowmobile. "That's mine," he says.

He's directing my attention to a full-sized adult Skidoo. I smile, thinking "How cute" and go on talking with Jay, thinking the child is showing off with a fib.

"Where are you guys staying?" he asks.

"Out by the airport, camped on the ice."

"How about if I bring the box out to you, it'll be easier than taking it over there on your skis with that sled."

"Sure, thanks Jay – we'll see you in a bit."

John and I ski back across the ice to our tent and wait for Jay to appear with our box of food. I break out a clove cigarette to share with John, but he declines. I traditionally bring these aromatic, sweet-tipped Indonesian cigarettes on trip to split with my partners in the evening. I discovered these while travelling in that country years ago and only smoke them on trip, and only a single one daily, passing it back and forth with my trip partners. It's a nice ritual to end each day. I know Dave loves it, but John is obviously not a fan. I pull a kretek out of a pack and light it, the clove crackling in the chill of the evening.

It's 9 p.m. and still bright out. A few kilometres across from us the Baffin Mountain Range rises straight out of the sea. If all goes according to plan, we'll be on top of them in a week or so. A speck appears in the distance and eventually becomes more visible. A man on a *qamatiq* rides behind his dog team, gliding silently past us a few hundred metres away. We find out later that this is the only active dog team in Qik. The Inuit are a practical people, and snowmobiles don't have to be fed anything but gas and can cover ground far faster than a dog team. As a result, across the North the practical use of dog teams has almost completely disappeared. It's mostly non-Inuit people that raise teams for recreation and racing, while the Inuit don't seem quite so nostalgic about their mushing past. Dogs in these towns tend to be chained to the ice all winter long, languishing in purgatory, unable to fulfill their destiny and desire to run. Many of these animals have a lineage that goes back to the original people who came over the Bering land bridge to populate the North. They are hardy, strong runners. Chained and sedentary, living in their own feces, their existence now seems miserable. The Inuit view them only as utilitarian. They are primarily used now when people go out on the land to camps and the dogs are chained outside the tents to keep polar bears away. Any dog not chained up and running loose around town is quickly shot as they are seen as a threat to children. These are not pets.

The musher disappears around a distant jumble of ice, headed to the backside of town. The distinct whine of a pair of snowmobiles breaks the silence of the evening. We turn to see the machines coming toward our camp. Sure enough, it's Jay. Right behind him follows another snowmobile that looks from a distance like there's no driver at all. They come in fast, about 50 km per hour and then slow to a smooth halt at our camp. I laugh when I see who the second driver is. It's little Lucas, the 4-year-old with his hands up on the steering bars like he's riding a Harley chopper. He wasn't kidding me – that was indeed his snowmobile that he pointed out back at Jay's house. They raise kids differently up here.

Jay steps off his machine and grins, then walks back to his *qamatiq*. These 25-foot-long, hand-built wooden sleds are based on a dogsled design and are used by the Inuit to haul gear, game, and anything else you can imagine behind their snowmobiles.

He grabs the box and places it by our tent and then turns to John. "Um, you have that bottle of whisky for me?"

"Oh, for sure...absolutely."

John goes into one of our duffle bags and digs for the Johnny Walker. Jay turns to me in explanation, a sheepish look on his face.

"My wife doesn't allow any alcohol in the house; she's pretty religious...but I like a sip here and there." Jay is a much-sought-after guide in the area, with a solid reputation of safety and knowledge of the land. Having met and chatted with him today, I doubt he'll go off the rails with the Johnny Walker. At least I hope not. Besides, he's an adult, and a gift is a gift.

John gives the bottle to Jay, who tucks it away in the *qamatiq*.

I'm a bit disappointed, as an unexpected windfall of whisky is now gone. Little pleasures are much appreciated at the end of a hard day on the trail, and the combination of whisky and clove cigarettes is something I look forward to. No matter what happens during the course of a trip, there's always a contemplative puff and sip to finish each day.

"Okay boys, I'm going to go for a ride with Lucas. Good luck on your trip."

The two of them race off down the sea ice and soon bleed into the horizon.

John and I boil up some water and have a quick freeze-dried meal each. Shortly after that, we're snuggled into our sleeping bags. The mercury has dipped below -20°C and the sky is clear so it will continue to drop through the night. We fall asleep quickly, saying little. Dave is our mutual bond and we've not had any common experience that frees us to do anything more than be polite with each other.

CHAPTER 9

Gliding out from Qik
The town disappears behind
Into the Great White

The next morning Dave's flight arrives, and all of his luggage has made it with him. It's always a worry whether your checked bags arrive with you on these Arctic runs, as the flights will arbitrarily hold back baggage that is considered nonessential. Food and other supplies for the Northern and Co-op stores are prioritized, as the flights are the only lifeline to the outside world. You don't find out whether your bag hasn't arrived until you land at your destination. It happened to me the previous year in Pond Inlet, when a bag of essential gear was held back and then sent in on the next day's flight. I saw crates and crates of Pepsi come off that flight, but no bag. They do indeed have a sweet tooth in these communities. Thankfully, all of Dave's stuff is on board and we're fully assembled to get going that day.

The only order of business before we leave is a mandatory Parks Canada orientation at the office they have in Qik. As Dave works for Parks, everything has to be "by the book." A young Inuit man named Matthew gives the orientation, more or less reading the points we have to be aware of from a sheet we all hold. As with Pond Inlet, which is the gateway to Sirmilik National Park, we have to watch a polar bear safety video. It's actually not a bad little video, but they show the people dealing with the bears armed with shotguns as a last resort. Ironically, you're not allowed to carry shotguns in any National Park in Canada so the video seems to be delivering a mixed message.

Outside the Parks office, we're assembled and ready to go. We all wear plastic telemark boots with light, metal-edged touring skis that have waxless "fish scale" bases that allow us to kick and glide on flat and moderate uphill sections, but still perform like alpine skis on the downhills. We also have skins for some of the steeper climbs we'll face as we ski from sea level up to 6,000 feet on the Penny Ice Cap. All of our food, camping equipment, glacier travel gear, and other amenities fit into our pulks – essentially plastic orange toboggans that we tow with flexible fibreglass rods connected to a harness that we wear outside of our jackets.

Lunch has just started at the local school and a group of kids on bicycles gather around to pepper us with questions.

"Where are you from? Where are you going? Why don't you use a snowmobile?" We laugh and answer their questions as well as we can. Self-propelled travel is something that is rarely done in these communities. Why would you walk or ski when a snowmobile will get you there faster and easier? It's simply practical thinking. That's why little Lucas has been trained so young to drive a snowmobile – they're considered essential to life up here. There certainly isn't any ski culture in Qik, though the area is shrouded in snow most of the year and they gaze at the tantalizing Arctic Cordillera mountain range across Broughton Channel.

We ask around town about the Penny Ice Cap and if anyone had been up there. Even the Parks staff who did our orientation hadn't seen it. Again, very practical. In the town of Pond Inlet, which Dave and I had used as an access point when we skied to the highest summit of Bylot Island the previous year, the story was much the same. They too stare across at a spectacular mountain range. After walking around that town trying to get information about Bylot Island from locals, I could find nobody who'd set foot there, despite the fact it dominated the horizon to the north, only 25 km away.

A man named Methuselah set me straight. He sidled up beside me on the frozen dirt streets of "Pond." I remember snugging up my down jacket in the chill May air while this wiry, craggy fellow looked relaxed and warm in his cotton, one-piece orange jumpsuit.

"*Comment ça va*?" he asked me, thinking I was one of the many Quebec contractors who work in town.

"You speak French?" I asked back.

"Only a little." He grinned, then stuck out his hand. "My name is Methuselah."

We exchanged greetings and I commented, "Methuselah? That's a unique name, very Biblical."

"Yup, from the Bible, that's me..." He paused for a moment, as if stuck on that thought, then continued, "Where you from?"

"Vancouver...and you?"

"Here."

"Have you been to Bylot Island?" I pointed at the jagged, snowcapped peaks jumping from the horizon across Eclipse Sound. Everything on the Pond side is gently rolling terrain, but Bylot resembled a huge chunk of the Alps torn out by a giant and dropped into the Arctic Ocean.

"Nope, but I grew up looking at it."

"How come you've never been?"

"No seals or caribou there, nothing to hunt...but I did go around it once in a snow machine – took a week."

"You heading out on the land this weekend?"

"Nope, I'm a builder – gotta work." He grinned again and pointed at his chest, to the orange jumpsuit with safety reflection that he wears.

"Have a good weekend anyways, Methuselah."

"Ya, you too." He gave a happy nod and walked on.

So that was it, no game, no fish – so why explore for no practical reason? On the face of it, it makes perfect sense. I would question my own motivation, but I have an inexplicable, deep-seated wanderlust and need to experience new landscapes. It's a tic – an obsession that's driven my wilderness travels. A disease, perhaps, but better than most afflictions.

We ski along the streets of town. It's bright, sunny, and crisp, with the air a relatively balmy -15°C. Along the way we stop at the Co-op store to fill our fuel bottles with 12 litres of white gas. Every other thing up here costs a princely sum, but white gas and other fuel are ridiculously cheap. It's heavily subsidized by the government, as it's seen as an essential item for survival up here, not only to power snowmobiles but to gas up cooking stoves. Pretty much all of the outlying cabins at remote fishing and hunting camps have the classic two-burner Coleman stove as the mainstay for cooking and heating the cabins. As a result, a four-litre can of white gas that would cost $30 in Vancouver is only eight tax-free dollars in Qik.

Finally, the three of us stride away from town. Months of planning and group emails have culminated in this. We spend the first couple of hours getting in the groove of pulling our 80-pound sleds along behind us, becoming used to the glide of our skis on the cold, grippy snow.

John and Dave drop back in conversation and I pull ahead, already savouring the bright surroundings. This is what it's all about. It's always worth it. Setting off to explore a new landscape where every stride brings a fresh horizon is sublime. I always remind myself, especially when times are tough, "I shall not pass this way again." That thought always puts me in the moment, makes me absolutely present. It's a very addictive thing that keeps me coming back again and again.

We camp on the sea ice that evening, 16 km out of town, and Dave breaks out the bear fence. He has meticulously modified the stock model to make it work effectively after rigorous dry land testing. It's the first time he's set it up on the ice, so he and John go about putting the thing together. I decide to deal with other tasks, like setting up the tent and getting the kitchen area prepared. It takes them over an hour to set it up but it looks great. It's a hassle for sure, but on the sea ice we don't need to take chances, as there are lots of polar bears in the area.

Not too far from where we're camped, on the outer coast of Broughton Island, is an area known as Iceberg Alley. The pack ice is always broken up there so there are lots of air holes for seals to come up for a breath. It also means there are lots of polar bears there hunting them. Like us, these predators are wanderers and very curious, so the sight of our tent is sure to spark their interest. The bear fence has a blank 12-gauge shell inserted below a firing pin attached to each corner pole. The firing pin is prevented from deployment by a small plate attached to a string that runs 15 metres over to the next corner pole. The idea is that if a bear crosses any of the eight lines (two per side) it will trigger the firing pin and the blank will fire, most likely scaring the bear off and definitely waking us up so we can deal with the bear accordingly.

The whine of two snowmobiles rises through the crisp evening air and in minutes they've pulled up beside our camp. The lead sled is driven by a burly sealskin-jacketed man with a shotgun and a chest belt of slugs slung over his chest, like he's just praying for a polar bear to cross his path. His hands are covered in wolfskin gloves. Behind him sits a young Inuk in a Canada Goose jacket. Another young man pulls in behind on his own sled. The wolfskin glove guy is a white man, craggy and weather-worn, with a blonde beard. He looks to me like someone who's spent a good period of his life outside.

We shake hands over the top of the bear fence and he introduces himself as Scott Thornhill. He's obviously the leader of this small group. The other two look very soft and city-like, possessing fluorescent tans rather than ones earned from the sun.

"We have a camp over by Iceberg Alley, a big communal tent with a heater that gets up to 30°C inside when it's really going," Thornhill explains.

"Who goes to Iceberg Alley?" I ask. "Hunters?"

"Nope, photographers from all over the world. Professionals, hobbyists, you name it. Lots of those close-up polar bear shots you see in all the magazines were taken here."

Scott scans our camp set-up. Dave sees this and asks, "What do you think of our bear fence?"

He nods his head in approval, then says, "It's good…I'd maybe move the lower wire down to about six inches off the ground. You'd be amazed at the tight spaces a polar bear can squeeze under. They're like giant mice and can compress their bodies to an amazingly small size if they have to."

Despite the suggested alteration, Dave is pretty stoked. His bear fence has just been "Scott Thornhill Approved."

CHAPTER 10

Bear tracks by our camp
Like a ship in the bright night
It passed as we slept

We wake up after our second night of camping on the sea ice. I'm up first, and step outside to get the stove stoked. We keep our kitchen set up outside, dug into the snow. In colder, windier conditions we'd cook in the vestibule but avoid it if possible. Cooking in the vestibule creates too much condensation that wets everything out over time. Of particular concern are the sleeping bags. Once the down gets damp, the loft disappears along with the warmth.

I pressurize the MSR stove by pumping it, then ignite the priming fuel in the cup at the base of the stove. This in turn heats up the fuel line and within a minute the stove roars to life. A bit of water survived the night in my insulated water bottle and I pour that in the pot, and then start adding snow. We need to make enough water every day for two litres each on the trail, plus enough for our morning granola and coffee. No one goes anywhere until they get two cups in them. That's my rule anyway.

Usually after the first cup, it's time to do your morning business. Ideally the bear fence has already been disarmed or else you have to gingerly step over or high jump the fence and hope you don't trip it. Nothing like a shotgun blast to get the morning started.

Dave and John are pretty aligned in how they approach the wintertime dump. I have my own method. I never bring toilet paper on trip, any trip. I don't like the extra bulk it adds, but more than this I hate putting bleached paper with a brown skid mark into any environment. I find the sight of this left-behind waste aesthetically and ethically distasteful. People lived without toilet paper for millennia, so why is it necessary now? In the summer, ideally I use a nice sphagnum moss. Soft, antiseptic, moist, and with a little grip, it's the ideal toilet paper. If I could, I would use this stuff in my bathroom at home, but I don't think my wife would go for a big stack of moss beside our toilet. It wouldn't quite match the décor. Moss isn't a choice up here; all around us is snow. So I use what's available.

This morning, the second cup of Starbucks instant goes through me like Drano and I scurry 30 metres off from camp with a shovel in hand. When it's -20°C out, you usually don't want to linger too long with your ass in the wind, so you wait until the absolute last minute to make sure the whole process goes quickly. I dig a two-foot-deep foxhole down to the surface of the ice with the shovel – a cozy little nook with a bit of wind protection. Once settled, I lay down a good-sized cow patty. The windblown surface of the snow is a hard crust and I use the diamond-shaped broken pieces of firm snow to clean up. The first wipe is always the toughest. It feels like a cold burn on my asshole, but every subsequent wipe improves until there's only numbness there. I shovel snow over the hole when I'm done so it barely looks like I was there at all. My turd will be frozen solid until a fox comes by to claim it, or until breakup to be gobbled up by whatever sea creature may come upon it after that.

Dave and John don't bother with the foxhole, they just drop a deuce on the snow, then wipe with toilet paper, which they then burn down to ash. Whether I notice them stepping out for the morning ritual or not, I'm soon alerted to it by the smell of burning paper. Their shit freezes instantly but the shit stain on the bleached landscape will linger until drifted out by transported snow.

We finish filling our day's water supply and break down camp. Our first day and a half was spent mostly following a snow machine track that heads out to Iceberg Alley as well as to the entrance to Akshayuk Pass further to the south. Our route now veers directly into the wall of mountains we've been skirting to this point along the sea ice. Our doorway is Coronation Fjord, a 20-kilometre-deep notch in the range that will lead us to the toe of Coronation Glacier, which will lead us up and over the Penny Ice Cap. Our travel rhythm is to move for an hour, then stop together for a 15-minute break of eating, hydrating, and chatting. It keeps the team together and breaks up the daily routine nicely. Five or six of these pulls per day should get us to Pang in about two weeks' time to catch our flights home.

The snow is clean, unbroken alabaster. We begin breaking a line through it toward the distant gap where the fjord begins. Dave strides away from camp and John and I settle in behind him. After only 50 metres, he stops and crouches down. I come up behind him and see what has drawn his attention. The unmistakable tracks of a polar bear run in a breadcrumb line from Coronation Fjord, past our camp and across a broad, open expanse toward the southern tip of Broughton Island. This particular individual's tracks veered from its intended course toward our camp. The apex predators of the North, polar bears are eternally curious creatures, and the site of our big orange dome tent in the middle of the ice would naturally draw its attention. It ranged in close enough, got a good sniff, and decided to move on to more familiar prey. Despite their man-eating reputation, healthy bears by and large avoid human contact. The Inuit have hunted them for millennia as a source of food and fur, so they generally know better than to engage with people.

When I was rowing the Northwest Passage with a group in 2013, we came upon an Inuit beluga hunting camp in Darnley Bay, not far from the hamlet of Paulatuk. I walked around the camp with Steve Ilisiak, a hunting guide who was there with a group of his friends from town. Ambling through a row of beluga carcasses lying on the beach, I came upon the huge, skeletal hind leg of a polar bear. I asked him, "Wow, what's the story behind this?"

"It's the hindquarter of a ten-and-a-half-foot polar bear I got last winter. Got it right out here on the ice."

"What did you do with it?"

"What do you mean?"

"Did you use it for anything after you shot it?"

"Oh yeah, I used everything…we eat all the meat, even the shot-up parts, which we feed to the dogs. Nothing ever gets wasted. It's so expensive to eat anything from the store; we need the country food. It's a matter of survival. We've been hunting up here for thousands of years.

Inuit are part of the food chain – when we take a bear or a beluga, it's all part of the regular cycle. We're an important part of the ecosystem up here, like any other predatory animal."

"Do you ever worry about polar bears, about them stalking you like I've heard so much about?"

"No, not at all. Bears are smart; they stay away from us. Just the other day I spotted one about a kilometre south of camp here, walking along the shore. It suddenly stopped when it smelled the camp, then swam a whole kilometre out to sea and a kilometre past the camp before it headed back to shore. It avoided us on purpose. It was a matter of survival for that bear too, and it knew it."

I stopped to take a few shots of the big prints in the powdery snow. Both of my feet would fit in the space of one of its paws. John has brought along a little mascot for our journey: a small stuffed toy penguin his son named Waddles. He wants to tell his 5- and 7-year-old kids about his big trip in the North when he gets back through the eyes of Waddles, so he poses the stuffy in one of the big tracks. This may be the first time an Antarctic Gentoo penguin has been recorded lounging in the track of a polar bear.

We set off again, now following the bear track in reverse toward Coronation Fjord, suddenly more alert than we'd been a few minutes earlier.

CHAPTER 11

A furious wind
We ski against its sharp teeth
To the glacier's toe

I wake up with fabric smacking against my face. It's 3 a.m. and the whole tent is flexing up and down and rumbling like thunder. We've just been hit by a wall of wind funnelling down off Coronation Glacier and over the ice to where we're camped halfway along on the fjord.

When we went to bed last night it was dead calm, as it's been everyday of the trip so far. Lulled into a sense of security, we pegged the tent down but not the guy lines that support the upper structure of the tent. The poles for the tent are made of a material called Syclone, a virtually indestructible and flexible synthetic material that is now being put to the maximum test by this sudden blow. All three of us are up, bracing the tent from the inside with our hands.

"We need to get out there to anchor down the guy lines!" John shouts over the flapping of the fabric.

"One of us needs to stay in the tent while two of us do the anchoring, otherwise it might blow all the way back to Qik!" I respond.

A quick game of rock, paper, scissors determines Dave is the winner. He grins and stays snuggled in his sleeping bag.

"Have fun out there, boys. I'll keep it locked down in here!"

John and I quickly dress, put on our camp booties, and step out into the maelstrom. It is bright outside though the sun has yet to peek over the line of mountains to our northeast. It's the first of May and darkness only presents itself as a couple of dusky hours at this time of year. Snow crystals driven by the breeze sting my face as we step around to the windward side. We tie off the guy lines to our sleds, shovels, and skis – basically anything that's solidly set in the snow. We also arrange our three sleds to provide a wind barrier that will take the edge off of the blast. The tent is solid once again and seems to be holding. We step back into the relative quiet of the vestibule and then into the tent. Dave is already fast asleep, thanks to his adeptness at Roshambo.

I'm a light sleeper, always have been, and particularly when I'm out on a journey through a landscape I've never experienced before, when it's light almost 24 hours per day. My body is wired to go. Dave and John are heavy sleepers, and snorers. They drone on all night, in and out like accordions, alternating snores. It's like a sonorous language of its own and I know who's snoring by their distinct tone. Dave's snore is deep and guttural, like a thunderstorm parked directly over the tent. John is higher-pitched, like an approaching snowmobile that never arrives. I counter the snoring by double-stacking those ubiquitous orange foam earplugs you get at the drugstore in each ear, then wrapping the arm of one of my fleeces tightly around my head so the earplugs stay in place. For the light I use an eye mask. Then I bury myself deep in my sleeping bag. I am such a princess. Even with all of these measures I can still hear the snoring drone, though it sounds like it's coming from a nonexistent tent next door. Plus, my own heartbeat now pounds in my ears. The next step is to calm the excitement in my mind, the excitement of being on trip, which ironically robs me of valuable sleep. I find if I get four hours per night, I'm good to go for weeks on end…the energy coursing through me makes up for the rest. Whether it's true or not, there's the common legend that Einstein and Hitler only slept four hours per night, and they were markedly accomplished at completely opposite ends of the human spectrum. A certain degree of manic obsession is involved when you don't sleep, as the mind just keeps on running, and this obviously presents itself in very different ways.

I calm my mind, push out thoughts and try to think of nothing. I say to myself a few times, "Everything is perfectly perfect." Somehow this mantra helps and soon all I see behind my closed eyes is something like the aurora borealis – pulsing, shifting colours, and then nothing. I'm asleep.

The blast that came in last night at 3 a.m. continues through the day. We cook outside in the lee of the tent but don't linger. The stiff breeze makes it feel like -30°C and we break camp quickly. The cutting wind has us wearing our Gore-Tex shells over our light thermals. The trick is to stay warm but not sweat, so that when we stop it doesn't freeze on our bodies. Beyond his shell and long underwear, Dave packs an extra toque into his briefs to insulate his John Thomas.

I ask him, "You circumcised?"

He replies, "Yep."

I nod. "They stole the natural toque from your Johnson."

He laughs.

Sometimes you have to put yourself in uncomfortable situations to realize why evolution made us how we are. In urban life, circumcision's not a terrible idea. It arose from Judaism and eventually became standardized as an easier way to keep your Tom Collins clean. But in the wild, when people used to be naked or close to it, it was for protection and warmth. So now Dave looks like he's packing a Ron Jeremy-like unit down there with the toque laid over top.

We ski slowly, steadily, into the biting wind all day long. Goggles protect our eyes from the stinging snow as we take turns breaking trail. Slowly the end of Coronation Fjord materializes and we can see the distinct white ribbon of the glacier snaking down through a deep rift in the mountains where it meets the sea. We camp a couple of kilometres from the end of the fjord. The toe of the glacier is a wall of broken ice, though it's hard to tell how high it is, or how difficult it will be to get around it until we actually see it up close. This is one of the crux points of our journey. It looks from the topographical maps that the best route is around the north end of the toe, but we'll confirm that tomorrow. Right now, it's another day under our belt, another 18 km travelled. All that matters is putting the tent up, erecting the bear fence, and getting the water going for hot tea and freeze-dried food.

CHAPTER 12

We've already established our rhythm around camp. Dave and John do the bear fence, I do the tent and then set up the kitchen. After our meal, we all share a clove cigarette and take a few tiny sips of whisky from my flask. We've determined that if we take two mini sips each per evening there's a chance our scant whisky supply may just make it through to the end of the journey.

In the tent, John and Dave sleep facing the same direction. I sleep in the opposite direction, to get as far away from the snoring as possible. John and Dave look at the next day's route in the evening while I write in my journal. On a 75-day canoe trip I did in 2007, my partner Taku Hokoyama – being fluent in written and spoken Japanese – decided to do a daily haiku in Japanese characters. I followed suit in English using the typical 5-7-5 syllabic structure. Ever since then, on every journey I write a haiku in the evening that captures a moment of that day or the essence of the day. It's a simple way to reflect on and process my daily experience.

John and Dave used to do three-week trips together with no communication device whatsoever, immersing themselves in wild, remote journeys through the mountain ranges of North America. Things have changed for them now. Dave is married and has a 13-year-old daughter. His wife runs the only yoga studio in the town of Banff, which Dave built with his own two hands. John is also married and has two young kids.

For this trip, John and Dave each have an inReach satellite-messaging device. It acts as both an emergency beacon and communicator and is the only way they can communicate with their families. We're posting daily location updates so friends, family, and anyone else can follow our progress on a tracking map. We also have the ability to attach a message to our daily camping location in the form of a 160-character text. The haiku is a perfect way to communicate our experience within the parameters of this medium, so I recite my haiku to John every evening and he sends it out to the world...or our immediate family anyhow.

This is John's first significant journey away from his family since the kids were born. Dave only got back into these types of journeys with me on Bylot Island the year before. Part of the deal with their being away is daily, personal communication with their loved ones – quick back and forth messages are the lifeline to home life. I doubt they would come on these journeys without some kind of link. Constant communication is assumed – it has become an inescapable part of the fabric of modern life, even up here.

It's comforting in many ways to be able to communicate even when so far away, but something is lost when something is gained. An inReach or satellite phone doesn't let you fully step into a new world, to fully immerse. My wife understands this, and she doesn't expect to hear from me while I'm on a journey. I tell her how long I'll be away, giver her the map link, and let her follow the haiku journey like anyone else who might be interested.

Until a couple of years ago, I didn't give any updates whatsoever. All I carried with me was a personal locator beacon (PLB), which had no communication capability. It's a small, compact device that you would only turn on if life or limb were threatened. When activated, the PLB sends an emergency signal to the nearest rescue service, which would theoretically instigate a search via the pinpoint satellite signal it emits. Perhaps only a psychological safety blanket, it seemed to satisfy the anxiety of my wife, mom, and whoever was my trip partner at the time. It also allowed me to mentally disappear into a journey, with nothing to jolt me away from a new, ever-changing and dynamic wilderness reality.

On past longer journeys I might write a postcard or other note if we were picking up supplies en route. I was canoeing across Canada in 1995 when my sister got married. She was hoping I'd take a break in the middle of that 171-day trip to attend the wedding, but I couldn't...I couldn't break the rhythm, and we were trying to beat out Old Man Winter before he locked up our travelling water in ice.

In lieu of a gift and my attendance, I mailed them a congratulatory note on a piece of birch bark I found on the wind-whipped shores of the upper basin of Lake Winnipeg. The stamp stayed on, it arrived at the wedding on time, and was a hit. A thousand Denby dishes couldn't top that.

I've missed most of the weddings I've been invited to because I'm away most summers. Weddings, though, are as repetitive as a 9 to 5 workday. For the bride and groom, the day is memorable, stressful fun. For everyone else, it's a party, a blur; then it's over. Make out with someone you met on the dance floor after draining half a dozen rum and cokes from the open bar. Puke on someone's dress. Wake up the next morning hungover and self-loathing…or so I've heard anyways. I don't go to weddings; I go on trip.

Each of my long journeys is as unique and distinct to me as someone's child is to them. They are experiences that are forever burned into my soul and will be with me until the day I die. That's more than I can say for most wedding unions. All ceremony and fluff, weddings are mere simulacra – a cookie-cutter event that's little more than people milling around the faint hope that these people pledging their vows will actually stay together. The ritual is mostly anchored around idealistic vows that don't take into account human complexity. The simple experience of a long self-propelled journey, time and time again, delivers so much more. My sister's marriage dissolved over a decade ago but that cross-Canada canoe trip is with me to this day.

It's interesting how group dynamics shift from trip to trip depending on the mix. All three of us get along, but John and Dave have a giggly and easy rapport from years and years of having known each other. I kind of stick to the periphery of conversation, reading, writing, and smiling along. I'm definitely the third wheel…and not grudgingly so. It's nothing I do consciously; it just feels right for the group mix. I generally do things by feel, carving my place in the hierarchy depending on what will be best for this thing to go forward smoothly, without friction.

CHAPTER 13

The wall of ice looms
We watch a huge shard cleave off
Humbled by nature

The next day we ski to the toe of the glacier. It seemed insignificant from our campsite, like we would be able to just step up onto the glacier and ski onward to the Penny Ice Cap. However, as we approach it, it seems to grow exponentially with each stride so that by the time we finally reach it, a 50-metre wall of solid ice blocks our path. The behemoth pops and pings, a thing alive with cracks and fissures that run in a haphazard pattern across its cold, blue face.

John and I are standing only 30 metres from the base of the wall when a bus-sized section suddenly peels off and explodes onto the sea ice. It happens so randomly and suddenly that we both hoot and holler at the top of our lungs in the moments afterwards. We're both exhilarated at witnessing such a feat of power, and joyful that we weren't standing directly beneath the massive chunk when it peeled away. Another 15 metres closer and we would have been pounded into pancakes, prepped by the glacier for the next roaming polar bear. It would have been a unique way to enter the local food chain, to be certain. A cloud of ice particulate rises from the freshly settled rubble, then dissipates. Then the glacier continues its grumbling, brewing up the next calving. John and I take a few strides back and wait for Dave to join us.

Our plan is to make our way through the moraine on the north end of the glacier where it meets the side of a mountain. This moraine is composed of rounded boulders, some as small as a tennis ball, others as big as a house. We each work our way up, going back and forth twice through the punchy ground. There seems to only be a thin skiff of snow over the awkward, steep, uneven ground so we try at first to take our skis off and walk through. After each of us has post-holed up to our crotches a number of times in the first few metres, we abandon that plan. Our balls can only take so much pounding. Instead, we put skins on our skis, half the load on our sleds, and beat a slow, winding path through the boulders. Each of us has to do a couple of trips, covering several hundred metres through the moraine until we reach a spot up top. It is hard work, and we strip down to our base layer.

The day is bright and sunny, and since we're in the lee of the glacier there is virtually no wind for the time being. I'm sweating by the time I finish my second trip. From our fresh vantage I look back to where we've come from. The endless parallel tracks of our skis can be seen far below on the sea ice of Coronation Fjord. Dave is near the bottom, working his way through the moraine with his final load, resembling a tiny ant crawling through a pile of driveway gravel.

Once on top of the moraine we take a break and have a bite to eat. We can see the first few kilometres of the glacier curving off to the west, framed by the Baffin Mountains. The surface of the glacier is pocked with boulders and dips but then looks like it settles into solid, unbroken ivory a kilometre inland from the toe. After lunch, Dave is in a jovial mood. He squats on top of a huge boulder in the moraine and releases an epic bowel movement. I take a picture of the event – to be shared for future giggles rather than public consumption, of course. Men really do become boys on these journeys. Torn from the responsibilities of adult life and into the simple joy of a journey, the silliest, most juvenile things seem absolutely hilarious.

John and I are almost crying with laughter and my stomach hurts from the uncontrolled convulsions. I take one more image of the giant turd, framed in the foreground, with Coronation Fjord in the back. Dave makes his own beef jerky and has brought almost a garbage bag full of the stuff with him, perhaps the equivalent of an entire cow. I'm surprised he can fit anything on his sled beyond the meat. He's been shovelling handfuls of it in his mouth at every break, and as a result his excretions are enormous. This particular display is a monument to that, though I doubt it will last very long as a hungry Arctic fox will be sure to find it soon after we leave. Second-hand jerky is manna from heaven for these barren land scavengers.

Dave realized how much he had overloaded himself with said jerky early on and has already been forcing it on John and me in order to lower his sled volume and weight. I always tend to go pretty tight on my food, just enough to get me through, but never enough to get me full. Having gone with Dave to Bylot, I figured I could rely on him for a top up and happily take a bag of his homemade to supplement my stash. It's one of the joys of the trip – being limited by what you can carry food-wise makes everything taste better. You savour every morsel.

Roping up, we head out onto the glacier. The first few kilometres, closest to the edge of the glacier where it calves into the sea, will tell us the nature of the crevasses on this particular expanse of ice. I'm the least experienced in terms of glacier travel so I'm in the middle of the rope sequence. If any of us collapse through a thin sheet of snow covering a maw in the ice, the other two will hold that person fast. Once anchored, the person in "the hole" will be aided by one of the safe party to get out. I despise this position…being pushed and pulled by, and managing, the ropes feels so constraining. You can't move at your own rhythm and pace, always having to move at the pace of the person in front, like a loaded donkey being led by a halter. It's the opposite of freedom, but necessary in this notorious section of glacier.

The wind-blasted, sastrugi-dappled surface of Coronation seems rock solid, but we are being cautious. Eric McNair-Landry's wife Kate fell armpit-deep through a thin veil of snow while on skis in this very same area. She, Eric, and Eric's sister and husband were crossing over this same glacier the previous July. They were roped up and safely got her out, but their experience served as fair warning.

An even more relevant example was given to us by Jay in Qik. A pair of European skiers attempted the same route as us a couple of years earlier around the same time of year. Not too far along on the glacier one of them fell deep into a crevasse.

They weren't roped up, in fact didn't have a rope with them at all, so the one member of the party had to ski back toward Qik and luckily for them flagged down a local on a snowmobile. They went to town, got a rope, then went up on the glacier and hauled the man out. The pair abandoned the trip after that.

We travel for a few kilometres along the glacier. All seems solid, with no evidence whatsoever of any big cracks in the ice. The breeze from the west is still in our face but lighter than the day before. The sun circles around the mountaintops, staying high in the northwest.

Before setting up camp, Dave probes the area to ensure we don't set up over a hidden crevasse. It would be a rude awakening to have the three of us wrapped up in the tent hurtling downward into an abyss in the middle of the night. There are cracks around, but they are inconsequential. They run right across the glacier but none are more than a few inches wide. Now that we're on the glacier, we dispense with setting up the bear fence, which makes for a quick camp. The Inuit don't come up here because there's nothing to hunt in this lifeless expanse of rock and ice, and it's an impractical travel route. The same goes for the bears – we are far away from where the seals hang out.

CHAPTER 14

Lined by dark towers
Three specks linked by nylon rope
Albescent glacier

The wind eased the next morning but it was still -25°C. I wiggled out of the warm cocoon of my sleeping bag and sat up. Before fully emerging, I slipped on my down jacket and thermal pants, which had been warmed by my body inside the bag during the night. John groaned, Dave moaned. I slipped out of the vestibule and into the light. The glacier this low down is still flanked by a line of peaks on each side. Though it's light out, the sun has yet to peer from behind the greys and whites of the range.

I stamp my feet against the thickness of the cold, then hunch down to pump the MSR stove until it's pressurized. I take my gloves off to light the fuel in the primer cup. I keep a lighter in a shirt pocket every night so the butane will function for just this occasion. You don't fuck with morning coffee – it's an essential starting element on every expedition morning. The hiss of the stove energizes Dave and Johnny and they are soon outside, mugs in hand, sipping black gold. We are quiet, going about our tasks of melting water, making morning "deposits," and taking turns clearing our sleeping bags and pads out of the tent.

The sun finally peeks above the mountaintops and everything seems suddenly relaxed and easy. Conversation thaws out too and we crack a few jokes as we pack up the tent and eat our granola. Ahead of us lie thousands of feet of elevation, the glacier seeming to ramp endlessly to the west, climbing up and over the Baffin Mountain Range. It's warm enough that Dave doesn't need to accentuate his man-region with a toque today.

We put in a long day, 18 km of uphill travel on the glacier to make up for the short five-km day when we worked our way through the moraine to the top of Coronation's toe. It takes us six pulls during which we cover around three km per hour, each of us taking turns breaking trail as we inexorably move forward. We are down to our base layers by the end of each pull, but when we stop, we quickly throw on our down and sit on our sleds munching jerky, trail mix, and cheese. The 15-minute breaks go by quickly. Dave keeps an eye on the time and starts to get moving, breaking the inertia of rest, forcing us to move again. We unroped a couple of kilometres into our second day as it became obvious the glacier was solid ice and completely benign from that point onward – a surface as sturdy as stone.

CHAPTER 15

Sparkling dust landscape
Atop the Penny Ice Cap
Lonely Ecstasy

The next morning we break from the tongue of Coronation Glacier where it joins with the vast expanse of the Penny Ice Cap. This feature was named for Captain William Penny, a whaling captain from Aberdeen, Scotland. He pioneered overwintering with the Inuit at Cumberland Sound in order to be able to start whaling much earlier in the season. This 6000-square-kilometre sheet of ice forms the heart of Auyuittuq National Park. We have to ski up and over its 6,500-foot high point before we're able to descend to Akshayuk Pass on the other side. We continue to climb steadily throughout the day, ascending rolling white benches of snow along the way. The sun is cooking so Dave and I manufacture nose guards from cardboard and duct tape to save our beaks from the close rays and reflective surface of the snow. John outdoes us with a custom leather nose guard that he affixes permanently to the bridge of his sunglasses. Always crafty, John just always seems to have his shit dialled a little bit better than us.

We break out onto a flat expanse of white, with the occasional bump here and there indicating an ice-encased peak that has yet to break from the frozen grip of the glacier. Though the sheer size and scale of the glacier makes it seem like it's a fixture as old and long-lasting as Earth itself, the Penny Ice Cap – like all the glaciers on Earth – is slowly but surely diminishing so that one day these encrusted pinnacles will be released. For now though, they remain entombed like mummies deep inside a sarcophagus of ice.

We ski onward until we see that the terrain before us is about to drop steadily downward, indicating we've reached the high point of the cap. We gather up and pause for photos, breaking out a celebratory kretek to commemorate the moment. I feel like Neil Armstrong, standing atop an alien, lifeless moonscape – we three just specs of dirt on an endless, crisp, and immaculately clean sheet. The clove cigarette crackles between my chilled fingertips, which I stuff into my pocket between deep, brain-tingling drags. The sweet aroma – from tobacco and cloves grown in Indonesia – somehow doesn't seem out of place here. In fact, it is perfect.

We ski down about a kilometre from the high point and set up camp under a spectacular sun halo, the light reflecting and refracting off airborne ice crystals to form a golden outer ring. I look back at our tracks – a thin blue, ephemeral line showing where we've come from. It's all downhill from here.

CHAPTER 16

Shroudeded in cold mist
A Norse spire reaches skyward
Mt. Asgard Splendour

The next day, we look for a way off the Penny. There are several spurs that run down to the south that look like potential access points to a lower glacier called the Turner Glacier. We ski across a snowfield toward what we hope will be our exit slot. Ideally, it's smooth, unbroken terrain that's not too steep. Our pulks have rods that keep the sleds behind us so they won't run up on our skis when we go downhill, but the unwieldy weight still has the potential to wrest control from us on excessively steep slopes, particularly if we're forced into tight turns.

As we ski toward the slot, wispy clouds arc across a deep blue sky, resembling a distant mountain range. By the time we cross the expanse these mountains have magically melted into the ether. The slot is a gap in the cliff band, a hundred metres wide, and it's somewhat steep but definitely manageable. It drops through walls that are hundreds of metres high. Far below we see the Turner Glacier, which eventually flows to Akshayuk Pass. There is no wind, the air tangibly still.

We ski down one at a time. Dave going first, followed by John, and then me. There's a nice light layer of snow about 20 cm deep that makes it easy to control your speed and steer down the slope. I take pictures of Dave and John as they descend, a couple of gliding ants across a white picnic blanket. I drop in, controlling my speed with a slight snowplough, making sure to keep my heavy sled directly behind me so it doesn't roll over. We all hoot and holler as the slope quickly drops us down a couple of thousand feet before flattening out onto the Turner. All that climbing for days and days and we drop about a third of our elevation in about 20 minutes. We definitely earned these turns.

As we begin to skin across the Turner Glacier, we are stunned by what comes into view. A vertical wall, impressive in its own right, had been obscuring what lay on the other side of Turner. As we ski beyond it, a flat-topped cylinder of a mountain with a 1000-metre vertical face looms before us on the edge of the far side of the glacier. It's a moment where we all stop, wrapped in awe, followed by whoops of joy that express how we feel to be in the presence of the spectacular formation known as Mount Asgard. Rarely seen from the back, where the full breadth of the mountain is visible, this view stops us in our tracks. It is only mid-afternoon, but we decide to bask in its glory for the evening. We ski up to within a couple of hundred metres of its base and set up camp. Asgard is one of several spectacular peaks in the Baffin Range that comprise the Norse Mountains. These peaks, named after various Norse gods, contain the largest vertical rock faces on the planet. Our little orange tent, placed in front of Asgard, looks like something from out of a Wes Anderson film. The scale is exaggerated, cartoonish, and hyper-beautiful. Asgard is not a Norse god but rather where the Norse gods lived, looking down on the planet from their heavenly perches. The vertical wall that had originally obscured our view of Asgard is actually the flank of Mount Loki – named after the trickster god who only decided to reveal mighty Asgard when the time was right. With Asgard on one side of us, and Loki on the other, the three off us stand, chat, and grin. On this fine evening, we smoke double-rations of clove cigarettes. The gods demand it.

Dave had been in contact with Grant, a Parks Canada mountain guide he knows from Banff. Grant has been down in Akshayuk Pass teaching mountaineering skills to staff gathered from National Parks across Nunavut. While we camped in our tent up on Turner Glacier in front of Asgard, he and his crew were snug in a Parks Canada cabin down at the west end of Summit Lake, somewhere below us. They'd been texting each other with the inReach. Apparently, they're heading back to Pangnirtung by snowmobile today so we won't see them. Grant's lone piece of advice to Dave is, "I hope you brought crampons… the Weasel River is a 30-km-long skating rink."

CHAPTER 17

Blustery Glacier
Pinballing through the moraine
Enter Akshayuk

After our bluebird evening spent at the base of Asgard, we awake to find that all the mighty mountains around us have disappeared. A thick blanket of fog shrouds the giants and shrinks our world to about 100 metres of visibility. Our goal today is to get off of Turner Glacier and down to Summit Lake in Akshayuk Pass. We don't have much information as to the best route down but the contours on the map showing the toe of Turner were much broader than Coronation so we don't expect vertical ice fall or crevasse issues.

We ski our way steadily along the east side of the benign glacier until a large boulder field comes into view. This is the end of the glacier – a lumpy, bumpy moraine-strewn exit to Akshayuk Pass.

Johnny is probably the strongest downhill skier of the three of us, followed by Dave, and then me. John has a Whistler pass and still skis a ton at the resort, while Dave grew up downhill skiing as well. Me, I duffed around Ontario on cross-country skis, but pretty much shuffled around rather than employing any sort of technique. Once I came out west, I learned to be a pretty decent skate skier, and then a proficient telemark skier as well. I've spent many days in the backcountry telemarking the steep slopes of the coast. I'm not into hucking cliffs (not intentionally anyways), I'm just out there to enjoy myself and through experience over the years have learned that I can get down just about anything.

John deftly skies through the moraine, around the large boulders, somehow avoiding the holes and dips all over the place. Dave and I trail behind, getting hung up with rolled-over sleds that we help each other right as we bash our way through the haphazardly clumped rock, ice, and snow – the final excretion of Turner Glacier.

We spill out onto windblown Summit Lake. Half-covered with a thin layer of snow, the rest of the lake is glare, aquamarine-coloured ice. We turn westward, pushed by an easterly wind. On the icy sections, all we have to do is spread our arms out, point our skis and let the wind sail us across the friction-free surface for the five-kilometre distance to the far side of the lake. An orange speck, so out of place in this land of black rock, blue ice, and white snow, catches my eye. As we get closer it becomes apparent that it's a small hut. We ski up to it and see that it's an emergency shelter cabin, built for summer hikers and climbers to duck into to escape inclement weather. There is apparently a string of them throughout the pass. A couple of hundred metres beyond the shelter cabin lies a much larger cabin. For use by Parks staff only, it's fully equipped with a kitchen, sleeping area, and gas. Unfortunately, Dave's friend had been gone for hours and the cabin was locked. No matter, meeting a big group of people out on a trip like this is always awkward. In our bubble of three we've fallen into a nice routine over the past 11 days and are happy to hole up in the little shelter cabin, out of the wind. It's tiny indeed – four walls, a roof, a small closet and two bare wooden bed benches flanking a tiny table built in below the east-facing window. The rock, paper, scissors came out again and this time Johnny loses and is relegated to sleeping on a spot on the floor between the two raised beds. All in all though, it's luxurious – out of the wind and bear-proof, this is easy living for us. No need to set up and take down the tent either.

We cook in the lee of the shelter cabin that evening. The fog has lifted and we have a clear view down the valley. The Weasel River does indeed resemble a skating rink…glare ice gleams like the moist back of a snake, winding down the valley and out of sight below the towering peaks of Mount Odin and Thor Peak. Alpenglow bathes everything in a pinkish hue as we savour our freeze-dried Pad Thai. Once you're well into a journey, everything tastes like the best thing you've ever eaten. My one mandatory accessory for food is cayenne pepper. I apply it liberally to my freeze-dried food every night, so much so that every one of my meals turns red. It adds zest and warms my insides like nothing else. It's also apparently great for the blood and fends off colds.

Anything you bring on a weight-limited journey ideally has multiple levels of function, and cayenne pepper fits the bill.

After dinner, we stand and gaze at the spectacular surroundings, the sweet aroma of clove in the air as we pass around a kretek, hear the crackle of the ember, and feel the nicotine buzz roll over us like a quick-closing wave. Years after this trip is over, I'll remember this. I know I will. These journeys are all about these punctuations, these highlights – snapshots of motionless serenity snatched from a state of constant motion. It is what it's all about. It's why these journeys are always worth it, despite the initial resistance created by the inertia of comfort. The planning, the hassle, the work to get to this point are swept aside by the broom of these moments.

The light dips and the thermometer drops, so we retreat inside the shelter. It's by no means warm inside this simple, uninsulated wooden box, but with the three of us dressed in our down, and with the addition of a lit candle inside, there is at least the perception of warmth. John poses a couple of shots of Waddles looking out the window, and Dave shows us various funky ways to coil the glacier rope. The mood is light – we've gone up and over the Penny Ice Cap and are safely down in the valley. It's all downhill and flat from here, tromping our way on crampons and skis to Pangnirtung, now just 60 km away.

CHAPTER 18

A river of ice
Coasting down like giddy kids
Nature's perfect slide

The next day we awake to brilliant sunshine, the temperature a mere -15°C. We don crampons and tromp down the glare ice of the river. I keep my sled in front of me as it slides resistance-free down the ice, pulling me lightly and effortlessly downhill. As we approach the base of Thor Peak, the scale of this mountain is staggering. Its 1250-metre face is the largest vertical face of any mountain on Earth. Whereas Asgard looked like something from a Wes Anderson movie, this looks like something from *Lord of the Rings* – huge, menacing, and monstrous. The top of Thor hooks prominently over the valley, the monolith seemingly a gargantuan vulture looking over us as we pass below its immensity.

Dave and John experiment with different ways to descend the giant slide of the Weasel. John lies on it belly-down like an Olympic skeleton driver, gliding somewhat out of control, using his hands to maintain some sort of trajectory. Dave continues with the Olympic theme, sitting on his sled with his legs pointed straight out in front of him and using his ski poles to angle and propel the sled. He reminds me instantly of a Paralympic sledge hockey player. I tromp onward contentedly, snapping pictures of them and letting my eyes drift to the tops of the surrounding peaks.

The next day we work our way through a frozen gorge of dirt and boulders called "The Rock Garden." For a few months of the year the Weasel River is liquid and this is a rumbling rapid but now it is only a benign gully that we tromp through. When Eric McNair-Landry came through here on his way paddling and hiking across Baffin, his brother-in-law, a professional whitewater kayaker and adventurer named Erik Boomer, dragged his kayak to this point and paddled these burly rapid sections by himself. We're still framed by mountains on each side, but the spectacular peaks of the Norse Collection are behind us.

We pause at an inukshuk that marks the Arctic Circle, and the three of us and Waddles pose at the sign beside it. It seems odd in this valley to mark a manufactured concept like a line of latitude. It doesn't physically exist, and yet here's a sign by this pile of rock marking its existence – creating it in fact. It's quite possibly the first time that a penguin has been photographed at the Arctic Circle so at least there's that. We do another side-trip to something called "Crater Lake," a perfectly circular lake up on a ridge that does indeed look like a meteor hurtled down from the skies, smashed into the earth, and left this behind. And yet, it's not – it's merely a glacial lake. Somehow attaching it to an astrological phenomenon makes it worth visiting...otherwise it would just be another lake. The temperature is steady at -15°C, but a funnelling headwind makes it feel much colder.

Our final night in Akshayuk Pass is spent at the mouth of the Weasel River where it meets the sea at Overlord Shelter...a wooden box with a floor, nothing more. It sits at the base of a mountain named Overlord, which has a somewhat amorphous Jabba the Hut blob-like shape to it, lacking the sharp edges and spires of the inland peaks. Though we have 32 km yet to ski it feels like the end of the journey. We look out on the braids of the Weasel River delta, where the alabaster sea ice of Pangnirtung Fjord stretches into the horizon beyond the black wisps of the river's terminus.

CHAPTER 19

Sunny Skies today
Easy gliding and no wind
Finally Springtime

We're a little ahead of schedule now but none of us are lingerers. The whole anticipation and build-up for this journey was about getting up and over the Penny. When we first arrived at Akshayuk Pass, it was beautiful and the ice was a novelty, but now that we're out of the Baffin Mountains and into the delta of the river, it is time to plod on to town.

We put our skis back on after two days of hiking with crampons and the extra bit of free distance found in the glide of each stride is welcome and liberating. There isn't a breath of wind and it's only a few degrees below zero, our first really spring-like day.

In the delta, the gravel braids of the river fan out into the fjord, and for the sake of efficient travel we try to stick to long, straight runs of ice through the gravel. We all end up taking different channels, each convinced that our route through the delta is the best, and yet we arrive at the open sea ice at the same time. I feel strong, and my skis run nicely as I fall into a smooth rhythm. We put in our biggest day of the trip, covering 22 kilometres in an easy four pulls, savouring the moments along the way today, knowing that tomorrow is a short day to Pang.

We stop short ten kilometres from town and a couple of days before our flight leaves. Camping for our first night on the sea ice since Coronation Fjord, we look back at the seemingly impenetrable mountains of Auyuittuq. It's satisfying to think we've come right through the range and ended up here – a town-to-town, sea-to-sea journey, by fair means. It's a two-smoke evening – I've brought plenty for the team – and we enjoy the calm, nightless evening. We've rationed our 500 ml of whisky perfectly too. I've topped up my old narrow-mouthed hip flask all the way along and we've limited ourselves to two small sips from it each for 13 nights. This evening the final drops are drained, an internal warmth appreciated by explorers for centuries. A little treat to acknowledge another good day lived, another day on the trail in Mother Nature's embrace.

Though there is no Iceberg Alley on this side of Akshayuk Pass, bears do occasionally wander from one side to the other so there is the remote possibility of a curious *nanuq* coming around. John and Dave set up the bear fence for the first time since Coronation, efficiently having it up in half the time it took them that first night.

At about 1 a.m. we're awakened by a loud "Bang!" and then another "Bang!" I immediately think a polar bear has penetrated our fence and triggered the blank shotgun rounds at the corners. One more "Bang!" from within the tent tells me the sound wasn't coming from outside, but rather from John. The baffles of his air mattress were exploding one by one. Apparently, it's not ideal to inflate these by mouth in cold temperatures as the moisture inside freezes and destroys the glue in the baffles, resulting in failure. John's mattress now looks like an anaconda that's swallowed a pig, as one end of his mattress now sports a huge, unwieldy bulge. A couple of reasons to be positive about this gear malfunction: (1) it was our last night before we got to town, and (2) a polar bear was not trying to eat us.

CHAPTER 20

The last stride is here
A hamlet tucked in the hills
Our long journey's end

We casually shuffle the last ten kilometres, an easy-breezy feeling on a bright, sunny, and mild day on Pangnirtung Fjord. A small, dark cluster of rectangles becomes apparent at the base of the distant ridge. With each creeping step, the town becomes more prominent, the squares and rectangles becoming more numerous and house-like.

We ski the last few strides into the hamlet, past boats sitting on the sea ice, waiting for breakup that's still a couple of months away. Snowmobiles and ATVs buzz around – like in Qik, there are many people going somewhere in a place where there's really nowhere to go. Making our way through hard, brown snow mixed with the gravel of the road, we end up at a prominent green building on the west edge of the settlement.

As an employee of Parks Canada, Dave is hoping to leverage his position into free accommodation. The Parks manager is not presently in town. An older, funny fellow named Billy Etoongat is there, sipping coffee at a large round table in the main office. Beside him is a younger Inuk man, Matthew, who is in charge in the manager's absence. The electrical power in the whole town just went off when a transformer blew. The coffee in Billy's hand is the last warm mug for the day.

He tells us there's a Parks-dedicated house in town, but that's where the new manager is going to be living. She'll be here in a week and some of her stuff is already in there.

Dave asks, "Any chance we can stay there a night? Have some showers? We'll be out of here in a couple of days and will use our own sleeping bags."

Matthew – his round, squat face crinkled in thought for a moment – answers. "Hmm, I don't think I should let you. She'll be here in a few days...I don't think I'd feel right about letting you stay there."

Billy chimes in with an impish grin. "Looks like you boys are sleeping out on the ice again."

Dave doesn't push it any further, not wanting to give a bad impression as a fellow Parks employee. I respect that, and don't overstep my bounds. We linger for an hour chatting. None of the stores in town are open anyways because of the outage so we hang out, in no rush to be anywhere.

I go to the darkened bathroom to take a birdbath. The water merely dribbles out, as power is required to pump it. It is still lukewarm, just enough to wash two weeks of ski touring from my pits, asshole, and balls, using paper towel to dry up afterwards.

Without power, Matthew and Billy decide to close up the Parks office early, which means we'll have to shove off back to the ice for another couple of nights as the flight John and I have to catch isn't leaving until the morning after tomorrow.

Billy smiles at us as we get up to leave. "I'll have coffee ready for you boys when we open up tomorrow at 8:30. Hopefully the power's on by then." He also offers up the name of a B & B in town, but with no power that would be like paying a princely sum for a glorified and less snug version of our tent. For us dirt bags, it's got to be free or we're headed back to the ice.

We reassemble outside, clicking our sleds back on and dragging them a few hundred metres out onto the sea, intentionally a little far off and out of the way so we won't be bothered and have a decent sleep. There's no rush, nowhere in particular to be, and this close to Pang no bear fence to set up. Only a suicidal bear, willing to risk a hail of gunfire from a well-armed town, would dare come anywhere near us.

Our bright orange tent is quite conspicuous once set up…it can be seen from every angle in Pang. We're impossible to miss and the curious soon arrive. Three kids – two younger boys around 12 years old on bikes and an older kid, around 17 or so, walking beside them – come out to see what we're up to. They have a little Corgi/Husky mix that darts between the three of them. The white and brown dog is so full of energy I think it will explode. The kids are as quiet as most Inuit are, smiling shyly.

John says, "Hi guys!" and they continue to shyly smile. Or is it shyness? I think rather it's our interpretation of the interaction. Dead air in conversation in our general North American society is considered awkward and uncomfortable. People will blurt out just about anything – no matter how frivolous – to fill that space and avoid the sweat-inducing silence. The Inuit seem to live in that quiet space. In a vast land of sound-absorbing snow, quiet is the norm, the preference, the comfort. It's the conversation that's awkward. It's why they're so brief and to the point. They say what needs to be said and nothing more. Talk of the weather if you're in town is irrelevant as they're inside warm houses. Weather doesn't matter. That sort of talk is saved for when they're out on the land, where the weather actually means something.

We ask the kids their names and find out the two younger ones are named Glenjay and Joseph, the older boy Jake. Glenjay and Joseph go to school. I ask Jake what he does and he says, "I just sleep all day."

There isn't any ski culture among the Inuit – they used to snowshoe and dogsled but never skied. Nowadays it's all about the snowmobile. I always thought it was because of lack of wood, but Indigenous North America, even in the boreal forest, never utilized skis for travel. We let each of the kids try on our skis, and they shuffle around our camp with big grins on their faces. The two younger kids are naturals, but tall, lanky Jake was straight-legged and stiff as a board, teetering on the edge of collapse the entire time. He's still smiling though…perhaps he just discovered something to get him out of bed every morning.

John and Dave ride around on the kids' bikes, two oversized men on undersized steeds, looking like clowns on tricycles at the circus. Once the swap has been played out, I get everyone together for a shot. Glenjay poses with Dave's skis leaning on each shoulder, logos out like an Olympic skier doing a TV interview after a race. John poses on Glenjay's bike while Joseph sits on his own bike. Jake is crouched down, grinning and holding the little yappy dog.

They disperse back to town, leaving us on the ice. We resignedly cook up our last evening of freeze-dried food. Alas, the dream of eating a Delissio deluxe frozen pizza from the Northern Store disappeared with the power outage and lack of an oven. Sigh, maybe tomorrow. First World problems, indeed.

CHAPTER 21

The next morning, we awaken and brew up some coffee. Somehow, we don't trust that the power outage is sorted, so don't want to rely on Billy's offer of coffee at the Parks office. The snow around the tent is quite thin, and we scrape down to the ice surface to bunch up enough of a snow pile to melt into water. Pouring the boiling water over the instant coffee packet, I take my first sips and discover it is unpalatably salty, the snow obviously having mixed and merged with the seawater ice.

The next round is fine, and our morning granola does the trick. Soon we're back on our way to town. Nothing to do, nowhere to go, just waiting for a plane. Once in town, we discover the lights are back on and we wander into the Parks office. Billy isn't around, so I get the first pot brewing in the Parks office kitchen myself.

Matthew and an Elder saunter in and I pour them coffee. I've decided I'm going to get us into that Parks transient housing unit someway, somehow. I sit down with the two men in the kitchen, while Dave and John are using Wi-Fi in the boardroom. The Elder is a vibrant, weathered old Inuk with gnarled hands and a dark face from decades spent outside. He doesn't speak English but has bright, inquisitive eyes. He smiles broadly when I pour him a cup of coffee and nods appreciatively. Matthew says he is one of the premier sculptors in town. A couple of his pieces, intricate and beautiful, are displayed in the boardroom.

Matthew asks some more about our trip and other trips I've done in the Arctic. I mention that last year Dave and I were in Sirmilik and the manager of that park, Carey Elverum, let us stay for several days in the transient unit there.

"Oh, so you stayed there last year? Carey let you stay?"

"Yeah…you know that Dave works in Banff? Carey let him stay because he works for Parks, just like you do."

Matthew rubs his chin thoughtfully. "Hmm…maybe I better let you use the house in town. If Carey let you use the unit in Pond, I better let you use the one here."

I grin and reply, "That'd be great, thanks so much. We really appreciate it."

Matthew brightens, now seemingly excited to set us up at our new digs, "Yeah, no problem. If you guys go back and pack up your stuff, then come back here, I'll drive you to the house."

I walk into the boardroom where Dave and John are hanging out. "Well boys, how do you feel about hot showers and a soft bed tonight?"

Dave looks up, "What do you mean?"

"I chatted with Matthew about the transient unit and he said we could use it. I dropped Carey Elverum's name and that seemed to do the trick."

Dave grins, "You've got a way with getting your way."

Within the hour we are packed up and sitting in the cab of Matthew's Parks truck. He drives us the few blocks of frozen dirt to a house at the edge of town. It has a small Parks Canada sign by the door.

Matthew opens it up and gives us a tour. It has a kitchen, three bedrooms (one for each of us) and a bathroom. The Parks manager has left a pile of her belongings in a corner of the living room but otherwise the house is furnished and clean. John and I leave tomorrow so we only have one night here, while Dave has two. Far better than being in a tent on the windswept ice. It's funny how the mind works. During the course of a journey the tent is a paradise – a place where you shelter from the elements and a warm, cozy bag is all you need to be satisfied. Once a journey is over, though, the mind adjusts to easier things. Staying in a tent beside a town of warm houses seems unfathomable, almost unfair. The luxury of a heated house instantly separates you from the harsh environment outside and the weather no longer matters. Survival is easy and you bask in that ease. More than a few days of this though and you get antsy, somehow craving the engagement of survival again. At least I do. But for now, things can't get any better than this.

Once we've settled in and chosen our respective bedrooms, we all have a hot shower and do laundry. Besides wind-chapped faces, we are back to the state in which we started. We head to the Northern Store and pick up two large, frozen rising crust deluxe pizzas. Back at the house we devour them and luxuriate in the torpor brought on by the oversized meal.

Throughout the day, we notice a group of young kids, four in total, perhaps 4 to 6 years old, sledding up and down a small slope by the house. Their enthusiasm seems never-ending, bright smiles spread across their faces. They take turns using two sleds. One sled resembles a snowmobile, with a single ski up front and two behind, steered by handlebars. The other sled is a miniature wooden *qamatiq*. The kids are basically emulating the adult-sized snowmobile and *qamatiq* of their Elders. They use what they know. Unlike little Lucas in Qik, they have yet to graduate to the rumbling two-stroke model.

We have our three orange pulks that we want to give away in order to save on baggage overages for the journey back. Dave already promised a couple to an older woman he bumped into in town…these youngsters are the perfect candidates for the third. I bring out the sled and the kids are wide-eyed. It's big enough for all four of them to fit into. I line them up at the top of the hill and they go racing down, their momentum carrying them more than twice as far as their old sleds. It's a revelation to them. They run back up the hill giggling and grinning, stumbling over each other like a group of puppies. They abandon their old sleds, and the orange plastic rocket is what they spend the rest of the afternoon riding. As seen in their switching from dog teams to snowmobiles, the Inuit seem universally to be very practical people. Use what works best, tradition be damned.

John and I fly to Iqaluit the next day, stay in an Airbnb there, then onto Yellowknife for another couple of days with Eric McNair-Landry. Dave's flight is pushed back four additional days due to weather – the unfortunate nature of the game sometimes in the North. He emails us pictures of himself eating seal and narwhal with the baggage guys at the airport…the advantage of staying somewhere for a while and getting to know the locals, who seem always willing to share.

On our way in, John and I slept in Eric's main house – a one-floor wooden bungalow typical of Old Town. Eric described how he had to jack up the corners of the house every spring thaw so everything inside wouldn't crack apart. Apparently, everyone in the neighbourhood has a jack – it's just part of living in Old Town, where 100-year-old houses are the norm. They have character, but character requires maintenance.

On the way up, John slept on the floor, I slept in the den. Eric and his wife Kate had the only bedroom in the house. But on our double-back through town, we have been shifted next door into Eric's workshop. Inside the shop hang traditional design skin-on-frame kayaks he built. It's also heated and insulated so actually a nice, private space for us to lay our mattresses down and sleep. Eric has a couple of friends in town, John and Genevieve, and they got the main house digs. It makes sense – they were old friends, and John was a fellow kite skier. We'd met him briefly on the way through, and while we were traipsing across Baffin, he and Eric spent a week kite skiing 250 km from Yellowknife to the Dene village of Łutselk'e at the east end of Great Slave Lake. After that, they caught the daily hopper flight from there back to Yellowknife. Just an average week in the life of Eric McNair-Landry, I suspect.

I'd been to Łutselk'e almost nine years earlier, when Taku and I stopped there for a few hours on our way to Rankin Inlet, 2000 km away. The people in town were friendly; people from all walks of life there greeting us warmly; a really tight-knit community. I shot a film about that trip and interviewed Chief Steve Nitah at the time. He thought at first we were from Greenpeace or something, wanting to confront him about hunting and trapping – a funny notion from the 80s, I thought. He was a big man, with a heavy presence. Not someone to be fucked with, but he warmed up to us pretty quick.

He told us he lived on the land in skin tents until he was 10 years old, and then moved to the village, that caribou no longer migrated near the town due to a series of mines that had sprung up across their migration routes. "We lived off the land for thousands of years and then in a couple of decades were thrust into modern society and expected to fit in. It's a transition we're still working on."

In Yellowknife, you can see the disconnect between these worlds, and the difficult transition Nitah talked about. Drunk locals stagger around the downtown core, living a dead-end life. Several ask us for money as Johnny and I walk by. Meanwhile, just down the hill there's a microbrewery that might as well be in Vancouver. It's populated by transient, well-off white hipsters and other young folks. There are seemingly two different societies living in this city that don't seem to have any connection with each other whatsoever.

Communication and connection between people is always tricky. Back at Eric and Kate's place, we haven't quite clicked with them beyond polite conversation. It's understandable as we're really just getting to know them. They had offered me their place to stay when I met them back at the Wilderness and Canoeing Symposium, but perhaps didn't think I'd follow through…or be staying for a couple of more days at the tail end of our journey. This is their home, their place, and these are their friends…and suddenly these two drifters show up in their lives.

John and Gen are super easy-going though – very open and friendly. Perhaps it's because they're guests like us, though invited and not drop-ins. John and Eric go out on the ice to play around on their kites while Gen takes Johnny and me around town to show us the sights. She and John have lived in Yellowknife off and on over the years so she takes us to lunch at Bullock's Bistro, which has currency bills from around the world tacked all over the ceilings and walls. Afterwards, we go to the Woodyard Brewhouse (the hipster brewery) for a pint.

Gen gamely hobbles around with us on a bum knee. She is super cool, like hanging with a dude. Originally from Quebec, she says when she met John a decade earlier in Fort Smith, she barely spoke a word of English. Now there's nary an accent. They make their living as Arctic guides, and on Arctic cruise ships, as well as on the whitewater of the Slave River near Fort Smith where they live.

CHAPTER 22

The next morning Kate, Gen, and Johnny drive 100 km west of Yellowknife to drop off John and Eric so they can kite ski back to town. I elect to stay and glide out on an experience of my own. There's a phenomenon that happens every spring around this time, when the temperature during the day stays above zero degrees and dips to around freezing at night. The snow is long gone from the vast, thick sheet of ice that covers Great Slave Lake. By around noon the entire frozen surface is "candled," when about a one-centimetre thick, soft layer sets up and the lake becomes the ultimate skate skiing track. I've skate skied for years and love it. It feels like flying and is a great way to travel wide-open lakes like Great Slave Lake. Eric was kind enough to lend me his skate boots and skis, so I dress in my base later in the early afternoon and walk the 50 metres down to the shoreline from his house.

Walking out a few feet, I stand atop a couple of metres of ice. The fringe of "little sticks" formed by the boreal spruce on the far side of Yellowknife Bay are outlined clear and hard against a turquoise sky. I click into the skis and push off, instantly gliding 20 feet with my first stride. Getting into a rhythm, I see the small ticky-tacky houses of Old Town blur by. I soon snake through the colourful collection of boathouses that sit just offshore. The number of these houses has doubled since I was last here in 2009. With an exploding population and limited housing leading to exorbitant real estate prices, these houseboats are a way to live in town but be free of municipal taxes and interference.

Soon the boathouses and the town itself are but a memory as I fly away into the distance. There is no one else around on the ice and I drive my poles powerfully, propelling my skis along with little effort. There is no wind; the conditions are perfect. The skis are running great and I feel like I could go forever.

Fit from a couple of weeks of dragging a sled, I find this unencumbered skiing liberating. After an hour, I enter into an archipelago of islands near the mouth of Yellowknife Bay. I recall Taku and I paddling through here years ago, my first trip into the barren lands ahead of me. Now I want to push out beyond the islands, to the great expanse in the middle of the lake so I can glimpse where I'll be going in a mere six weeks' time. Somehow, almost inexplicably, this ice will be gone by the end of June and I'll be in a canoe, plying these very same waters. I wonder if breakup will be late this year, as it seems impossible that the two-metre-thick ice I now glide on can possibly transition by then. The tickets are purchased, though – me and Bougie are committed. Hopefully, Eric and Kate will submit to being our gracious hosts once more.

I break out past the last island and come to a stop. I look to the east and see the white expanse bleeding into a green and brown backdrop. That's enough, that's all I wanted – this view of my summer line. I'm an hour and a half in and it's time to turn around. I loop back and continue the push-glide-glide-push rhythm with the skis and poles. By the time I get back to Eric's place I've covered 55 kilometres in under three hours. Almost a quarter of our entire Baffin distance covered in the time it takes to have a leisurely lunch. I'll be back when the sun is at its apex and winter is but a memory – when solid is liquid, when dark is light, when skis are replaced by paddles.

CHAPTER 23

Yellowknife in May is brown. The last vestiges of snow melt in muddy trickles into a matrix of sewers and creeks, the only life being the hearty, stunted black spruce that drape the fringes of the city. North Vancouver, by contrast, is always alive. Winters are a dark green, often wrapped in a grey cap of misty rain that only allows a dusky light to penetrate its layers. Glistening sword ferns and dogwoods mix in beneath towering Douglas fir, western red cedar, and hemlock – a veritable temperate rainforest that is most alive when it rains the hardest, when a labyrinth of creeks and rivers storm down forested slopes, hissing and roaring amid a patter of fat droplets reflecting and deflecting off every square inch of exposed earth.

When May comes, the days are longer, and the sky brightens. It still rains, but the sun is stronger behind the clouds, and when the clouds break, an explosion of bright emeralds mixed with flashes of colour reflect back in a cornucopia of light. Cherry trees explode with blossoms – pinks and whites that bring Instagrammers out from the coffee shops to dress up the backgrounds of their selfies…to show how very amazing their lives in Vancouver are, to show how very good it is to live there. Rhododendrons are the best, in my opinion. Reds, blues, whites, purples…their flowers are not limited in colour. From the ground spring delicate lady ferns – a lighter, brighter shade of green unfurling for their annual appearance, softening the hard lines of the hearty evergreen sword ferns that surround them, waiting for them to awake from their hibernation in the dank, moist soil.

Spring is a time for renewal, when longer days hold promises not only for the flora, but for the fauna. Deer browse a diverse buffet of green, bears awake to feed on the first of many berry cycles – salmonberry, blackberry, and blueberry will come in staggered stages to sustain the bears and the inward-migrating birds throughout this warm time of plenty.

Humans also rejoice. They play, they frolic. There is an energy and vibration. Men and women shed their winter coverings, heads turn, mating season commences. But not for me. I'm in a good relationship – a long-term inset bond with a person I love and who gives me the freedom I desperately, passionately need. But there is…another.

I'm in a sort of twisted, open relationship. Shannon is my winter lover, but adventure is my summer fling. One cannot exist without the other. The darkness and the light. Which is which, who is who? I'm not even sure anymore. It's an annual cycle, like the seasons themselves. And so I go again, flee back to Yellowknife and a waiting canoe, back to adventure – my other true love.

PART TWO
WILD WATER

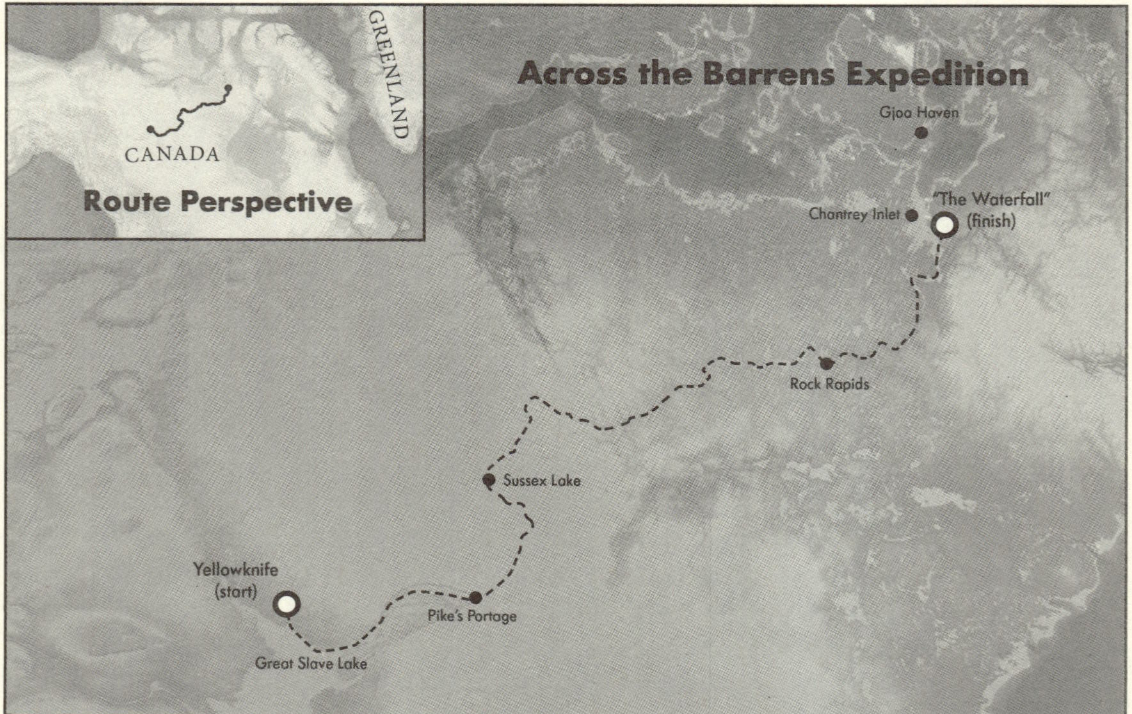
Across the Barrens Expedition
Route Perspective
CANADA
GREENLAND
Gjoa Haven
Chantrey Inlet
"The Waterfall" (finish)
Rock Rapids
Sussex Lake
Pike's Portage
Yellowknife (start)
Great Slave Lake

CHAPTER 24

It's 8 a.m. on June 27 and the white minivan pulls up in front of the condo building. Ryan has already texted me about their arrival and I'm waiting with my dry packs all ready to go. There isn't too much stuff, only a checked bag each beyond our carry on. I've already shipped my canoe, paddles, and all of our food to Eric in Yellowknife. Ryan steps out to help me load up the bags, we hop in the van, slam the doors shut, and off we go. All the planning and packing is done for now. I hate that part, going over gear and checklists again and again when, really, it's all so simple. All the details and preparation claw at you until you're finally en route and there's nothing left to do but accept your fate.

In Vancouver we wait at the gate for our flight to arrive. There's a chance we may see my mother and sister connecting through from Toronto on their way to San Francisco for my aunt and uncle's 50th anniversary. Yet another family occasion I'll be missing due to a journey, and I regret it not a bit. Hot, dry California, with its crowds of people compounded with a lot of sitting around and milling about chit-chatting. It would drive me completely, batshit mad.

I check the gates and see that indeed they'll be disembarking right by where we're waiting. Ryan is dressed up like he's going to Hawaii, wearing a floral T-shirt and a straw hat that he grabbed from the wall of his grandmother's house after she passed away a while back.

My mother comes out using her walker, which she's used since getting hit by a car at a crosswalk and breaking her leg badly a year earlier. She's actually recovered quite well with dedicated rehab and a stubborn disposition but found out you get to go on the plane first and get extra special service when a walker is involved, so she takes full advantage of that perk.

They emerge from the gangway and we hang out and chat with them for ten minutes. My mother is overjoyed to have some bonus time with her son. Ryan is friendly and chatty and they both laugh at his Arctic apparel. She would love it if I lived at home still, but I haven't since I was 18, and she understands I have to live my own life. I do manage to spend a month every summer at the family cottage near Parry Sound with her once the expedition season is done – a great way for me to transition out of the journeys and spend time with one of my favourite people. I hug her goodbye and we board the plane.

Ryan and I have to connect through Edmonton to get to Yellowknife. A tall, heavyset tween moves slowly in front of us on the tarmac as the line of passengers shuffles toward the waiting connector flight to Yellowknife. He suddenly freezes in place, pats himself down in a panic, and then explodes into an audible wail.

"My iPad! I don't have my iPad!' he cries.

His eyes are wide with horror as Bougie and I step around him. It's as if someone has executed the boy's mother in front of him. But, in fact, she's quite alive – she's the one trying to settle him down.

Soon a circle of airline workers and security move in around him. He tries to bolt back into the airport to hunt for the device, but they manage keep him on the tarmac for the time being. He rages on inconsolably, cursing the workers for not being able to find the precious tablet. The flight is delayed for 20 minutes as everyone tries, as politely as possible, to either get him on the plane or get him and his family members to check off the flight.

Finally he boards, slumping in the seat behind me. He kicks the back of my seat and swears loudly, completely oblivious to the fact that he's held up a plane with a hundred people waiting to depart. I suppose it's not all his fault. He's probably been attached to that device since he was a toddler and it's become a psychological extension of his being.

Man, I think, *I can't wait to paddle away from all this.*

Our addiction to technology seems almost inescapable in the civilized world. It's one reason I'm headed back to Yellowknife to begin a 1750-km canoe journey across the wilds of Nunavut and the Northwest Territories, where the only functional use for an iPad is as a cutting board – and a poor one at that.

This poor kid on the plane – so disturbingly attached to a small metal and glass object – brings to mind the writings of Ray Kurzweil. Kurzweil is a famous contemporary futurist who for years has predicted, "The

Singularity is near." The "Singularity" being a time in the near future when humans and technology will assimilate. Kurzweil sees it as a utopia where, among other things, microscopic robots called nanobots will exist in the bloodstream of every human, diagnosing and fixing any illnesses that may strike, allowing individuals to live for hundreds of years.

His positive spin on this unity of man and machine confuses me. We live in a finite world. If everyone were to live forever, wouldn't we quickly use up all the resources on the planet and perish of starvation, war, and other calamities associated with scarcity? As far as I can tell, there's no technological escape from the unavoidable. No one gets out alive. Death has been around as long as life. The two are, and always will be, inextricably linked to each other. That bond will never be broken no matter how many nanobots you throw at it. Our limited time on this planet creates an urgency in me to make the most of it.

Summer is in full swing in Yellowknife, the air still and warm, the days exceptionally long. The big lake I skied across only six weeks earlier is now wide-open blue water. Ryan and I take up residence in Eric's workshop, just 50 metres from the landing where we'll start the journey. In his backyard is our canoe, still wrapped in the packing plastic like when I saw it in May on our way Qik. My paddles and all of our freeze-dried meals also arrived at Eric's place and they are stacked in boxes in the workshop. We only have to shop for a few extra snacks – oatmeal for breakfast, and tortillas, peanut butter, and honey for lunches.

Ryan had the idea to ship a bunch of the stuff from Yellowknife ahead to an outfitter on a lake not far from the headwaters of the Back River so we'll have a lightened load for the Pike's Portage, a long series of carries to get from Great Slave Lake to the interior. Depending on price, I'm willing to investigate that possibility. A quick walk from Eric's place is Air Tindi, a charter air company that, among other things, services remote fishing lodges in the region. When they tell us it will be over $1,000 to send a large bag of food to the lodge in question, I politely decline. The cost is part of it, but they won't fly in for a week, and if they get waylaid for some reason then we'll have no food for the latter half of the journey, which is a risk I don't want to take.

We spend the morning of our first full day outfitting the canoe with a spray deck and knee pads, then do all of our shopping in the afternoon. By evening we're pretty much packed and ready to go. Ryan and I head out to the Black Knight pub for food and beer, then continue on to the Woodyard for a couple of nightcap beers. We are right buzzed by the time we hit the sack around midnight.

CHAPTER 25

With wide-open arms
Great Slave Lake welcomes us back
The summer begins

The next morning, we're a bit hungover and have breakfast with Eric at a nearby Old Town restaurant called the Dancing Moose, where he tells us some tales from an incredible journey he did with his sister across Mongolia with kite-powered land buggies. He tells it in his usual low-key way, making an otherworldly adventure seem like a walk in the park. Back at his house, we portage our canoe and all the gear to the dock at the landing at the bottom of the street. We pack it all up and everything fits beneath the gunwales and under the deck. Eric takes a few parting shots of us with my camera and, without any more fanfare, we canoe away from Yellowknife.

We paddle past the ubiquitous floating houses in Yellowknife Bay, the colourful, eclectic off-the-grid community that looks like a floating version of colourful downtown St. John's. In May they were locked in ice, but now they bob peacefully in a resort-like setting.

We cross over the bay to thé east side, pass the Indigenous village of Dettah, and melt into the islands I'd skied through only weeks before. We camp on a rocky islet, only 18 km from Yellowknife as we left in the late afternoon. It was good to get a few kilometres in and the trip underway...I always get a bit antsy in town, wanting to get the tedium of chores out of the way and get going, so it's good to be free of that. We have 50 days of food on board, fully self-contained for the foreseeable future. And man, is 50 days a lot of food. We'll get through about a week of it before the bludgeoning Pike's Portage, but it seems like an interminable amount of weight. At least we'll have a buffer.

Ryan rolls up a joint. "You want a hit?"

"No thanks, just a bit of whisky and an evening kretek are all I need."

"Suit yourself. It's here if you need it." He takes a deep drag of the joint and settles into himself like a couch. Ryan was a ski patroller at

Whistler for a dozen years, a place where it's stranger not to smoke weed than to smoke it. It appears he may be high for a good portion of the trip, as long as the weed lasts anyways. He's a chronic smoker, though, so I doubt it'll negatively affect him – it's just what he does.

I'll do the cooking – basically boiling water for freeze-dried food, oatmeal, and coffee/tea – while Ryan will set up our tent, sleeping bags, and sleeping pads. On this first night I show him how to peg out the tent with sticks and rocks when you're on a slab of granite. I like a nicely pegged out tent as it maximizes floor space and sheds rain and wind more efficiently. Ryan doesn't really seem to care, or just does a shoddy job to needle me, the only semblance of an authority figure around.

We settle down in the tent and snuggle into our sleeping bags. I'm starting a book called *Paddlenorth* by Jennifer Kingsley, about a group that paddled the Back River a few years back. I also borrowed a copy of George Orwell's *1984* from Eric, thinking I didn't have enough reading material for the full journey. It was the best choice I could see from Eric's eclectic library that seemed more like school reading and deep philosophy than something truly enjoyable to read on trip. He had two copies of *1984*, so I figured I'd try out the spare. I read it in high school but have completely forgotten it, so it will be fresh once more. I scribble in my journal, the first notes of the journey. After the late night of drinking and then breaking the inertia of Yellowknife to start the trip, I'm tired.

Ryan and I are set up head to toe in the tent and I glance down to see he's got his earphones on and he's watching his phone. Hmm, I've never seen this before on an expedition.

"What're you watching?" I ask.

He glances up. "An avalanche seminar."

Ryan is an avalanche technician, assessing and evaluating avalanche danger onsite for resource extraction companies that work in the mountains in winter. I nod, still more curious.

"Did you bring a book?"

"Nope, I've got a couple hundred YouTube videos downloaded on my phone...bunch of movies. That should get me through."

"Oh. My. God." I thought to myself. I was aghast. It dawned on me in that moment that his nightly ritual would be exactly this. I also realized that this was the first-ever expedition where I've partnered with...a millennial. That's right, one of *them* – those tech-loving, entitled kids born somewhere between the late '80s and early 2000s. That kid we'd seen screaming for his iPad in the airport was merely a younger version of Ryan. Heaven forbid if he ever lost his fucking phone, or if I happened to throw it in the cool deep waters of Great Slave Lake. But I wouldn't do that. That would be littering.

I came to escape superfluous technology, to read and write in the evenings to the sound of the wind and rushing water, and here beside me was a millennial gazing into his flickering phone. Not surprisingly, I discover he's also a fan and proponent of Kurzweil. He happily tells me that Wi-Fi will one day be available on every square inch of the planet – even here. To my horror, I was bearing witness to the fruition of the Singularity in the most remote corner of the North American continent.

I do use technology on trip too of course – but only practical items that serve the journey and allow me to navigate effectively. I use an inReach for weather updates and vital communication, a compass for direction, a map to see where we are, and a GPS to confirm position. None of these technologies distract or remove me from where I am though, from being present in the experience. Watching videos in the wild puts you far away from here, disengaging the brain from the experience.

CHAPTER 26

Canoe family
Tucked away from choppy wind
We stop and say Hi

For the next couple of days we manage to average over 55 km per day, getting in a good groove on the broad lake. On our first full day the water was calm and glassy but on day three a headwind has come up, though we still manage to make good time in spite of it. We pass by a family of five camped on shore. They're set up on a beach flanked by two rocky points. We stop to chat with the husband, who is on one of the points cleaning a big lake trout they'd caught.

"You're welcome to join us for dinner – we've got lots of fish here."

His wife sidles up beside him. They are in their 30s I'd guess, and their kids are between 5 and 10 years old. They're from Yellowknife and have a couple of weeks' holiday so paddled off from town and will go as far as they can in those two weeks. Wherever they end up, they'll call in a boat to bring them back to town.

She asks, "Where are you guys headed?"

"We're going to the Back River."

She instantly exclaims, "Oh…that'll be amazing!" Then she looks at her husband, who looks back at her. She goes on. "Maybe someday, but not with the kids yet. We used to do some bigger trips…before the kids." Her voice trails off, lost in another time of her life, when possibilities were limitless. She has a family now, and at least they're out here enjoying themselves. What she lacks in freedom, she gains in the engagement and instant community a family provides. It's not something I've ever wanted, but I can see the appeal.

We decline the dinner invitation as we've just started our trip and want to make a few more kilometres today – and also want to put a bit of a dent in our own supplies before Pike's Portage. The children have gathered around their parents, shyly looking at us, clinging to the legs of mom and dad.

"Have a great trip," I say, and we paddle off, leaving them to their dinner.

CHAPTER 27

Delayed by big wind
We paddled on 'til midnight
Whisky sip, then bed

On day four a heavy northeast wind kicks up and we battle along shore into the building blow. As we bump along, I notice a coast guard ship approaching. We're not wearing PFDs so I think they're coming to hassle us about that. Instead, they ask us if we're okay and warn us that the water is pretty big past McKinley Point.

We thank them and paddle on to McKinley, a rocky outcrop just before a long northeast-facing section of shoreline. I hop out and peer over the other side of the point, which is strewn with rolling whitecaps. We'll be exposed to the full brunt of this for 20 km until the protection of a narrows further up. I check the inReach for a weather report and it looks like the wind will die off in the afternoon. We could probably battle and bump along making scant kilometres but will make easy distance later on, so the choice is made. We decide to hang out in the protected lee side until that happens and then push on into the evening. Ryan rolls up a joint and I decide to partake. We'll be here for at least a few hours, it seems, so no big deal in getting a bit bent to pass the time and adjust my perspective for a while.

After having our puff, Ryan promptly falls asleep, face down on the rock. The sun is out and it's pleasant in our wind-sheltered nook. I wander around McKinley Point, exploring the rocky, rolling landscape interspersed with clusters of black spruce. Finding a nice mossy nook, I lie down and do some deep breathing exercises and then some headstands. It's something I do sometimes to centre myself and work on balance. The upside-down view, where the rock and water are sky and the sky is the airy land I'm standing on, is convincing enough with the THC floating around in my brain that I think for a moment I've crossed over to another dimension…if only for ten seconds.

I return to the nook where Ryan and the canoe lie, and read and write until about 4 p.m. The wind eases by 4:30 p.m. and we hit the water before 5, paddling until 8:30 p.m., when we stop on a small island to have a quick dinner. After dinner we paddle into the narrows before the East Arm of Great Slave Lake and pause for a break. We're in a cluster of islands just off of Narrow Island. The water is glassy calm now, with the flaming clouds of an eternal sunset reflected all around us. Ryan pulls out his yerba-maté gourd and we pass it back and forth, drinking the energizing tea to get us through our last push. It's a simple, cherished pause – breathing in the landscape and surroundings, content and in the moment, nothing existing for me but the here and now. When you're fighting wind, you're focused, strained…and then you get to sections like these, paddle this endless glass, and your whole body uncoils, transitioning from a tightened spring to a loose pile of rope. One cannot be appreciated without the other.

Just past midnight we pull into camp in the sheltered narrows before the lake opens up into the East Arm. It's July 2 and always bright, so time is somewhat meaningless anyways, though I like to keep to a consistent daily rhythm of travel. We set up the tent on a small pocket gravel beach, share a kretek and sip some whisky with a horde of mosquitoes, then fall promptly asleep at 1:18 a.m.

CHAPTER 28

On the evening of day five Ryan and I come through Taltheilei Narrows and into McLeod Bay in the East Arm of Great Slave Lake. We glide along the base of sheer, jagged yellow cliffs hundreds of feet high. The waters here are crystal clear and over 2,000 feet deep – making it the deepest lake in North America. We're nearing the tree line in this aptly named Land of Little Sticks, and the spruce forest spreads out in a sparse, stunted patchwork over the surrounding hills.

Our canoe hits the gravel beach with a *hissss* and we hop out, unloading our myriad packs in order to set up camp for the night. The lake is dead calm, and a brilliant double rainbow emerges from the vapour of a passing storm, lingering for our viewing pleasure as we erect our tent and tarp.

Perhaps more momentous than the rainbow is the burning of four illicit rolls of toilet paper in our fire that evening. I have never, ever used toilet paper on any of my wilderness journeys. If Indigenous Peoples of the past and wolves of the present can do without it, why bring along another superfluous piece of technology that takes up valuable cargo space? On the Baffin ski trip with Dave and Johnny I used shards of snow; in the summer I have more luxurious choices.

I recall the joy in Ryan's eyes when he held up the toilet paper while we packed up our food in Yellowknife a few days earlier.

"I got the toilet paper!" he beamed.

I stared at him, dumbfounded. "What's that for?"

"It's…toilet paper," he replied back, confused.

"I don't use toilet paper on trip – I use moss, sticks, and stones."

"Really?" he gasped, unable to comprehend this concept.

"Yes, really." I said, and then returned to packing.

Ryan remained undeterred, squirrelling away the bleached rolls of luxury into one of the packs. I would have to wear down his resolve. So for the past few days I've been needling him about the TP and introduced him to the wonders of sphagnum moss and smooth pebble stones as superior replacements. At our camp this evening he finally relents – partly due to my efforts, but maybe more so because the Pike's Portage is looming at the end of the lake. The prospect of carrying anything extra over the two-day slog around the cascades of the Lockhart River is perhaps all the motivation he needs. The curls of smoke from the fire carry away the last bits of particulate from the offending sheets, and I am content.

CHAPTER 29

Translucent water
Distant shimmering mirage
Butterfly Effect

On day six we cruise the north side of the Kahochella Peninsula, the sheer cliffs slowly backing away from the shoreline as the day goes on, revealing fans of rocks and trees that seemingly spill into Great Slave Lake. It's another virtually windless day and we groove along at a good clip. Yesterday we covered 65 km, and today will probably be similar. I love putting in good, solid days on a lake like this...you strike while the iron is hot, as at any time a big wind can come up and grind progress to a halt, like it did a couple of days ago. So besides a lunch stop, we keep eating up kilometres. It's hypnotic and meditative, the water is so clear here it feels like we're paddling in the sky. We can see a hundred feet straight down to the sandy, rocky bottom through a hue of glimmering jade.

The clarity reminds me of the eastern section of the Northwest Passage, where the water is similarly crystalline. On that occasion, I dove off our custom rowboat wearing a pair of goggles so I could immerse myself in its splendour – to feel for a moment that I'd been jettisoned from a space capsule and shot into icy, brisk, airless space. I held myself suspended, ten feet underwater, and peered across the endless sweep of the ocean floor, feeling small and insignificant in the midst of all that immense beauty before driving for the surface and hauling my naked self from the cold liquid.

Ryan and I paddle over a field of multicoloured boulders that reflect sunlight in the shallow waters. Our boat comes to a stop on shore and we have lunch on the pebble beach. The air is still and warm and I put together our lunches – meat and dried sausage with a bit of mustard and cayenne pepper on tortillas. While we lunch, a butterfly joins us and flits about for ten minutes, constantly circling and landing on us, completely unaware and unafraid. It keeps our attention and makes me reflect on the Butterfly Effect, where the single beat of a butterfly's wings ripples through time in a chain reaction that affects everything. Take this butterfly, for example...with it keeping our attention, we'll be leaving this beach a couple of minutes later than normal, which could synchronize later on with an incident on the trip – good or bad – that wouldn't have happened otherwise.

We chat most of the day, talking about family, skiing, and whatever else comes to mind as we pass the time of steady movement through the suspended space of the lake.

As we paddle through the afternoon, the vast horizon in front of us is framed with a shimmering mirage that we keep paddling toward but could, of course, never reach.

"If we ever pass through that mirage, I think it'll be a time portal that will transport us back a thousand years," I say.

Ryan smiles. "Yup, that could very well be." He'd smoked his usual joint at lunch, I was simply high on trip, but our minds were in the same transfixed state – bent and made pliable by Great Slave Lake.

CHAPTER 30

It begins to tear
Wilderness repairs the fray
The fabric of time

We pull into the beach at Fort Reliance, in front of an old RCMP detachment building, now abandoned and listing. Across the way are a couple of rotted log buildings that would have been part of the small settlement that George Back wintered at between expeditions down his now-namesake river.

The day is sunny and calm once more, by evening turning into one of those warm summer nights that wistful childhood memories are made of. With several hundred pounds of food and other assorted gear on board, we clip along efficiently, our 17-foot T-Formex Esquif Prospecteur carrying us inexorably to the end of the lake. The efficiency of the canoe is one of the reasons it's such a great way to travel long distances through the wilderness. We're packed with 50 days of supplies, but the seats support our body weight and all we have to do is set a nice steady rhythm throughout the day. I carry five paddles with me on an expedition. I bring two whitewater paddles – the Grey Owl C-1 – whose large, straight, reinforced blades can bang off rocks and efficiently manoeuvre the canoe down whitewater rivers all day long. They're my longest paddles at 58 inches and also double as the centre pole when setting up the rainfly. Because of their weight and shape, you wouldn't want to be paddling all day with one of these paddles, but they provide confidence and assurance in any moving water scenario. The other three paddles are Grey Owl Touring bent-shaft canoe paddles, which we use 95 per cent of the time on trip. The blade is bent at a 12-degree angle from the throat of the paddle (where the blade meets the lower end of the shaft). These paddles arose from the sport of marathon canoe racing – long-distance events on courses set through canoeing regions that require maximum speed and efficiency. The science behind it is that your paddle enters the water slightly more forward than a standard paddle and then doesn't pull water up at the end of every stroke like a straight blade does. The stroke is highly compact, with little wasted movement. I've used this type of paddle ever since I crossed Canada by canoe in a single season back in 1995. If you want to paddle effectively with the least amount of effort, you should use these. I'm amazed they haven't completely taken over the canoe paddle market, but people are stuck on tradition and like to work harder and less efficiently in a canoe, I guess. If anyone would paddle for five minutes with a bent-shaft paddle and then switch to a straight paddle right after, the difference in ease and efficiency would be remarkable. They'd never go back. It's one reason I cover terrain generally twice as fast as the average canoe tripper, and that Ryan and I have been covering over 60 km per day on this big, broad lake.

Though paddling a canoe is as gentle and low impact an activity as any, there's still always a break-in period for anyone on a long trip. I have years of muscle memory and know my stroke. I make subtle adjustments in technique, focusing on using my large stomach and back muscles, twisting at the waist and using my arms as fairly stationary attachments to the paddle. That way I don't stress the small ligaments and tendons of the elbow and shoulder, which can become aggravated with daily ten-hour paddling days and no planned rest days unless the wind tells us to stop.

On day three Ryan complained of a bit of shoulder soreness. I shared my technique tips with him and gave him a demonstration. He quickly went back to his own way, with too much shoulder movement. I can see everything from my perch at the back. I again suggest that he shift technique, but still no adjustment. I'm not surprised – most of my partners in the past have had tweaks they've had to deal with but ultimately revert to the poor technique that caused the problem. So now, on our seventh day, Ryan complains quite a bit about his shoulder, saying it's getting worse when he paddles on the left side. So we spend most of the day paddling on one side only to rest it. Ideally you switch sides every ten minutes or so to stay fresh and balanced. Luckily, we are about to get some paddling rest for his shoulder with Pike's Portage coming up.

A couple of days of portaging with minimal paddling will give him a break.

After poking around the ruins of the RCMP station, we paddle the last few kilometres to the start of Pike's. It's late evening when we hit the perfect crescent beach of golden sand. A wispy cloud stretches over the lake we've just paddled, reflecting a perfect airbrushed streak of orange, yellow, and red over the glassy water. We've done our biggest day so far, covering 70 km. We've also managed to paddle the 390 km from Yellowknife in only six and a half days.

Pike's is a historic route, comprised of eight portages connecting nine lakes – it was used for centuries by the Dene, Cree, and Inuit, then later by European explorers and trappers. It is named after Warburton Pike, an English explorer who travelled through the area in 1899 and wrote about his experiences on that journey.

There is no one around at the trailhead when we arrive, though curiously there is a perfectly good red Royalex canoe sitting on the beach. Evening is upon us so the owner isn't likely to show anytime soon. Maybe it was a person who'd been rescued and had to leave their canoe behind. After our usual dinner/kretek/whisky (and Ryan's personal doobie), we scuttle off to bed, eager to start the next phase of our journey in the morning.

CHAPTER 31

Seventy Years Young
They're paddling to Baker Lake
Inspirational

At 6:30 a.m. I'm scribbling in my journal, wrapping up the thoughts that I'd been too tired to finish the evening before, when I hear soft footsteps in the sand just outside the door, then a "Hello!"

I pop my head out and look into the face of a bearded man wearing the ubiquitous Tilley hat of recreational canoeists; he's looking down at me and grinning. He seems excited to see other canoeists. The abandoned canoe made sense now.

"Oh, I guess that's your canoe," I say.

"Yes, I was selected by our group to come and get it. We spent all day yesterday shuttling our gear to the first lake on Pike's. It's a brutal portage." He paused. "Oh, my name's Lorne."

"Hi Lorne, I'm Frank…and this is Ryan."

I've stepped out of the tent by this point, as has Ryan.

"We didn't quite get it done yesterday. The rest of the group are shuttling the last bit to the lake and I came back for the canoe. It's not even mine. The woman it belongs to said she could portage her own canoe. But she can't…so now I'm getting it."

Lorne didn't seem particularly happy with his lot. He was part of a group that ranged in age from their late 40s to him, the oldest at 64, but perhaps also the fittest. He's from Ontario, and he'd joined up with this group of six through a canoeing chat room. Obviously, an interesting social experiment. He further mentions there's also an older Australian couple on the trail who camped halfway along the first portage.

"We're on a 4 a.m. to 4 p.m. schedule…get up at four, pull into camp at four, y'know?" He went on. "How was the lake for you? Did you get caught by the ice too?"

"Ice? No…no ice at all. It was smooth sailing all the way pretty much. Took us under seven days to get here from Yellowknife."

"Seven? Really? It took us 16 days. Did you do the portage?" He tells me about the portage across Kahochella Peninsula that avoids the northern exposure on the East Arm of the lake. It makes no sense to me to portage 50 days' worth of food when you can canoe across the prettiest part of the lake.

He tells me they're doing the Hanbury-Thelon route to Baker Lake. I'd paddled part of that back in 2009. Lovely country. In return, I tell him we're going to the source of the Back River, then to the Kaleet, and up to Simpson Strait and across to Gjoa Haven.

"Wow...that's a long way." We pass a few more pleasantries before Lorne walks over to the canoe, rolls it onto his shoulders, and ambles slowly up the trail.

Ryan and I have a leisurely breakfast and then get down to packing up and prepping everything for the portage. Our burden includes a 115-litre pack, two 70-litre packs, a 60-litre barrel, a 35-litre pack, and the canoe. While we were in Yellowknife I'd fashioned a thick yoke pad out of cheap blue camping mat foam to take the edge off the canoe's weight on my shoulders. I strap our five paddles under the seats of the canoe – the two heavier whitewater paddles under the front seat and the three lighter, bent-shaft paddles under the rear seat so it is nice and balanced for portaging.

By 8:30 a.m. we're ready to go. It's a hot, still day with the sun already high overhead. The trees on the whole first section of the Pike's Portage – a five-kilometre uphill stretch with 600 feet of elevation gain to Harry Lake – had been completely burned off by a large fire three years earlier. The path is a dustbowl, with charred and fallen spruce as far as the eye can see, interspersed by the bright greens of the poplars emerging from the ashes.

When tackling a big portage you need to approach it tactically if you want to get it done in a mentally and physically tolerable manner. I figured this out back on my cross-Canada canoe trip of 1995 when we were faced with two 32-kilometre portages going up the Saint John River where the ice was still in above a couple of dams along the way. On the first portage, I tried to just generally grunt along as far and as fast as I could until I couldn't anymore, then take a rest. The portage was along a road and took nine hours to complete until we got past the ice. It was completely miserable as 18-wheelers raced by and their passing wind would catch the canoe, leaving me struggling to keep from getting knocked over. I switched tactics on the next portage a couple of days later, approaching it like an interval workout. Using a countdown timer on my digital watch, I would trot with the canoe for ten minutes, then rest for five. I did this continuously, mostly along an abandoned railway track, and completed that 32-kilometre portage in only 6.5 hours. I felt far more refreshed than after the first portage. I went very light on that trip as there were towns every few days and I could move along without doubling back.

Using a similar approach on the uphill portage to Harry Lake, I moved for 20 minutes at a time continuously with the canoe, and my rest would come via the jog back to get the next pack. I would then trot that pack up to where the canoe was, then run back for the final pack. Ryan took whatever time he needed to get to the shuttle point, needing to only do two loads instead of my three. In this way, we were able to complete the section up to Harry Lake in five hours.

At Harry Lake, we don't run into Lorne and his crew but do meet the two Australians he'd mentioned. We pass by some of the couple's left-behind bags (they shuttled too), and first catch sight of them when I pass a man carrying a yellow Esquif Prospecteur 17 outfitted with a North Water deck – the exact same set-up we have. He's moving slowly through a rocky rise in the burn. The trail is wide, so I move by him on the left without stopping. I'm midway through the last 20-minute pull, which I hope will get the canoe to the end of the portage before I have to double back twice more for the other two loads. As I pass, I get a look at the fellow – a tall, lanky, white-haired man with skin burnt red from the sun and wind.

"Excellent choice of canoe and spray deck! Keep it going – you're looking great!" I call out as I go by.

He flashes me a weak grin and returns to his labours. Further down the trail, I pass a small pile consisting of two red gas cans, a large beige waterproof duffle bag, and a smaller backpack. My calculations are luckily bang-on and the third "pull" with the canoe nets us Harry Lake. Kate, the female half of the couple, is sitting there resting with their things. She's wearing a wide-brimmed hat from which curly white hair spills around her bespectacled face.

"Hello, I'm Frank," I greet her.

"Oh, hello, I'm Kate…just taking a rest before I go back for the next bag…how far back is John?"

"He's getting here."

"Good…he's knackered. It took us all day yesterday to get halfway over this portage, and we hope to get it done today. How about you?"

We started a few hours ago…we'll see where we end up by around 7 – that's when we usually stop. I'll see you on the trail – got to go back for another load."

With that, I run back to get the next bag. Ryan isn't far behind. "Almost there!" I say as we pass.

He smiles nonchalantly. "Sounds good." He's enjoying the pleasant THC-brightened hike.

I next come upon John sitting and resting by his canoe and this time I stop to chat. He apparently purchased the canoe based on a review I did of it in a paddling magazine the year before.

"What's your plan for the trip?"

"Well…" he pauses and wipes his brow, "we started in Yellowknife and planned on doing the whole Back River, but we got stuck behind a big section of ice in the narrows before the East Arm for nine days. It pushed us so far off of our schedule we're now doing the Hanbury-Thelon route instead."

"You have the maps for both?"

"Oh yeah, we came prepared with a contingency plan."

"When did you start?"

"June 13."

Wow, I thought. They began a full 16 days before us and we'd caught them only a week after we started. This proves the point that the very end of June or early July is the time to set off from Yellowknife on this sort of trip, no earlier. The key to doing long trips in the Arctic successfully is to start a bit later so you don't run into ice, but then move quickly and efficiently enough that you beat out the big north winds that develop later in August.

Anyways, John's a great guy, possessed of the self-deprecating wit and a great energy typical of Australians…and he's 70 years old! I can only hope to still be tripping at this level if I ever reach that age. But then, I thought the same thing about canoe-tripping into my forties, and here I am going on 48 and still feeling good with a canoe on my head and paddle in my hand. Once a tripper, always a tripper.

John groans, "Man, this is a tough portage. I did the Chipman Portage in northern Manitoba a few years ago, but it was nothing compared to this. This just keeps going uphill."

I've been to similar areas and done similar trips as he and Kate. They paddled from La Ronge, Saskatchewan, to Baker Lake in two seasons a few years earlier. I'd also done a trip from La Ronge to Baker Lake in 2016 in 44 days, though via a different route. I have much more in common with these older folks than I do most people my own age or younger.

"I'll see you on the trail – still have two loads to do."

"Yes, you will – see you shortly."

I trot off, eventually passing their pile of goods. I continue on for another five minutes and get to one of my packs, hoist it up, and start back. As I approach their pile of things, I think of them, of how kind they are, and how tired they are. I'm sure they'd appreciate a hand, so I grab both of the Jerry cans, one in each hand, and bring them through. On the way, I see Kate, who'd gotten to their pile but only grabbed the small pack. She's moving slowly uphill, using a walking stick in one hand. In that moment I thought of my 77-year-old mother and couldn't imagine her taking on a trip like this. I suddenly feel protective, like I need to help these people in whatever way I can.

"Keep going Kate, you're doing great!"

She sees the gas cans in my hands and exclaims, "Oh, you saint! Thanks for grabbing those!"

"No problem at all. I had two free hands anyways," I reply. "See you shortly!"

I pass by John one more time. He's almost there with the canoe.

"Oh man, you grabbed the gas. Thanks, mate!"

I plop the gas by their bags, set by a flat spot they intend to camp at that night about 50 feet from Harry Lake, then continue with our bag to the end of the lake.

One more trip. I run by John, who's just about at their drop spot with the canoe. A bit further, I trot by Ryan, bringing in his last pack, and by Kate, then by their remaining beige duffel, and finally to our pack stash. I hoist the heavy 70-litre pack onto my back and start speed walking back. When I get to Kate and John's big duffel, I hoist it over my head and pop it on top of my 70-litre pack.

Sloshing through swamp and fire-scarred rock, I come over the final rise that gradually levels off to the lake. Kate and John are sitting and resting, having a bite to eat. I walk up to them and lay the duffel at their feet. John is ecstatic.

"Mate! I was just trying to sum up the energy to go grab that. Unbelievable – thank you."

"You're a life saver, thank you!" Kate adds.

I grin. "No problem…and now your portage is done."

"That's great…I think we're going to camp here. We'll need to rest up after that one."

I feel so good that I could help them out, and they were so appreciative I think I got a lot more out of helping them than they did. It felt like good trip karma. After a little more banter I head down to where Ryan is smoking his post-portage joint. We pack the boat up and paddle across Harry Lake to an island at the far end that has a nice bug-dampening breeze and full sun exposure. Once there, we strip off our sweat-soaked clothes and plunge naked into the cool waters. I feel like my whole body sparkles once I emerge, refreshed and re-energized to the core. Planting my butt on the warm stone, I air-dry and enjoy our last ration of Hungarian salami and cheese on a tortilla before we move onto peanut butter and honey for the remainder of the journey.

At the end of Harry Lake, we have a 300-metre portage to French Lake. Ryan, who's seen me hup the canoe over the five kilometres of the first portage, insists he be allowed to carry the canoe this time. Carrying a canoe, though, is an art. First, you have to smoothly pick it up and pop it on your shoulders. Once on, you have to become one with the canoe. Like on the water, the canoe is merely an extension of you when being portaged. You have to manoeuvre it over rough, uneven terrain, allowing yourself to flow naturally over any obstacle you may come into contact with. Our Prospecteur 17 canoe is definitely the toughest, most capable tripping canoe out there. It is amazingly stable, fast, and nimble – able to negotiate the roughest lakes, the most technical whitewater, and driest boulder fields. However, it is not light. I always choose durability and performance above weight. Unloaded, it is 76 pounds, but once I strap in the paddles it's over 90 pounds.

Ryan has a touch of skier snobbishness, as if any other outdoor activity is exceedingly simple compared to what you'd face on an extended mountain ski traverse. When he asks to portage the canoe, I say, "Sure… let me just give you a quick technique lesson on flipping it up onto your head." I prop the belly of the canoe onto the top of my thighs with my hands on the yoke. In one action I snap it onto my head before I roll it down and rest it on the ground again. Ryan then tries it. He rolls it onto his thighs but when he tries to snap it onto his head, he only gets halfway before teetering awkwardly in the transition as he strains to get it up from that position. I grab it and stabilize it until he's able to get under it.

"You got it?" I ask.

"Yeah, I'm good."

He then proceeds to walk across the marshy, lumpy trail. I can see him struggling, the canoe tipping back and forth like a teeter-totter, with Ryan's head the pivot point. He weaves from side to side, cursing, and his whole body quivering with effort. About halfway through the 300-metre portage he drops the canoe on the grass and stands huffing with his hands on his hips. I walk up to him with the big pack.

"I can't believe you carried this thing over that first portage. It's bloody hard...I don't think I can do this canoe-carrying thing."

"It's just like any sport – you have to put in the time, become one with it. Why don't we trade? You take this pack; I'll grab the canoe." With that, we swap and I snap the canoe over my head while Ryan follows along with the pack. Like with the toilet paper, a teaching moment for sure. I suspect there will be many more of these to come.

We do one more portage into Acres Lake and set up on a nice point on an island. The thunderheads have been building all afternoon but hold off until we've set up the tent, eaten our meals, and finished with a *saveur* (my name for the evening whisky sip and smoke). We're hit by a deluge of thunder, lightning, and rain that rolls over us like B52s carpet-bombing the Hồ Chí Minh Trail. We scurry into the tent and lie in our sleeping bags, listening to the booming echo of the thunder, the splatter of heavy rain on the tent fly, and the wind rippling its fabric as the tent lights up with every flash.

The storm has almost passed, with just a few stray droplets still hitting the tent. I'm dozy but finish my haiku about John and Kate. Ryan is already fast asleep. We've covered a total of 18 km today, which is decent considering the big portage at the start. If we duplicate the distance tomorrow, we'll be close to getting off of Pike's Portage.

CHAPTER 32

The Boreal Wanes
A vast landscape opens up
Behold the Barrens

The next morning, at the end of Burr Lake, we see a cluster of canoes at the beginning of the portage to Found Lake. It turns out to be Lorne's crew. As I run back and forth on the portage, I get to meet everyone in the group.

"It's just great to be out here," Lorne glows, with his manicured dark beard, brimmed cap, and all-round great attitude.

I also chat with Murray, the group leader. He's done the trip to Baker Lake via the Thelon twice before. I'd actually spoken with him and his wife Vicky at the Wilderness and Canoeing Symposium where I met Eric McNair-Landry. They live north of Temagami and have constructed an epic 130-km hiking trail through the region. When Murray sees me running along, he smiles and says, "I remember I used to run this portage...I did the first five-kilometre section in four and a half hours years ago." Suddenly I feel competitive. It took us five hours. Too damn much stuff...either that or Murray's just a plain old hard-ass. He does seem to possess a quiet, grounded confidence – a man out here simply to be out here. He grins and then throws us a compliment. "You guys are moving pretty fast...Lorne said it only took you a week to get to Pike's."

"Well, conditions were great for us on the lake; we got lucky," I reply self-deprecatingly. He smiles as I continue, "I guess this trail isn't going to portage itself...see you on the double-back." With that, I trot off.

The other three members of the group are all women: Marilyn, Sandy, and Randy. Randy was the woman who couldn't portage her own canoe. Perhaps Lorne was sweet on her, who knows. "Romance on the Barrens" would be a great title for a Louis L'Amour novel.

I'm glad I'm not on their trip though – it would truly drive me nuts. I can't stand the drama and inefficiency of such a large group. They had planned for a 50-day trip and it seems they'll need every single one of those days to finish. Also, Murray is doing this trip for a third time. Why? There are so many other worthy trips to do out there. I understand he probably had an awesome journey the first time and wants to recapture the magic; or perhaps there's comfort in the known. However, you have enough known where you live day-to-day and all the familiar comfort you need. For me at least, these journeys are about stepping away from that comfort, seeing the new and the fresh every day. The old saying "life begins outside your comfort zone" rings true for a reason. To each their own though...even though the Thelon is as busy a route as there is in the Arctic, it still is relatively rarely travelled. It also allows you to experience the North via a very straightforward, technically simple route.

We move past Murray's group, leaving them to the portage, while we paddle out to a small island for lunch. Ryan tries to carry the canoe again on the next portage, and again only gets halfway before dropping it. That will be the last go-round between him and the canoe, I suspect, but good on him for trying.

We keep flowing through the day, doing numerous portages between small lakes until we reach the end of the final lake before Artillery Lake. Once at Artillery, we will be free of Pike's. We are also now clear of the boreal forest. The little sticks of black spruce have been replaced by broad, rolling plains of rock, dwarf birch, and dwarf willow. From our high perch above Artillery our view seems to stretch on forever. We can also see dark clouds building and coming toward us from the north – a sure sign of a cold, hard system coming right for us.

I lay the canoe on its side, back to the incoming wind, and drape the fly taut over top of it with a paddle providing a peak in the middle, while small boulders hold the corner lines. I prop my PFD against a boulder I've selected that fits the lower curve of my back. Our packs rest in the canoe and act as comfortable backrests. It's a great little system I devised for cool windy days...but doesn't work as well on warmer days as it will give the bugs refuge too. As we eat our freeze-dried Pad Thai dinners, a few drops hit the fly but there is no deluge, and the temperature only drops a bit. The mosquitoes appreciate the wind block and join us for dinner. Ryan bats and swats at them, while I let them be. They can have their pound of flesh today, for tomorrow I'm sure they'll be gone.

CHAPTER 33

The end of the grind
Back to the big lake country
Pike's Portage is done

I awaken at 6 a.m. to a steady rain pattering on the tent. As per usual, I pack away my sleeping bag and Therm-A-Rest while Ryan sleeps. I like to be out of the tent and get the stove going for coffee and oatmeal before my partner rouses. It's a time I can write in my journal or read to those first few sips of coffee.

The air has a damp chill to it, driven by a brisk northwest wind. There are no mosquitoes at all as the cool temperature has quelled their bloodlust and sent them hiding in the nooks and crannies of the tundra. I light our WhisperLite stove and the flame licks the priming bowl for a few seconds until it's ready. I turn up the gas, and it hisses to life. Sitting inches away from the stove, with a pot of water set to boil, I feel as warm and cozy as if I'm by a roaring fire. I pop in four tablespoons of coffee in the water, cover it, and settle into my book.

Ryan appears 15 minutes later and tucks under the tarp with me. He shivers in his black, delaminating cycling jacket. The jacket has no hood, and he wears only a thin merino wool base layer that is as much hole as fabric. He has a pair of wind pants on, but no rain pants. He sits for a minute, staring at the stove. Turning to me, with a quizzical look on his face, he says, "Man, it's pretty cold and wet today, isn't it?"

"Yup, it's the Arctic," I confirm.

He looks at me, cozied up in my layers, my burly rain jacket, and my rain pants.

"I don't have a rain hood…or rain pants," he says with concern.

I stare at him blankly for a second. We've had lovely weather up to this point and I didn't really notice his inadequate clothing. I figured with his extensive mountaineering experience he'd be dialled in gear-wise. I even offered to hook him up with new apparel before the journey began and he said, "No, I've got everything I need."

"Why don't you have that stuff? What about all your shell layers for skiing?"

"I didn't want to wear them out on a paddling trip."

Great, I think. *He brought his $1,000 iPhone and yet isn't prepared for Arctic weather. Unless that device can magically cover his body in a waterproof layer, he brought the wrong piece of technology with him.*

"Well, the tundra is like being on a horizontal mountaintop. You have to expect mountain weather out here – I told you that."

He shrugs his shoulders, nonplussed. "Guess I'll have to make myself a rain hood."

He proceeds to dig a large heavy-duty freezer bag from one of the packs and cut open one side of it, then ties in a piece of shock cord so it will stay on his head in the wind. It looks ridiculous, like he's a grandma protecting her blue rinse perm from the rain. I laugh as Ryan poses proudly with his new garb. I doubt it will work very well, but I appreciate his innovativeness.

As we start getting ready to pack up, we check the inReach for weather and it's calling for a strong northwest wind all day long. Looking down at the lake a few hundred metres below us, we see some light whitecaps showing. Artillery Lake itself is 80 km long, its west shore relatively straight with only a couple of small bays. I figure that even with a strong wind we can work it up that shore with a bit of a lee.

"Should we maybe leave the tent and fly up so we have a place to hang out in case it's too windy for us to move?" Ryan suggests.

"No, man, let's take it all down and pack up as per usual. We can move in this."

Ryan trusts the technology of the forecast so much he doesn't even want to break camp. A forecast is merely one part of the movement equation. It doesn't take into account the way the geography of this lake lines up favourably for us, and doesn't take into account experience, craftiness, skill, and determination. These assets will overcome a stiff headwind in most cases.

Over the years I've learned that there aren't too many conditions that can stop a canoe. I've only once had to lose a full day to the wind in well over a 1,000 days of canoe-tripping, and that was because we were stuck at the bottom of a 15-km-long section of Kasba Lake in Nunavut in 2016 by a northwest wind that hammered the fully exposed east side of the lake we were on. The wind at the time was rolling right across the 20-km-wide lake and the full fetch of it was hitting the coast we had to travel along. Today we have geography in our favour.

Ryan's primary paddling experience is as a packrafter. The tiny little rafts can't move effectively against much more than a light breeze, so his perspective on what can and can't be paddled is seen from the view of a much different craft. It would be like me standing at the top of a 50-degree couloir and thinking, *There's no fucking way I'm going to ski down this,* while Ryan would daintily drop into it like he was going for a walk in the park. It's all about perspective gained from experience.

The portage is all downhill, with a steep uphill double-back. We get everything down to a beach landing and survey the lake. The steep sides in this initial narrow section of the lake provide a great lee so the first few kilometres will be well protected. We load up and paddle on, getting into a nice groove, and when we enter the broad section of Artillery, we stick close to shore. As long as we stay within 20 metres or so, we should move along nicely and avoid the brunt of the wind. If we drift out further than that it will try to grab us and blow us out to the exposed middle. Our progress is steady and we fall into a comfortable rhythm. The only moment of concern from Ryan is when we have to do a two-km dash across a bay.

"Ready, Ryan, we have to dig in here to get back to the lee."

"I don't know man…I don't think we can move in this wind."

I laugh. "Trust me, this won't be a problem."

And sure enough, we easily outgun the wind and make it back to the straight-running shore on the other side. Ryan is impressed, having learned we have more capability than he thought we did.

"See, Ryan, no problem."

"Yeah, a packraft could never have done that."

A breakthrough moment. His "packraft mind" will become a "canoe mind" by the end of all this. The capability of two people in synchronicity with their canoe is limitless, proven out by millennia of use.

A third of the way up the lake we spot a cabin at the base of a long esker that juts and curves out from shore. We land on the sandy, pebbly shore, pull the canoe up, and amble over to the structure. The plywood building has a sign outside the door that reads "Roger's Rat Cabin." The door itself has been busted clean open by a bear, who'd gone in and torn the place apart. It probably happened not too long ago as it didn't seem like snow or rain had penetrated to turn the place into a mildewy soup like I've seen in other cabins. Roger was in for a surprise whenever he decided to come out here again. There are a bunch of fuel barrels lined up around the corner so he's bound to come in by plane sometime – probably from Łutselk'e or thereabouts.

Inside the cabin, there is some treasure to be had. Firstly, there are a couple of four-litre tins of white gas, so we top up the litre we'd used to this point, which gives us a nice measure of comfort as far as fuel to use for cooking goes. Also, there's a copy of *The Orenda* by Joseph Boyden among a pile of books in the corner. I wasn't too jazzed on *1984* – I'd read it in high school, and like my journeys I'm not into repeating myself. I don't mean to disparage classics, but it was a bit of a dated read. I need adventure in my reading like I need adventure on my journeys. Repeating oneself in anything is anathema to adventure. So I dug up *1984*, whispered apologies to Eric, and traded it in for Roger's copy of *The Orenda*. It looked like it was well worn so I figured he'd read it and wouldn't mind a nice fresh copy of *1984* to read when he next got here. A barren ground book swap. *The Orenda* was much more appealing as I'd read Boyden's *Three Day Road* and loved it. This one detailed the bloody rivalry between the Iroquois and Huron First Nations at the time when Europeans first began to encroach upon their lands. It seemed a much more appropriate trip book than Orwell's dystopian masterpiece.

CHAPTER 34

Long Hair in the Breeze
Grazing the grass as they please
Twenty Musk Oxen

The next day, we cruise in a nice, light southwest wind along the shore and then face a five-km crossing over the top of the lake to get into the Lockhart River. With 80 km of fetch barrelling up that side we have to negotiate big breaking rollers coming at us sideways. They've built to their maximum size and velocity at our crossing point. We take them one wave at a time, hitting them at 45-degree angles, up and over, again and again until we finally frogger our way over and into the calm waters of the Lockhart River. En route, we watch a tern viciously attacking a duck, forcing it to repeatedly dive. Eventually, the duck never resurfaces and the tern flies away. Nature can be cruel, but ducks are not the smartest creatures, and people eat them, so it's just the way of things.

The Lockhart looks more like a lake initially, spread broadly and thinly over sand with a deep hidden channel that's tricky to follow on its upstream course. We come upon a cluster of faded white structures surrounded by an electric fence that either no longer works or just isn't hooked up. I imagine it's there to keep barren ground grizzlies from going in and ransacking the place like they did at the Rat Cabin. Inside the perimeter, the four buildings are in various states of disrepair and disuse. Judging by the hundred or so caribou antlers stacked into eight-foot-high piles and bleached out by the sun, this was once a caribou hunting camp. Caribou rarely if ever migrate this way anymore.

When I spoke with Chief Steve Nitah of the Łutsël K'é Dene First Nation back in 2009 about the caribou, he thought that three diamond mines to the north might have changed their migration patterns and pushed them far to the east. Others say climate change has thrown off the synchronized calving that happens with the coming of the spring. Standing here between two giant stacks of caribou antlers and knowing that First Nations and Inuit hunt caribou without limits (males, females, pregnant females) with the aid of high-powered rifles, snowmobiles, motorboats, and ATVs, it seems overhunting is part of the problem, if not the main reason, for their decline.

I understand the argument about traditional hunting rights and subsistence living as it relates to their culture, but I'm just doing the math. More people, plus highly efficient and excessive hunting, equals less caribou. A simple equation. If people want more caribou around, they have to stop slaughtering them beyond their needs. It's a traditional, healthy food source for the folks up here, but better to have less of that food than have absolutely none in a few years' time. Whether First Nations or otherwise, people are ultimately just people and act on instinct. We think in the present, about what we want right now. If we don't get it immediately, someone else will. It's an impulse hardwired into our DNA that worked when we were hunter-gatherers but doesn't work in the modern world where wild animals are an extremely finite resource.

A few minutes after we head away from the camp, dark lumps among the surrounding sandy, grassy hills catch my eye. Looking closer, I see it's a herd of 20 musk oxen. They gaze at us blankly through their Barbie-doll-hair horns as we paddle by. It's exciting to see our first large mammals of the journey…we'd seen the hoof prints of these beasts on the Pike's Portage but no actual visuals until now.

I tell Ryan, "I'm going to step out and get some shots."

We pull over and I hop out of the canoe. The herd continues to stare as I creep up. They allow me to get within about 40 metres of them before they decide to move away over the hilltop. A large bull stands his ground for a minute longer until he too reluctantly wanders after his group of ladies.

The Lockhart eventually narrows and we have to portage about 400 metres around a big set of rapids with a ledge. There's a rough trail through a thicket of thigh-high, tough dwarf birches that takes us to an eddy above the rapid. We load up and from there paddle a small lake to the next rapid, which we're able to line up to the next lake. We paddle the couple of kilometres to the end of it, where we set up camp in sight of the next rapid, which we'll negotiate tomorrow morning.

I'm happy with the day – we've cleared Artillery Lake and made it up a-ways on the Lockhart. As we set up camp and get water boiling for dinner, I notice we're short one of our bent-shaft paddles. I dig around, and look everywhere, but nothing. There's a reason I carry a spare, but to be down to a single paddle each so early in our journey is unacceptable to me. I look back and think that we must have dropped it or left it somewhere along that portage.

"Ryan, we have to go back for it. Now."

Ryan casually looks up at me, smoke from his joint curling by his face.

"Why don't we just go in the morning...if it's there, it'll still be there."

"No, man, it's going to bug me all night. I need to resolve it now. It may have dropped in the water or something and will be long gone by morning. Let's finish eating dinner and make sure we're all set up in the tent. We can do a dash back to the portage. It'll be quick with an unloaded boat."

He rolls his eyes, takes another drag, and says, "Sure, if that's what you want."

We finish off dinner and hop in the canoe. There's not a puff of wind in the air and the lake is pure glass as our unloaded canoe lightly skims over the water. The ever-circling sun is dipping toward the western horizon through a thin haze of cloud, the life-giving orb brushed with gold and red. We easily run the first light rapid that we lined earlier and break across the next small lake to the portage at the top of the big rapid. When we hit shore, I scan around in the eddy and on the edge of the shoreline there. Nothing.

"I'm going to run down the portage trail to see if we dropped it along the way."

Without waiting for a reply, I bolt down the trail with dwarf birch lashing at my shins. My eyes are focused, scanning back and forth as I run, looking for the distinct golden colour of the ash and cherry wood paddle, which should stand out like a beacon in this green and brown world.

Nothing, nothing, nothing. Not a sign of it. I get down to the start of the portage and scan the shoreline there. My hope starts to fade as there's no sign of the paddle anywhere. I fear it may have slipped into the water at the top of the rapid while we were loading up from the portage and then washed down to the big eddy at the bottom here, but there's no sign of it bobbing in the water anywhere. It could have drifted across the lake already. I walk to the river's edge at the bottom of the rapid and look across the whitewater flume to the eddy on the other side of the river. My eye catches something out of place. The distinct angle of the shaft where it bends into the blade is bobbing around in the still water there, just feet from shore. I look again, just to be sure. Yes! There it is, there is no doubt.

I sprint back up the portage trail where Ryan is waiting in the canoe. "I found it! It's at the bottom of the rapid, in the eddy on the other side. Let's paddle across and I'll bushwhack down and grab it."

We paddle along the top of the torrent and pull in. The ritual evening mosquito horde descends as I thrash through knee-high birch and head-high willows and, sure enough, there it is still bobbing in the eddy. I wade in knee-deep and grab it. Clutching my prize and accompanied by the whining horde, I make my way back to Ryan.

We paddle hard in an attempt to lose the mosquitoes but many of them deftly tuck into the lee inside the canoe, looking for an opening in our clothes to exploit. We both have our bug jackets on, our faces half-blackened by the accompanying scourge. Swiftly lining back up the light rapid, we hop in once more for the final couple of kilometres to camp. I'm relieved and buoyed by the successful mission. We roll into the tent at 11:15 p.m., which is awesome, as this paddle boondoggle hasn't delayed us at all. We'd be right back on track for tomorrow.

CHAPTER 35

A lone Austrian
Subsisting on fish and grit
On a Vision Quest

The next morning we line the final rapid of the Lockhart River and enter the broad expanse of Ptarmigan Lake. The wind is blowing steadily at our backs, giving us a straight push north up the lake. Wind is the be all and end all of showstoppers or goers in the Arctic. If a big bad North kicks in and you're in the wrong spot, you can be pinned for days. The bottom of Ptarmigan Lake is not a spot you want to be in when facing this bitterly cold spectre. Today though, it's irrelevant. The surrounding landscape of low, bare hills provides no resistance to the warm southerly breeze, giving it a broad berth to push us along. It's easy living in this sort of weather. We ride the beautiful tailwind – an unobstructed nudge urging us onward through a sparkling, sun-splashed basin.

Your eyes become accustomed to the static, treeless landscape, and any movement or feature out of place is noticeable. We're following the eastern shore of the lake, and up ahead a flapping green material draws my attention. As we approach, I see that the flapping is from a single-pole A-frame shelter tent. Just up from it, a man is taking down his sleeping tent, focused on his work and unaware of us. The wind quickly brings us alongside his camp and we pull in just below him.

I step onto the beach and call out, "Hello!"

He turns, sees us, and smiles – then scurries down to greet us.

His name is Bernie Kohl, an Austrian solo canoeist who began his journey ten days before us in Łutselk'e, about three-quarters of the way between Yellowknife and the start of the Pike's Portage. He was paddling a folding canoe. These canoes have become popular over the years as the cost for air transport of hard-shell canoes like ours has become exorbitant. With a folding canoe you simply break down the aluminum frame, roll up the vinyl skin, and put it into a bag. That way you can transport it via planes, trains, and automobiles quite efficiently. They're also relatively light.

I own one and used it to go to Europe and canoe across Norway, Sweden, and Finland back in 2004. The big disadvantage is that they're quite delicate. It's fine to take one through deep water, but god forbid you hit a rock in a rapid or pull it fully loaded over rough terrain. They also don't manoeuvre as nimbly as a hard-shell boat. I prefer something that can take massive amounts of abuse and won't leave you stranded in the Arctic. You have to tread lightly with these boats, and the Arctic is a hard taskmaster on such equipment. But Bernie is solo and moving slowly and carefully. He flew with his canoe by plane from Yellowknife in order to skip most of the big lake. We compare notes about our trips and find out he's behind schedule. Bernie did a two-km portage north of Łutselk›e to get to the East Arm of Great Slave Lake but was trapped in Shelter Bay by lingering ice for five days, which melted away by the time we passed that section. His goal, like ours, is to continue to the Back River and paddle it to the Arctic Ocean.

Bernie has some alternate plans in mind depending on how his trip goes, and his five-day delay, like with John and Kate, may reroute him in another direction.

"I might go north to Paulatuk via the Western River if I get too far behind, but I will try for the Back."

Bernie has also sent food ahead to Aylmer Lake Lodge instead of having to carry it over the Pike's Portage. We'd considered doing that but balked at the price and the uncertainty of our food getting there in time. With Pike's done for us, I was happy we'd decided to stay self-contained. Besides, a detour to the lodge to pick up food would kill half a day for sure, and we were grooving along nicely now.

With this lovely following wind, I ask Bernie why he isn't taking advantage of the conditions to claw back some of his lost distance.

In his strong German accent, he sighs. "I have to de-bone ze fish."

"Excuse me?" I reply.

"I'm getting all of my protein from fish. I caught a bunch yesterday on ze Lockhart River," he points to the rapid we lined up just a half-hour earlier, "but have to debone them all before jarring them." Bernie lifts the top from a big metal pot to reveal a pile of whole trout, already boiled and salted, sitting in brine. "Once I debone them, I put them in jars. I can eat them like this for a week," and again he emphasizes, "I need ze protein."

Ryan and I shoot each other amused glances.

"Would you like to watch me debone ze fish?" Bernie asks hopefully.

I look down at the pot of fish, then feel the beckoning breeze on my cheek. "No thanks, Bernie. We're going to keep on paddling. Good luck."

On one hand, I see Bernie is living a completely different kind of Singularity than that proposed by Ray Kurzweil. He is literally single – a lone person depending largely on the bounty of nature, not technology, to sustain himself. It's very pure in its intention, but perhaps not practical if you actually want to finish the route you set out to do.

I give Bernie a parting hug, and Ryan snaps a shot of us on the shore, standing arm-in-arm by his pot of fish. We promise to look each other up post-trip to see how things went. Ryan and I peel our canoe into the wind and are whisked away. I turn to give Bernie a last wave but see that he's already bent to his fish-cleaning chore. I could never do that – never just sit and let easy travel conditions pass me by – but perhaps with Bernie it's more about just simply being out here, not worrying too much about where he ends up.

I'm very mission-driven by contrast and am addicted to moving. The potential of the north wind holding us up, of us digging deep into our food supply as we wait, drives me on. I look for openings, for tailwinds like this, to give us a buffer. I love to put in ten-hour days, every day, eating up as much ground as possible through an ever-changing environment, revelling in the meditative flow of that movement. The north wind will inevitably slow us down at some point so you have to make hay while the sun shines, as the saying goes. Upstream, downstream, portages, big lakes…it's a chess match with the elements that I find enduring pleasure in.

A few months later Bernie reaches out to me. It turns out he eventually got stuck partway along his route due to sustained north winds and called in a plane to pick him up. I suspect he spent too much time deboning fish, and not enough time paddling – and I'm sure it didn't bother him a bit.

We rapidly cover the breadth of Ptarmigan and have lunch at the small, unnamed lake that connects Ptarmigan to Clinton-Colden Lake. It's warm on the rock, with a light balmy breeze to keep the bugs down. I dive into the crystal clear, ice-cold water and give myself a good scrub-down, then air-dry. It really feels like summer today.

We break from the small lake into expansive Clinton-Colden and begin to make our way into it. We pretty quickly run into a broad pan of broken ice, at least a hundred metres across, that we skirt around and then keep moving north. We cut toward the middle of the lake, eventually settling on a small island where we can camp. If ice drifts in from somewhere and blocks us, I figure we can escape from any side of the island.

As we set up camp in the evening, ice is suddenly on my mind. It occurs to me that we may be moving too fast for the ice to clear in time before us. We have one more big lake to cross – Aylmer Lake – once we're done with this one. I'm not too worried about Aylmer but think of the big lakes far to the northeast in the middle of the Back, called the Garry Lakes. In the book I'm reading now, those lakes were still frozen for the group that travelled there at a similar time of year. I'm not too keen on slowly dragging our canoe across the ice. It's doable, but not ideal.

More so even than the Garry Lakes, I'm thinking about ice up in the Northwest Passage. My planned route has us leaving the Back at the Garry Lakes and working our way due north to the Kaleet River, a small system that would allow us to follow a sheltered line of lakes and rivers to a point within 16 km of King William Island. From there we would wait for an ideal weather window and cross over to the island and then follow the shore to Gjoa Haven.

I'd planned this obscure line to avoid any kind of supplemental boat or plane pick-up. But now I was unsure what the ice situation up there was. I needed to find out. If it were still locked up, we'd have to continue down the Back right to its end and figure out a pick-up in Chantrey Inlet. I remember asking John how he and Kate planned to get out from Chantrey before they were forced to take their alternate route down the Thelon, and he said, "Oh, there are camps the Inuit have at the mouth. We're just going to find someone there and arrange a boat or plane ride out." He had seemed so casual about this part of their plan, like it was a sure thing, so I put that in my mental quiver of possibilities. In the evening I text Shannon on the inReach to have her inquire about ice conditions around Gjoa Haven, which could sway our plans away from the Kaleet and toward Chantrey.

CHAPTER 36

Low sun in the sky
Riding rollers on floe edge
Crystal Sharp Moment

Overnight, a light wind pressed pans of ice into the south end of the island we were camped on. It isn't too hard to get out as we simply push through for about 50 feet until we're clear. The pans are about a foot thick, sharp and jagged, and the few we bump through put some small gouges in the bow of the canoe. Once away from the island, we have no problem getting across the southern end of Clinton-Colden Lake. We can see a thin line of ice to the north so it seems the wind has pushed it all to that end of the lake. It's nice and warm when we get to the narrows before Aylmer Lake, so we have another refreshing swim at lunch. After lunch, the wind turns into our faces and we have to buck through the shallow channel against steep chop before breaking onto Aylmer, where there's quite a bit of ice floating about. We want to work around the north end of the lake in order to access the final arm that leads to the short Back River access portage.

The sky darkens as towering, black billowing clouds blow in. The wind ramps up quickly and large pans of ice float by as if propelled by silent motors. A hard wind line accompanied by a wall of rain comes across the lake toward us. In seconds it's on us and we're brought to a drenched standstill in an instant. Lightning flashes and thunder cracks. We pull over to the side and hunker down, snuggling into the tunnels of our spray deck as the deluge pounds us, like a firehose had opened up in the sky. In five minutes it's over. The roiling water returns to glass almost instantly as the slate wall of rain, cloud, and wind passes by and continues east across Clinton-Colden. We move through a thicket of islands, with large pans of ice everywhere. The opening to the bay where Aylmer Lake Lodge is located is clogged with ice. Had we sent our food there, we'd have been out of luck, at least for today. Looking all around the islands, it seems like the ice might have trapped us. The owner of the lodge had told Ryan they're usually open for business by July 1, but it's July 11 and it doesn't look like any clients would be fishing quite yet.

I want to get a better view of the ice conditions so we pull up on an island with a high point and scramble to the lookout. From there I can see the north channel is fully blocked with ice, but that we can sneak south around the ice edge and get to open water.

"Ryan, let's go around the south there. If the wind changes again, we could get surrounded and trapped by the ice."

"I dunno man…it's already 7 p.m.…Why don't we just camp here? I'm tired – we've already put in over ten hours today."

"I don't want to get stuck here…There's an opening so let's take it – the map shows it's about seven kilometres around to the opening of the north arm. Would be nice to get there and get away from all this ice."

Ryan grudgingly agrees.

"Right on. I think it's the right move," I say. We hop in the canoe, neglecting to put on our PFDs or wetsuits as we have done all day. It had been warm, balmy, and calm until that squall back at the narrows. Voyageurs and First Nations never used all that safety gear anyways. We seem to live in a Nerf society now, where everyone is overly protected against danger when in reality our best protection is always going to be our skill and experience. There's something very freeing about paddling unencumbered by the constraints of neoprene or a lifejacket. With just a thin veneer of clothing and your hands gripped snugly around the firm wooden shaft of the paddle, you attain a free, almost sensual, feeling.

It's yet another reason to come out to the wild, where you're beholden to no one's laws or rules, where you can do as you please, die as you please, thrive as you please. Once you're born, the inevitable conclusion is death, so why not do so on your own terms, as a consequence of your own actions? That is the essence of life, and death, for every species on this planet.

We walk down from the vantage point and hop in the canoe. There's a breeze, but no chop, and we head around the island and out to the edge of the floe. We follow it to the middle of the lake, where suddenly we face into the full fetch of the wind coming across Aylmer Lake. On one side of us is a jumbled, groaning pack of broken ice that is being battered by the breaking waves that pass beneath our canoe; on the other side are ice-cold breakers that I have to constantly angle the canoe over and through. There's nowhere to run or hide. If we swamp or tip here, we'll die quickly.

At first it's a little unnerving but once we get into the rhythm of it and take it one wave at a time while feathering the edge of the ice pack, it becomes exhilarating. We're on the literal edge, living in the moment, one stroke at a time out in the middle of Aylmer Lake in a blowing wind. It's a dynamic experience – cold spray from the waves slashing the boat sprays my face and arms as the ice tinkles to my right. The sun circles overhead, laying a squinting glare over the turbulent waters as the wind whistles in my ears. I smile and smile and smile.

This goes on for nine kilometres until we reach open water at the point that marks the entrance to the north arm. We're past the ice and set up camp on a rocky point. Though the south wind is warm, it brings the coolness of the ice pack we just rounded into our camp, like a fan in a refrigerator. It's now 9 p.m. and we're bundled up in our warm clothes, sipping hot tea with freeze-dried dinners that taste like the finest food a gourmet restaurant could ever serve up. It's a good day, and we're almost off of these big lakes and into the river. We've already covered 613 km of the big lakes and Pike's Portage in 13 days, have plenty of food, and are ahead of schedule.

In my journal I write, "We're way ahead of time now. I may pull in at 6 instead of 7 p.m. on the Back to enjoy it more, catch some fish for dinner, etc. We have lots of food and are in no big rush now that we're (almost) off the big lakes." But I know better; the Back will have plenty of tricks up its sleeve. I envision a fast-flowing river pushing us along the whole way. But there could be ice, could be long portages, could be lots of bad wind. And even if there isn't, I'll be driven on by eternal wandering lust for movement that makes my mind and body twitch when time on trip feels idle.

CHAPTER 37

Giant Tinkling Cubes
World's Largest Martini Glass
Aylmer Lake Ice Dodge

The ice seems to cover the north arm of Aylmer Lake from bank to bank. We paddle a few kilometres north from our campsite at the turn and see the thin white line ahead of us. To our left is a long, narrow island, to our right is the mainland. Everywhere else, there is ice in the form of hundreds of interlocking pans that sit together as one giant assembled puzzle.

We skirt the edge of the floe and head over to the island, which has a prominent ridge that should reveal the extent of the ice. Pulling our canoe up onto the moist sphagnum shore, we begin our trudging. The high point seemed so close from the water, but we have to traverse a series of damp ditches and sub ridges before we finally achieve it – a 15-minute walk that looked like five. Once up top, we can see right across the ice and also beyond it. There's a stiff northwest breeze that's moving the whole pan down the channel. A gap at the far side looks like it will give us passage past the floe. However, as the floe moves, it steadily blocks our route out. We hurry back to the canoe and, with our escape route partially stuffed, we push pans of the foot-thick ice out of our way for 50 metres until we achieve open water and then paddle on to the far side.

As we work through, we spot a lake trout lying atop the ice. It is quite dead, and we look around for an eagle that may have dropped it there, but see nothing. Also, there don't seem to be any claw marks on this particular lake trout. Perhaps the eagles here are like Labrador retrievers and they have a soft mouth, or in their case soft claws, that don't damage their dead prey in transport.

The rest of the day is grey and cool, the north wind having dispensed with the balmy south wind's weather and replaced it with a properly bitter Arctic summer day. Grey sky, grey water, grey mood. We battle into the teeth of the wind until we finally reach the top of Aylmer Lake, to the beginning of the unmarked portage to the Back River. Even if the wind turns and comes at us from the south tomorrow, the potential ice that would be brought with it wouldn't affect us anymore. We are free of the lake and hungry for river travel.

Shannon got back to me this evening on the inReach about ice up in Simpson Strait between the mainland and King William Island. The report is not good. Though it's only July 12, it's quite possible we'll reach the sea via the Kaleet in three weeks. The current report states that there is "thick first year ice" up there, which means that King William Island is firmly locked in still. The ice going out this year seems to be a week late everywhere from Great Slave Lake to the Northwest Passage, so we perhaps started a week early. Or else we're just too damn fast for our own good. I start to think that we should run the whole Back River down to Chantrey Inlet now and figure it out from there, like John and Kate were going to do. The catch is we don't have maps past the Garry Lakes, and my GPS malfunctioned a few days ago, with all the data disappearing into the clouds, so I don't even have the maps from that anymore. Bougie has a few of the maps past Garry on his phone so I figure I can make paper maps from those perhaps. Anyways, it's a river system, with a few big lakes mixed in there, mind you. Ultimately, we just have to go down it, and navigate without maps like George Back did 174 years ago. We shall see. I haven't quite given up on the Kaleet route yet.

CHAPTER 38

Choked with dry boulders
Dragging and portaging all day long
The source of the Back

I drag the canoe over the barren ground between Aylmer Lake and Sussex Lake. There's no trail, just low grasses, dwarf birches, moss, and rock. Like with most of my tundra portages, with no trees and a relatively smooth surface, I click the canoe into a line attached to my PFD harness and slide the canoe by pulling it behind me. The cool, stiff wind blowing out of the north would grab the canoe like a sail if it were on my head.

It's day 14, and Ryan and I have now travelled almost 650 km through a myriad of lakes and rivers to get to this landmark point in our journey. Sussex Lake is the source of the Back River, which flows for 974 km from this point to the Arctic Ocean at Chantrey Inlet.

It was originally named the Great Fish River by the Indigenous Dene People, but the British renamed it Back River after George Back, a commander in the Royal Navy who was the first white man to travel its length with a team of men in a 30-foot dory in 1834. Originally dubbed Back's Great Fish River, in typical colonial style the "Great Fish River" portion was dropped and all glory given to Back himself. The river is known for its remoteness, and the 83 sets of whitewater rapids that rumble along its course.

Ryan and I pose proudly, arm-in-arm, at the source of the Great Fish, with images of exhilarating downstream paddling dancing in our heads.

"This looks like the perfect place for granny's straw hat to be memorialized." Ryan takes the battered headgear and props it on a rock, marking the portage and paying homage to his grandmother, who will hopefully look over the source of the Back for years to come.

Full of enthusiasm and eagerness to feel the sweet pull of the river, we load up the canoe and paddle about 200 metres across the initial fattening of the watercourse before we're abruptly stopped by boulder-choked narrows.

Our map shows a clear, unobstructed river…if it was accurate, it would be pockmarked with "+" signs that indicate rocks on a topographical map. These maps are rarely used, though, and haven't been updated in decades. Either the river is just severely low this year, or it's been this way for a long time and just never accurately depicted. I suspect the latter. I had a similar experience "canoeing" over the Labrador Plateau between Nain and the George River in 2012. Wide-open rivers shown on our maps were mostly boulder fields and we ended up portaging much of a 200-km section there.

Ryan and I drag our fully loaded canoe over the first 100-metre section of rocks (a feat that's only possible with our near-indestructible Esquif T-Formex canoe), then paddle across a few hundred metres of shallow water before hitting a seemingly endless ribbon of rock where the river should be. I can't imagine how slowly Back and his unwieldy dory must have moved through this section. For some reason this beginning section is barely mentioned in his journal. Perhaps the river was deeper then, but this broad, flat valley could hardly ever hold deep water, and there just isn't enough source water to provide any sort of volume here.

We begin the first of two 1.5-kilometre portages over rough ground. On the map, this section is marked with a series of short lines across the river, which means these should be rapids, but we soon figure out that anything marked a "rapid" on our maps is essentially a field of dry boulders that requires portaging. The bushes are largely head height and the boulders extend throughout the higher ground. I do a combination of dragging and carrying the canoe, free-styling a route to the next fattening of the river. We leapfrog our gear, marking the point where we dropped the first load with a colourful life vest or dry bag. Ryan loses track of where he placed one of his loads but eventually finds it after backtracking and crisscrossing for 20 minutes. There are no signs of trails but we know someone's been here sometime in the past few years as we find the tattered handle of a reusable blue shopping bag with the word "IKEA" emblazoned across it. Nothing like a corporate logo to momentarily snap you out of feeling like you're the only people on the planet.

Putting in a full ten-hour day we only manage 14 kilometres, and camp by one of the wide bits of the river that's shallow, but at least not choked with boulders. While I settle the canoe on its side, back to the wind, and erect a tarp over it, Ryan sets the tent up broadside to the wind. I look at the tent with disbelief; it's fly strained and flapping on my side.

"Ryan, I don't mean to harp, but why did you set the tent up broadside to the wind? It's designed to be set up narrow end to the wind in exactly this scenario."

"It can take it."

"I'm sure it can take it, but the wind's going to have the fly flapping all night this way and put undue stress on the tent in general."

He rolls his eyes, but I press on.

"How do you set up your tent in the alpine?"

"I usually hide it behind some sort of barrier, like a rock."

"Well, look around." I gesture to the flat, treeless tundra. There are lots of boulders but none bigger than a backpack.

"If you don't mind, I'm going to rotate it in the right direction. You might be a heavy sleeper, but I'm a light sleeper and a rumbling tent fly will keep me awake."

And so the tent is rotated. Sheesh. Like pulling teeth sometimes.

Tired and bludgeoned, I retire to the tent and write a page in my journal, followed by reading a chapter of *The Orenda*. It's a fitting tale, telling of a time near the beginning of colonization when Indigenous Peoples were still independent and free. Back then the only way through the land was skill, craft and brute force, with no planes to hop you over difficult terrain. Few people do this route of ours – most take a plane in from Yellowknife and drop in on Jim Magrum Lake further downstream, or farther east of here at the Baillie River like the group from *Paddlenorth*, the other book I brought with me.

It looks like we'll have some more grinding portages and drags tomorrow morning before we're freed at Musk Ox Lake, which leads into a named set of rapids called Musk Ox Rapids. After that we'll be in the floatplane drop-off spot at Jim Magrum Lake, where deep water will prevail to the sea.

CHAPTER 39

True North Wind Today
We trudge through waving willows
A bug-free portage

I awake at 2:37 a.m. with the route on my mind. The Kaleet is a shallow river at the best of times and all this portaging around shallow rocks gives me no confidence in the navigability of that route. It may take us a week of portaging just to get through it, never mind the ice up in Simpson Strait. Also, I'll never do the Back River (or *Great Fish River*) again as I never repeat myself, so I feel that since we've taken the trouble to work our way to this trickling source, it would be an abomination not to run the river right to its end. We would be cheating this river and cheating ourselves. At worst, we'll have to paddle 170 km on the exposed Arctic Ocean from Chantrey Inlet to get to Gjoa Haven. At best, we'd run into an Inuit camp and arrange a ride back from Chantrey. It would be a roll of the dice, but our food supply is abundant so I figure we have a buffer to wait things out if need be. That settles it in my mind. I find an hour of sleep before waking again, eager to see what the Great Fish will offer us this day.

A few drags through rocks and some short paddles bring us to the next 1.5-km portage, marked occasionally with cairns that keep us on a generally straight track. It is a boulder-strewn, uneven carry, winding though low hills. The day is bright and sunny, with a cool north wind that makes the insects a nonfactor. A perfect day for a portage. Eventually, after the third load is through, we have lunch on the shore of Musk Ox Lake. We were so happy a couple of days ago to be off the big lakes and onto the Great Fish, but the slow, grinding siege through the boulders and thin waters of this river makes me appreciate the expanse of a broad lake for our afternoon paddle.

There's some chop on the lake, but overall good going. I'm happy to be paddling unobstructed water for the afternoon and we cover its 20-kilometre expanse and get to the very top of the lake. There's little protection from any kind of wind around Musk Ox Lake as it's almost dead flat. Not the best place to be stuck. The inReach says the wind won't get strong enough to stop us, but the north wind has fooled technology in the past. This ancient foil is what pushes me more than anything else in the barren grounds, and it gets us to the top of the lake, just before the beginning of Musk Ox Rapids, a five-km stretch of whitewater that leads to Jim Magrum Lake. It will be our first glimpse of the Great Fish River as a true *river*, in the sense that it will actually be a river of water, not stone.

Our tent and our camp are on a small rise of rock surrounded by damp moss and bog – a perfect locale for biting insects. We're like the feature of the day at the Chinese buffet and the customers are hungry tonight. The wind has died off and the mosquito and black fly patrons voraciously enter the restaurant. There's no lingering tonight as we inhale our dinners while pacing back and forth to create moments of free space outside our mouths to place food in there. Naturally, we get a mosquito or two in per bite, an extra bit of protein for certain. The black flies join the mix, getting in a few shots of their own before they retire for bed. Mosquitoes prefer the night; black flies prefer the day. Our dinnertime this evening coincides with that daily shift change where they're all present at once. I know when I've eaten a black fly with my meal because they taste like a dwarf blueberry as they pop in your mouth. A mosquito tastes like nothing at all, at best just providing the wispy texture of a very small blade of grass.

We'll not be denied our whisky and clove smoke, however, and stand on a metre-high boulder to catch even the slightest, lightest breeze that will keep them at bay. In combination with the exhaled smoke – which acts as a sort of mosquito coil – we get in our *saveur* and then scurry into the tent before peak witching hour. Soon enough, the fly is draped in a blanket of mosquitoes, the collective droning of their wings creating a comforting white noise that harmonizes with the distant, dull rumble of the Musk Ox Rapids.

The next morning is bright and sunny, but with enough of a chill to keep the insects at bay. Ryan smokes a couple of joints over the course of breakfast. One pre-oatmeal, and one post-oatmeal. It never really seems to affect him too much, besides making him exude a relaxed demeanour. We pack everything up under the spray deck and pull out the burly Grey Owl C-1 whitewater paddles and push off for the entrance of the narrows where the Musk Ox Rapids officially begin. The first set is an easy rapid that we run down the middle...a satisfyingly deep, rock-free wave train that whisks us around the corner and out of sight of the lake. We manoeuvre down through another couple of easier rapids and smooth sections until the whole river spreads out and turns shallow, weaving through a matrix of boulders. We pull out in the eddy above the constriction to scout a line. I hop out on a boulder for a better view and see we'll have to work our way through an extended bony section. The water is low – not pushy – and it looks like we can paddle through without having to walk or line the canoe.

I turn to see Ryan looking around in the bow of the canoe. He's left his sunglasses at the camp, but decides he'll be okay without them. I imagine myself without sunglasses, eternally squinting into the sun on these bright endless days, trying to read a rapid line through the glare. It's unacceptable to me.

"Did you bring an extra pair?"

"Nope."

I say nothing, but I'm sure the extra joint this morning didn't help his attention to detail when we packed up. I have an extra pair stashed away – I've lost and broken enough sunglasses over the years to be sure to bring a backup. Essential items need to be backed up if they're fragile in nature. However, I'm not going to give him my backup pair only to have him lose those too.

"Where at the camp do you think they are?"

"I'm not sure...maybe by the put-in...maybe where the tent was."

I look at the map and see we've come a couple of kilometres downriver. Going back upstream would take a good while, and I hate backtracking. I see that we've come around a wide bend though, and that if I ran overland and cut the corner it would be about 1.5 km back to the camp.

"I'm going to run back to the camp to grab your glasses."

"I can do it, I left them there."

I imagine Ryan weaving aimlessly back to the camp, only not to find them, and then coming back hours later even higher than now, a half-day wasted.

"No, man, I'll be faster. I'll run the whole way and follow a bee-line bearing to the camp. It'll be fun for me. You stay here with the canoe."

"Fine, if you want to do it."

I did actually want to do it. It was a mini-mission and navigational challenge, an opportunity to explore inland, though I knew from previous experience that the terrain would be anything but gentle despite the lack of trees.

"I'll be back in about 30 or 40 minutes, I'm guessing."

I set a quick bearing with the compass and take off over the bank at a run. I've left my long pants on to defend against the inevitable whipping from the knobby dwarf birches. The terrain rolls and rambles, a herky-jerky mix of boulder fields, hard tussocks of grass, swampy moss bogs, and the whipping birches. Almost certainly no one has done this little run or portage before, and though I'm backtracking, I find it quite engaging. It's an orienteering run where I have to make split decisions about following the bearing and finding the most efficient terrain. It is still cool enough that I haven't stirred up the great hordes of black flies from their torpor. I use my frustration with Ryan to drive me on, thinking, "Stoner, stoner, stoner…the guy rolls three to seven joints per day. I can't believe I'm tripping with a chronic pothead…and now I'm thrashing across the tundra looking for his glasses because of it."

After about 17 or 18 minutes, I get to our campsite. I run over to where the tent had been but see nothing there. Scanning over to where I'd set up the kitchen, I spot the sunglasses sitting on a small boulder where the stove had been. The brown sunglasses and black strap blend in perfectly with the surroundings. I grab them and quickly double back. The day is getting warmer by the second and the black flies are rising as I stir them from the bushes and mosses they'd tucked into for the cool night. The little buggers seem solar powered; the hotter it gets, the more energetic and bloodthirsty they become.

I get back to the canoe and Ryan is leaning against a rock, smoking a joint. I smile. It is what it is. At least I got the sunglasses and we didn't waste too much time. Plus I got to experience a piece of terrain that I otherwise would never have immersed myself in.

He turns to look at me, ultra casual. "You find them?"

"Yep, here you go."

"Where were they?"

"By the kitchen area."

"Hmm. Well, thanks."

I dig into one of the packs and hand Ryan the cord from my backup sunglasses. They're bright red, something that will catch the attention of even an addled pothead.

We head into the bouldery rapids, banging our way down. Our synchronicity in the boat isn't great and we get hung up on the rocks a few times, having to get out and push the canoe into deeper water. At one point, we're heading down a narrow flume between boulders and at the bottom a shallow, pointy rock is sticking a foot out of the moving water in the middle of the channel. I spot it at the last second and call for Ryan to "Draw!" so we can side slip it. He reacts too late and we hit it squarely so that it stops the canoe fully for a moment before we slide off. The impact is significant enough that I get out to inspect the bow of the canoe. Sure enough, we've taken a good hit. An indent the size of a grapefruit has pushed into the bow. Thankfully, it's a T-Formex canoe, so I use the butt end of the paddle to knock the indent out from the inside, and the boat seems no worse for wear.

Later in the afternoon, we decide to line around a drop in the rapid between boulders, as the current is piling directly into an unavoidable monolith just further downstream. I have the line in the bow while Ryan has the stern line. As we ease the canoe over the drop, the fully loaded boat shoots forward with force and simultaneously yanks the lines from both of our hands. I dive onto the canoe so I don't have to swim after it and manage to corral it into the eddy below and bring it back up to Ryan. It's a good day to brush off the rust and become a cohesive downstream team. Making all these mistakes when the river is low gives us a margin for error we won't have in the big volume stuff downstream.

All the tributaries we see coming into the river are bone dry, confirming my decision that we shouldn't risk taking my original Kaleet route. I want downstream push all the way to the ocean, not grinding weeks of dragging and portaging. Running this thing to the end, without maps, seems to be the most rational decision. Mother Nature ultimately tells us where to go, not our pre-conceived routes. What seems rational in a room full of maps becomes the opposite when you're immersed in the reality of wilderness.

CHAPTER 40

Little Red Canoe
Riding White Stallions all day
Pulled Ever Northward

The river fills in the next day and we run medium-volume whitewater all day, having to line just one drop. On Malley Rapids we sneak through a side channel and run a fun four-foot drop into a smooth pool, submerging the bow and letting it emerge like a breaching whale at the end of it. The day is warm and the winds light, and the river sparkles. Between rapids, we flow through sandy valleys, following the twists and turns of the flow, avoiding the shallow edges that spread out for hundreds of metres in water only a foot or two deep.

I'm getting a feel for the current, where a paddle stroke tells me if I'm in slack or moving water, where a riffle here and there tells me where to steer the canoe, where the darkness of a deep channel calls me onward and away from the golden shallows. We cover an easy 66 kilometres that day, and I relent to Ryan's desire to fish and we pull in an hour earlier than usual. It grates at my nomadic impulse, but we are making good time and have plenty of food. In many ways I wish I'd brought less food, so we'd be forced by scarcity to push faster and longer everyday, as that is what I love to do most. Moving, ever moving. I've paddled on the same side for the past two days again as Ryan's right shoulder continues to bother him. Rest is what I do in the city, not out here, so I'm okay with it. I'm in service to the journey.

Alas, Ryan doesn't catch a fish. Instead, he loses a valuable Red Devil lure to a likely lunker lake trout on his one big bite. Sigh. Much like my partner Peirson on a trip across northern Quebec a year earlier, Ryan doesn't help me put away the bags under the canoe and leave a tight and tidy camp before bed. He's happy just to leave things strewn about. Peirson, though, always had a great spirit and joy that overrode his obliviousness, and he didn't smoke reefers all day on trip. As I pack away the bags and put everything under the canoe, Ryan rolls another joint and stares at his phone. He seems to have little interest or curiosity about nature, focusing mostly on YouTube videos and games of Tetris. It's so, so strange to me. I'll have to vet out the chronic dope smokers on future trips – it's a habit of Ryan's that I had no idea of until we started this thing. Anyhow, *vive la différence* I suppose. Every partner is different – and I remind myself I'm on the beautiful Great Fish River and we're moving forward. I guess I'm nitpicking, and there's no one to pick on out here except Bougie.

CHAPTER 41

Mini vipers maul
Cloaking us in the canoe
Mosquito Posse

We run a couple of wave trains on the way into Beechey Lake the next morning – a 60-km-long body of water that forms the elbow of a sharp eastward turn from the river's northward course. The day is muggy, with a light southeast wind. The lake is broad, surrounded by a flat, featureless landscape. It is one of the few times on this trip I just want it done with rather than being in the moment and savouring a landscape I'll never pass through again. The forecast for tomorrow is a big northeast, so if we can get most of the way off this lake and into the intimate confines of the river proper again, we'll be set up much better for movement. Out on this big, broad, shallow lake we'd be sitting ducks to a big North, which will kick up large, steep waves.

The peculiarity of Beechey is that we have to be out in the middle of the lake even to paddle. Again, going by feel and looking for the dark water, we follow the subtle meander of the river through this lake. If we go off course, our paddles hit sand and we almost come to a halt. To compound this, I can still only paddle on my left side since Ryan's left shoulder continues to be sore. The problem with this is that the wind is coming directly from my right side and even this light wind weather cocks the canoe off course and pushes the bow toward the south shore, so I'm forced to draw with every other stroke to keep us on course. Under normal conditions, I'd be paddling on my right-hand side and be able to use a corrective J-stroke or pitch stroke to keep us moving forward and on course efficiently and with less effort.

The light wind and warm weather layers on a final bit of slow-dripping torture: a mosquito horde that accompanies us all day long, relentlessly doing what they do, harassing us all the way out here in the middle of the lake. We wear our bug shirts and long pants, dripping with sweat underneath as they hum and whine about us. They tuck into the lee of the subtle breeze created by the movement of the canoe. Like a conveyer belt, they come over the front, assault Ryan, tuck behind him, then assault me, then tuck behind me. Then they creep up along the edges of the canoe back to the front to do it all over again. There is nowhere to run, nowhere to hide. We are merely a mobile table of meat, drawing in the hungry mosquitoes from the barren grounds like portly gamblers to a Las Vegas buffet.

Fat, black clouds build and head toward us.

"Maybe we should pull in early to beat the rain," Ryan suggests.

I look around at the bleak surroundings, our mosquito companions, and the thought of the north wind tomorrow. We pulled in early yesterday and twiddled our thumbs after being skunked on the fishing. Negotiating a couple of kilometres of shallow water just to get to shore isn't a prospect I relish. I just want to get off of this lake.

"Let's keep going. I'd rather not be here when the North blows in tomorrow."

Ryan says nothing, and we paddle on.

It begins to rain, but with little accompanying wind it doesn't seem to disturb the focus of our small assailants, who whip us across the rest of the lake like we're at the oar in a galley. This morning we saw a lone caribou across from our camp – the very first of our trip. It offered me hope of seeing some more big mammals on Beechey today but all we see is a landscape seemingly devoid of life, save for us and the mosquitoes.

We pull into camp at the end of the lake after a 60-km day. The mosquitoes thicken as we set up camp, then are blown away by a sudden burst of wind that swings in from the north. The squall gives us a bug-free 15 minutes before they return and join us for the tail end of dinner under the fly. A consistent light breeze doesn't quite dispel them but keeps them out of my face as I eat, with them hovering and probing in the lee behind my head.

CHAPTER 42

Wet, cold day on trip
Paddling into the North Wind
Behold, a German!

The true, cold north wind blows in at 1 a.m., dropping temperatures into the single digits and driving the mosquitoes back into their hovels. Intermittent rain sweeps across Beechey Lake and we have a delightfully bug-free morning coffee and oatmeal. Cool and rainy versus warm and buggy? The choice in the North is exceedingly easy: Cool and rainy all day long, thank you. A few kilometres on down the river and we begin a two-kilometre portage, cutting a big bend overland and avoiding the class 5 torrent of the Beechey Cascades. In the temperate conditions, we amble over a combination of smooth rock and waving dwarf birch. I follow a direct-line compass bearing, which I share with Ryan. He ambles off course, losing the bright blue 60-litre barrel-pack for a while as it slipped off a rock he'd placed it on when he doubled back for the next bag. I shake my head at the inefficiency even though I am used to his antics by now. Soon he'll run out of weed and merge more completely with the land without the hazy barrier of THC interfering. In all, I triple back for bags while Ryan doubles back, and we get everything through in good time. The river burbles by the gravel landing where all of our stuff is piled and we hunker beside the overturned canoe to eat our tortillas with peanut butter and honey, hidden from the wind-driven drizzle from the north.

The rumble of the Beechey Cascades just 100 metres upstream creates enough white noise that we have to raise our voices just a couple of decibels higher than conversational to communicate. Not that there's much to say: the portage is done and we're quiet except for a "Please" or a "Thank You" here and there as the lunch is doled out. Downstream, we see the river does a hairpin turn. We'll get a couple of kilometres of current and wind in our favour before we abruptly turn north, where the irresistible force of the gale meets the immovable object of the river. It will be engaging if nothing else.

The canoe seems to fly toward the corner and each paddle stroke seems to move us a football field at a time. The wind quiets at the high bank where the hairpin begins and the wind in my ears goes silent. All we hear is the burble and hiss of the river. The inevitable turn back into the wind presents us with a seemingly endless line of jacked-up waves as the current collides with the invisible wall of the north wind. It seems like we're going against the river now. We rock wildly in the middle, going up each steep wave and then crashing into its trough. To even out this sudden ride on the whale's back, I slip to the inner edge of the river, where the current is slower, the water smoother.

Closer to the bank, it seems like we're moving faster. The piled boulders and sand move past as we feather the edge of the reverse-running eddies, catching just enough current to help us forward through the relentless wind. We plough ahead for a couple of kilometres, getting into our new groove until we come to a landing. Nestled in a depression in the bank is a red canoe – another folding solo boat like Bernie the Austrian had back on Ptarmigan Lake. Thirty metres inland, I see a small pup tent and another single-pole cook shelter like Bernie's. The set-up is eerily similar, but the colours don't match. We pull ashore to investigate.

I walk up to the camp and call out.

An odd-looking little man reminiscent of Marty Feldman's character Igor in *Young Frankenstein* pops out from the one-pole shelter. His big, buggy eyes seem to balance on top of a long green poncho.

His eyes grow wide when he sees me.

"Are you Frank Wolf?" he asks even before introducing himself.

"Uh…yes. How did you know?"

"Wow…wow!" he exclaims. "I was told you'd be coming and that I might see you, but wow! You are going reaalllly fast! I'm Karsten Iwers, by the way – from Germany."

First we meet an Austrian, now a German…we're in one of Canada's crown jewels and nary a Canadian to be seen.

"Who told you about us?" I ask.

"John and Kate. They saw you on the Pike's Portage. We were talking on the lead-up to this trip as we were both doing the Back River. I've been texting them by inReach. They said you were moving fast but... wow! How many days to get here from Yellowknife?"

I have to think for a second, and then check my watch for today's date. "We left on the 29th, so today would be Day 19."

He tells us he got dropped off by bush plane on Jim Magrum Lake, below the rocky Musk Ox Rapids, then asks if he can get our contact information.

"What for?" I respond.

He looks blankly at me for a second. "To contact you on inReach, to be in touch...I want to know how your trip ends up."

I smile. "Ryan's in charge of the inReach. You'll have to get his information."

Ryan rolls his eyes. I envision a daily pestering text from this eager little fellow and see that Ryan does too. Ah, technology, she giveth and she taketh away.

Despite tens of thousands of canoe-tripping days, I've never used a bush plane to skip over the difficult bits. The tough sections of a long approach always make the overall journey so much more satisfying. It's how people travelled these waterways for millennia, taking what the land gave them. It gives me an appreciation of water travel in its many forms.

"How did you find the portage around Beechey Cascades?" he asks.

"Oh, not too bad. It took us a couple of hours and about 2.5 double backs between the two of us. It was nice and cool too. No bugs!"

"It took me an entire day. I had to go over that portage six times to get all my stuff across. It was muggy and still – the black flies were terrible!"

He'd been portaging on the same day we crossed Beechey Lake with that horde of mosquitoes on that humid day. The poor bastard, he must have suffered like a dog. Now he was pinned in here by the north wind.

"Ah, you should see my paddle...you will be jealous."

He pulls out a black carbon fibre paddle and hands it to me. It's light as a feather, but also as delicate.

"Nice paddle, but I prefer wood. I always choose durability over weight. You can't paddle if your paddle's broken."

He thinks for a second. "But it's light, much less work."

"Then why aren't you paddling right now? You've got current in your favour."

"Too stormy, and I'm in no rush. I have 60 days of food. If I have time, I might try to paddle all the way to Gjoa Haven. Are you going to keep going into the wind?"

"Of course...we have current in our favour...and two strong wooden paddles to propel us along." I can't resist the dig.

He smiles and nods. "You'll probably be finished in a couple of weeks...I'm here for the whole summer."

We shake hands and say our goodbyes, then head off into the wind. Soon we turn a bend and Karsten disappears from sight.

Clipping along all afternoon with the current and a lee bank to our north, we make good time. A few read-and-run rapids break up the day nicely. After a 46-km day, we make camp in a sheltered spot below a rise, 20 feet from the river. I'm sitting under the fly with a view over the big, babbling river. The temperature is cool, with a light drizzle and no bugs. I sip a cup of hot, sweet tea and write in my journal, waiting for the freeze-dried food to hydrate. Ryan is in the tent doing god-knows-what...there's a high probability he's watching a Migos video or playing Tetris. But I'm out here. It's quiet, it's fresh. Life is good.

CHAPTER 43

Silver flash of light
Perfectly grilled over fire
Grayling for supper

The next day is warmer and windless so the mosquitoes hasten our exit from camp. There is little pleasure in lingering with them nagging us as relentlessly as an embittered spouse. On the water, there is good current and we travel quickly enough that the "skitters" don't stick around. It's a moving day. En route, we encounter three large rapids. On two of them we run through the side channels; on the other we drag the canoe over boulders along the edge. We have lunch below one of the rapids, nestled on a beach in the warm sun. I strip out of my sweaty neoprene and plunge in for a refreshing dip in the crystal clear water. Swimming out into the current, I let myself be whisked downstream for 30 feet before stroking back to the eddy and letting it take me back up to where I started. I ride this conveyer belt for a couple of laps before pulling myself out of the water and drying myself on a boulder like a snake. Sitting there naked, with the black flies on an apparent lunch break too, I look back up the burly centre of the big rapid. Had we gone down the middle, we would have swamped, flipped, and yard-saled below.

The Great Fish is broadening by the day. As the rapids get more muscular, they also become much wider, allowing for runnable options along the edges where the push, power, and volume of the river is minimized but still deep enough to run through smoothly. I light a kretek and delight in the head rush, which always seems so much stronger at lunchtime than at dinner. Must be something to do with dehydration, or the brightness of the day. Who knows? Whatever the case, the clove we split everyday at lunch is always the best.

At day's end, we pass the Baillie River, a major tributary of the Great Fish. We pass its mouth, after which the river grows by another third. Many people start their paddle down the Back by getting dropped off upstream on the Baillie and then connecting down to the Back. Either that or get dropped off at Jim Magrum like Karsten. In *Paddlenorth*, the group there did the Baillie access. Overall, it's a shorter trip with more consistent flow. I'm always a fan of running a river from the source down, so I can experience all its phases. To do otherwise only gives you a partial idea of the river. It's like watching a film from the mid-point onward – you miss the whole set-up, the meat of the plot, if you don't start from the beginning.

We find a good camp spot two kilometres past the confluence. Looking back up the river as I gather water for dinner, I notice a pair of canoes pulling onto the bank at the confluence. The paddlers get out and begin to unload. I doubt we'll see them again.

Our campsite has a rocky point jutting into the current, creating an eddy line that looks ideal for fishing. I cast the line out and let the lure drift into the eddy from the main current. Immediately the line goes taught and I reel in a two-pound grayling. A quick whack on the head with the butt of the paddle and we have a nice supplement for dinner.

I smile at Ryan. "My work here is done," I say as I offer him the rod. He grabs it eagerly and casts four times, bringing in two more grayling. The fishing here is just too darn easy. Ryan gets a fire going while I boil up water for our rehydrated Pasta Roma.

I've brought along a small grill for an occasion like this. Once the dried branches of the dwarf birch and willow have flamed to life and then settle to coals, Ryan grills the three fish until the skin flakes easily off the white meat.

Using his fork, he flakes all the meat into a freezer bag and tosses it with a bit of lemon pepper. Some of the meat goes into fortifying our pasta, while the rest will be kept to make fish tacos for tomorrow's lunch – a welcome change from the utilitarian peanut butter and honey I slather on for us every midday.

After dinner, we sit on the rock enjoying the cool evening. The fish we caught today were the first of the trip. Besides the one day a while back where we pulled in early so Ryan could give it a go but got skunked, we hadn't really tried. For me, fishing has to be easy and obvious…a spot by a nice deep eddy line on the river, like this.

"I smoked the last of my weed today," Ryan announces. "Lasted for three weeks but now it's gone."

"How do you feel about that?"

"Ah, it's fine. I knew I'd run out."

He does seem clearer this evening, more focused. The trip gods gift us grayling. Perhaps a coincidence? We shall see.

CHAPTER 44

Under puffy clouds
Following the thin blue line
Through golden sandbars

The next morning is strange. It's warm with a light tailwind yet there are no bugs. It's such a rare combination up here I think that the Arctic Trickster is setting us up for something. The Great Fish spills into a valley a couple of kilometres wide at points and spreads itself thinly over golden shallows rimmed by sand dunes. A ribbon of blue indicates the main flow and I have to focus on its path in order not to run aground. There is a marked difference in speed in the channel and we clip along surprisingly well all the way until lunch, where we pull onto a broad, seemingly endless sand bar. Clouds, once a friendly puffy white – like the clouds in the opening of the cartoon series *The Simpsons* – have turned dark and angry. It looks like these big thunderclouds will just skirt by us to the north. We continue on and it seems they've passed when they spot us on the river and turn on us. Big, heavy gusts of wind announce their arrival and we pull in to shelter from impending lightning strikes, but then the behemoths veer away to the west again.

We continue on for a couple more kilometres until yet another angry cloud bank turns and rolls over us with heavy wind and rain. We fight sudden whitecaps to get to the sandy shore, chased by bolts of chain lightning framed by black clouds, with heavy thunder following each strike. We scurry to a lone boulder and drape the tarp over it and huddle inside. The temperature seems to drop ten degrees as we're pelted with heavy drops of chilling rain, our butts and feet half sunken in the saturated sand.

Ryan shivers under the hastily constructed shelter. The old, tattered clothes he brought along are soaked through. He puts on his homemade freezer bag granny hood in an attempt to keep his head dry. He has no rain pants at all.

I may like to keep things simple, but I'm not a complete Luddite.

I fully embrace Gore-Tex and a three-layer clothing system to keep myself warm and dry in the elements. It's the current-day version of the caribou skins the inland Inuit used for the same purpose. A little comfort goes a long way.

Ryan puts his head between his legs and tries to catnap, while I read a few more pages of *The Orenda*. Ten minutes later, it's over. We slosh back to the canoe and then bail out the buckets of rain that entered through the spray deck cockpits. We paddle on for another hour and a half until camp, the wind now gone, the sky a brilliant pink, and the mosquitoes back to keep us company. Ryan's shoulder is still sore so I paddled on my left all day again. We also did our biggest distance so far – 75 km – so are moving well in spite of the storm delay.

We still haven't seen many big mammals yet, only that lone caribou days and days ago. Where are they?

CHAPTER 45

The hills are alive
Thousands of caribou stroll
Then fade into mist

Birthdays. Some people see them as a time to gather a big group together and celebrate themselves. I am quite the opposite. My birthday is July 21, the middle of the summer. Growing up, school was out and what friends I had were away. I was usually car camping in Killbear Provincial Park with my folks, or from my early teens onward, up at the family cottage across from that same park. My mom would bake me a cake, and my father would drift through for a slice, as would my brother and sister. And that would be that. No fanfare, no pomp, no circumstance. Perhaps because I never grew up with any sort of celebration around it, I prefer quiet birthdays. I love to be part of celebrations and parties and gatherings – but for other people, not me. I'm uncomfortable in the direct shine of a spotlight. I prefer to flit around mischievously on the edges, in the shadows. Celebrations are rarely for the person being celebrated anyhow – it's more for those throwing the celebration, so they feel good about not forgetting a momentous occasion like a birthday. The person at the centre of attention is almost pressured by others to allow them to do it. That's how I feel anyways.

Disappearing into the wilderness on canoe trips over the years became a convenient excuse not to celebrate my birthday. The third week of July is prime time for canoe trippers and no time to be in the city, so I'm out in the bush or on the barren grounds instead of stuck in the city having people sing "Happy Birthday" to me. To my wife's dismay, I always make sure I'm well gone by the time the 21st arrives.

And so it was again this year.

"When are you going on your trip this year?" she asked one rainy March morning.

"I fly out on the 27th of June."

She thought for a second, as if going through the motions.

"So you'll be away on your birthday again!"

"Yup."

Every year she asks, and every year the answer is the same. It's like she's Charlie Brown and I'm Lucy, holding the football for her to kick. But I always pull it away, and she falls into a heap. Again and again, year after year. Hope springs eternal I guess, but at some point she'll learn. Or not. It would be easier if she just didn't bring it up at all. Just a game we play – an annual anti-birthday tradition – an unremarkable way to mark a non-event.

Whether on my birthday or not, I'll often know months before I ever tell her what my plans are going to be. I think she secretly hopes I'll take a year off from my journeys, but that would be like taking a year off from life, from living. When I tell her, it's never "Okay, sounds good." It's always, "What? Where?" You'd think that after 25 years it wouldn't be such a surprise. Then she'll brood for a few days until acceptance fills in the darkness and we move on as normal. That's why I hold out as long as possible, as it's always a bit of an ordeal.

The long and the short of it is, the best birthday I can have is one on trip, in the wilderness experiencing a new landscape. It's a birthday that's unacknowledged, one that I might even forget, but certainly that the person with me is ideally unaware of. It's a game I play. With some people, the game is hard, as they know me in day-to-day life and have been burned on past birthdays in the same circumstance. My friend Todd, who's done several trips with me, never forgets any more, unfortunately. But Bougie has no way of knowing or caring about it.

We enter a twisting narrows, the water moving quickly around the corners through a hilly landscape. The only creatures we've seen on a consistent basis have been flocks of moulting Canada Geese, who come to the Arctic in thousands, shedding old feathers and growing fresh ones for the next year. Due to this shedding, they can't fly for several weeks, and scurry alongshore like turkeys when they see us, or "duck dive" with their big, buoyant bodies until we pass by. They are fairly helpless in their flightless state and provide a stable food source for wolves, foxes, and grizzly bears.

As we come around one particularly sharp bend that curves into the face of a hill, the scoured, emerald terrain of the tundra seems to vibrate. When I look closer, I see it's covered by small creatures that I initially dismiss as yet another group of moulting geese. But depth perception in the Arctic is skewed. Things that are far seem close, and things that are close seem far – there are no trees or other objects to give you an accurate perspective. I glance up at the hill again, and this time I see that these creatures have horns. They're caribou!

"Holy shit, a caribou herd!" I yell.

Ryan looks up vacantly.

"Let's hit shore and go check them out…I want to get some shots!"

I run the canoe up onto the gravel bank and hop out into the knee-deep water. Walking to the front, I pull the canoe up further. Ryan remains seated.

"You coming? I'm going to walk up there to get a better look."

"Naw, I'll watch 'em from here," he replies, taking a bite of his pepperoni.

"Suit yourself."

I don't understand why he doesn't want to come along, but I don't want to waste any time with an inquisition. I'm far too excited about the caribou – it looks like there are hundreds of them. I handrail the hill toward the herd and it wraps me through a valley along a small creek. The creek leads up to a lake, and as I follow it, the size and extent of the herd becomes apparent. Hundreds become thousands. It's a stunning sight, with the ungulates amassed into a herd, covering the entire valley around the lake. Comparing their numbers to a capacity audience at a Canucks game in my hometown of Vancouver, I estimate the throng to be around 10,000 strong.

I watch the herd alone for about 15 minutes. They bleat and grunt as they graze away. I move as close as I can to get some photographs and video. They pause to look up at me from time to time. Moving in unison like a flock of birds, they always stay just out of reach, as if there's an invisible threshold of comfort they won't let me cross. They don't panic, they simply keep me outside of a 20-metre comfort radius. Ryan finally appears at my side.

"Wow," he says, and then takes in the spectacle with me. A fog descends upon the valley and the herd begins to disperse into it. In minutes they are gone, evaporating into the mist. The land surrounding the lake is now devoid of life. We are suddenly by ourselves, as if waking from a dream. Were they actually here? It seems impossible that they could disappear into the ether so effortlessly. I double check my camera and confirm it wasn't just a hallucination.

The mist hangs just above the water for the rest of the day, providing a feeling of intimacy as the river snakes through canyons and hills. We run several high-volume swifts, with the highlight of paddling through the middle of Hawk Rapids, a deep series of smooth standing waves where the whole Great Fish River is squeezed through a slot-like canyon. The middle is deep blue, flanked by roaring holes and boils, shooting us through at what feels like 100 miles per hour, then settling us in the calm below.

By evening, we're through the rocky canyons and back out into the wide, broad river. We camp at a bend, on flat rock that resembles the interlocking stone of a patio or a Roman road. It's as if someone has painstakingly laid out the entire bend, perfectly flat, for our arrival. Those glaciers of 10,000 years ago were unparalleled stonemasons.

Dinner this evening is Pad Thai again – the heartiest of all of our freeze-dried selection, a meal that packs the most caloric punch. Afterwards, we enjoy our standard *saveur* of a nice clove cigarette and whisky. It tastes good this evening. When we're done, Ryan goes to lie in the tent while I remain under the fly, writing in my journal. It's a delightfully bug-free evening. A beautiful double rainbow appears in the dark clouds of a distant passing storm, the rumble of thunder faint and comforting music to accompany the lovely display. I tally up our distance: we've covered 79 kilometres, our biggest day so far.

It's been the perfect birthday for me. It feels good to have avoided the trap of hubris that comes with informing someone of your "special day." We've covered a vast stretch of land, satisfying my Tourette's-like urge for efficient movement. And of course, most importantly to me, I stood with a herd of thousands of caribou – the lifeblood of the land that came and went like ghosts. This ancient migration, this ritual pulse, provided me with a birthday gift that will be hard to surpass, one that I'll never forget.

CHAPTER 46

Spirit animal
Feasting on Canada Goose
White wolf on the beach

The Great Fish River spreads out into another of its broad sandy sections and we follow the thin blue line that snakes through the sandy shallows. After the excitement and speed of yesterday's narrowly laid out section of paddling, which required full engagement, the broad river leaves me feeling subdued…everything just seems so far away, as though we're merely a red speck floating disconnected through space.

Around midday, my eye catches movement along a broad beach at the base of a sandy esker 100 metres from our canoe. It's an Arctic wolf, busying itself over something lying on shore. I immediately steer the canoe into the golden shallows toward it.

When we get within 50 metres and our paddles hit the soft sand with every stroke, it looks directly at us. The canoe runs aground moments later with a hiss and the wolf immediately trots away from whatever was occupying its attention before. It moves parallel to the shoreline while keeping a close eye on us, pausing from time to time to lift its nose into the air, trying to get our scent. I shoot some video and take some stills. After a minute of casual trotting and sniffing, it finally catches our scent. It seems to hit the wolf like a charge from a rifle, and it bolts over the dune and out of sight.

I look at Ryan and point to where the wolf had been feeding. "I'm going to check out what it was eating. I'm betting it was a goose. You coming?"

He looks at the six inches of water around where we'd run aground. "Naw, I don't want to get my feet wet, I'll stay here."

"You don't want to check out the carcass? Because of wet feet? They're going to get wet at some point today anyways. You remind me of the Japanese campers I used to get when I was a summer camp canoe guide. They never wanted to get their feet wet when I took them on trip."

"Well, call me a Japanese camper then. I'm not getting my feet wet right now."

I shake my head in disbelief. Here we are on the Great Fish River and we'd just seen an Arctic wolf eating something on shore and he doesn't want to take a look because of some perceived discomfort. So, so strange. Any other trip partner I've ever had in the past would've been right there with me, shoulder to shoulder, to experience the moment. It was the same with the caribou the day before. I ran up to check them out while he sat in the canoe. More than wet feet, it seems to be pure disinterest.

When I was a summer canoe guide back in the day, the aforementioned Japanese campers would show up for a canoe trip with bright white sneakers and would become contortionists in their efforts to step out of the canoe onto dry land without getting their feet wet. We'd always get a group of these kids fresh off the plane from Japan to experience three weeks of summer in the wilds of Canada. Part of this experience was of course going on a week-long canoe trip.

I always put the weakest two campers in the canoe with me. When I first saw Yoichi and Ichiro daintily trying to get out of the canoe without stepping in the water, I walked up beside them, stood with my shoes on in shin-deep water, pointed to my feet, and then theirs, before telling them sternly.

"Step in the water."

They ignored me and nervously kept trying to stretch across the two-foot chasm of water to a dry boulder. Ichiro was toeing the rock, balancing precariously with one foot there and the other in the canoe. I gave him a light push and he was in the drink.

I then turned to Yoichi, "Wet feet…or I toss you in the drink next."

He reluctantly obeyed and stepped into the water with his bright white Stan Smiths like he was entering a bath of boiling oil. But he learned, and so did Ichiro. It was all part of being on trip in the early 90s. No coddling, no whining. Obey or get tossed in the drink and get the least amount of food at dinner. In the end, they had a great time because they were challenged, because they had to rise to the occasion. They came out of that trip reborn as canoe trippers. Sometimes it just takes a firm nudge.

It won't work to kick Ryan's ass like that. This is merely a small detail in the broad perspective of a grand journey. We are equals here and I can only lead by example. I leave him in the canoe and slosh down the beach to inspect the remains.

There's a line of feathers on the sand leading to the exploded goose. This must've been the final few metres as the wolf finally caught it and ended its life. The goose is torn open but there is still plenty of meat left – the wolf must've caught it just before we arrived. I look down the shore and up the bank to where the wolf darted off. I'm sure he's watching me, or at the very least he's aware of my presence by scent alone. I turn my attention back to the goose. Its head and neck are still connected to its body, the black, lifeless doll eyes looking up at me. I snap a couple of pictures and return to the boat, where Ryan waits.

The rest of the day goes well and we almost reach Pelly Lake, the start of a series of large lakes in the middle of the Great Fish before the whole river rumbles down Rock Rapids for 12 kilometres. After Pelly come the Upper and Lower Garry Lakes and Bulliard Lake. It's here that I half expect to find ice blocking our path, as many groups in the past have.

Ryan manages to paddle part of the day on his left side, which gives that side a break for me. It's a good sign that perhaps his shoulder has finally broken in and we can even out our days paddling on both sides again. It's been almost three weeks since he started having problems with it on Great Slave Lake, so hopefully we're over the hump.

CHAPTER 47

The river broadens
Spilling into Garry Lakes
Vast water vista

We slug it out across Pelly Lake all day, covering 60 km through a flat, sandy, and relatively featureless landscape. With little by way of natural features to key off of, I follow a bearing toward a distant dark line – islands we have to cut through to keep on an efficient track. Sometimes the wind comes from behind, sometimes from the side; sometimes it's shallow and full of sandbars, and sometimes it's deep. The sun is bright and cumulous clouds build through the day but never threaten to become thunderheads that will chase us off the lake with lightning.

We end up on a nice, rocky point where Ryan catches a burly lake trout and grills it up. We mix it in with our Mexican Cowboy Beans and Brown Rice and have plenty left over for fish tacos the next day. Whenever the weather is decent like this I go for a swim before changing into my dry, cozy camp clothes. The brisk, refreshing dip invigorates me and relaxes me before I snuggle into a soft cotton T-shirt, fleece pants, and thick socks. It's these small pleasures, like this scant hour of relaxation at the end of a long day of physical labour, that make it worthwhile. Stillness can best be savoured when contrasted by a day of effort.

CHAPTER 48

Surprise dinner guest
It walked right into our camp
Wolf at the table

A day-long light tailwind and side wind takes us almost all the way across both Upper and Lower Garry lakes – a fluid 68 kilometres. Once we got through Upper Garry, we were officially past the point where I'd originally planned to turn north and portage into the Kaleet River. With the low water on most of the tributaries into the Great Fish, I'm glad I'd abandoned the Kaleet plan. A report from Shannon tells me that Simpson Strait is still locked in ice, reaffirming my decision. Perhaps more than anything else, it's that this river is in my blood now. I'm in the groove of it and want to experience the whole thing, source to sea. Not far ahead of us lie the Rock Rapids, apparently the burliest bit of whitewater on the whole river, and I am eager to tackle them. From here on, we'll have to rely on the topo maps Ryan downloaded on his phone to take us to the turn-off to the Meadowlark River. My initial plan was to head up the Meadowlark and work our way to Baker Lake in the south, but now going to Gjoa Haven seems like a far more appealing line, as I've already been to Baker Lake on previous trips down the Thelon and Kazan Rivers.

As we paddle across the vast expanse of Lower Garry Lake, Ryan decides to put on his headphones and listen to a podcast.

What the fuck? It's bad enough he's inside that machine while in the tent, but now he brings it out in the canoe.

I say, "If you're listening to the podcast while you're out here, it means you're not engaged in the trip."

He replies, "Yes, I am engaged in it."

He then puts his earphones in and tunes me and the lake out. He becomes one with the machine, like his hero Kurzweil. YouTube, toilet paper, ear buds…what's next? I surmise that he must be coming off the weed, which used to distract him all day, and which he has replaced twofold with the drug of technology. That being said, I'm glad he downloaded all those maps on the phone. That's functional technology. Actually useful, not a distraction. There's certainly a distinction. For example, the T-Formex canoe: useful. Tetris: not so much.

After an hour, Ryan puts away the earphones. We're nearing the end of Lower Garry, which is marked by a high esker of sand jutting from its north shore. Suddenly two sets of horns pop up above the esker, 100 metres or so above the water. The pair peer at us curiously for a moment before they draw back, never to be seen by us again. They're the first caribou we've spotted since the big birthday herd three days ago.

We set up camp six kilometres short of the entry rapids to Bulliard Lake, on another flat plain of interlocking stone, backed by an esker that rises smoothly from camp to a ridgeline.

The tent is up, the Therm-A-Rests inflated, the sleeping bags unfurled. Our WhisperLite stove hisses lightly, boiling up water for our nightly ration of freeze-dried food and hot tea sweetened with brown sugar. I'm standing and chatting with Ryan, his back to the water, my back to the tent. He stops suddenly and looks at something behind my shoulder.

"Hello there," he remarks casually, as if someone he knows has just walked up behind me.

I turn around to see a large white and grey Arctic wolf standing beside our tent, observing us nonchalantly with its keen yellow eyes. The wilderness here is so expansive that this creature had probably never seen a human before, its curiosity drawing it in to inspect our alien presence. After about a minute – or what seems like a minute – it loses interest in us. We're neither caribou nor moulting goose. It starts to retreat, keeping its eyes on us as it zigzags up the rise slowly, pausing for a last moment on the ridge before slipping out of sight.

We jog up in pursuit to see where it's headed. Once on the ridge, we scan back and forth over the vast barrens stretching endlessly into the distance. To my eyes, there seems to be nowhere for it to hide. The wolf, however, is gone. Like the caribou herd dissolving into the mist, the wolf melded with the land and disappeared. A harmony of blood and dirt, of fur and rock – the creatures up here possess an ancient shape-shifting Singularity with the land that's born of evolution, not computers.

CHAPTER 49

On the hillside
Goose and caribou hang out
Prey stick together

We start the next day with a couple of snaking runs through the rapids before Bulliard Lake, having to line the edge of one particularly big drop. I'm in the rhythm now of quickly assessing and making decisions on how to negotiate the rapids of the Great Fish. I can look at a torrent and instantly visualize the best way to get the canoe down with the least amount of effort and risk. When we approach a rapid, its rumble notifying us of it far before we ever see it, my mind focuses. My eyes become sharp, looking for the first signs of the drop and the clues the river reveals about the rapid's character. You look for the soft spots, the quiet channels and clean lines through the powerful maelstrom, the calm in the storm. There are clean green lines through these rapids, a distinct path. The key is never to move faster than the water, to move at the speed of the current with occasional shifts to manoeuvre the canoe exactly where you want it to be. "Drift and shift," as I like to say. The last drop is not runnable as the whole river pushes over a recirculating ledge, the might of the water creating a sticky, powerful hole that would swallow up our canoe, churn it around, and spit it, our gear, and us out in pieces. A shallow, canoe-wide channel provides a sneak-route around and the canoe slides through easily. We are now in the calm water below. Looking back up at the maelstrom we've negotiated, it seems like there's no safe way down, but there is, there always is. Be open to the moment, to the opening, and it will come.

Bulliard Lake is intimate compared to the Garry Lakes. Somewhere along its edges is an old cabin where a priest once lived – the namesake for this lake, in fact. Much like the Great Fish being given Back's name, naming this lake after the priest is a way for outsiders, for people in general, to own something that's not theirs.

We're not exactly sure where the cabin is but in this treeless landscape any cabin should stick out like a beacon. We see nothing, and I've got movement fever; I'm not interested in looking at a dilapidated shack somewhere at the other end of this lake. Everything is ephemeral and fleeting in some way – even solid granite erodes into a pile of sand if you give wind and water enough time to work at it. This is even more so for man-made objects. Gravel roads grow over with vegetation, cars rust into the earth, wooden houses are eaten and absorbed by rot.

I spot a lone caribou on the shore. Oddly, it's surrounded by about a dozen geese, these two species of prey sticking together apparently, keeping a lookout for the next roaming wolf. As we pass by, the group moves away from us as a single entity. The geese crouch and honk, waddling inland with the caribou in tow. The Bulliard cabin is erased from my mind: this wild present, an ever-shifting constant, is far more interesting, tangible, and engaging than ruins from the past.

CHAPTER 50

The river's power
Rumbling like thunder all day
Rock Rapids descent

I've meticulously recreated the map of Rock Rapids from Ryan's phone on the back of one of the now-useless map printouts of my original Kaleet River route north. On the phone, I can see only sections of the route at a time, and having all the curves and angles of the river in front of me, with the rapids and waterfalls marked out, is a key piece of the puzzle of navigating these waters. You have to be able to see every section in context. I can guess from the map what my route will be through the rapids, where perhaps the best portage or lining or running section might exist. It's only an indicator though. I have to see how the river sets up in real life, in real time. We're going in cold: I have no information on the rapid and have read nothing about it. This is because I'd never planned on running this section in my original plan. I much prefer it this way anyhow. If you have a paint-by-numbers written guide of where the best place to run a rapid is, where a portage is, etc., it takes away the creativity of running a river. When your eyes are open to the big picture and not narrowed by someone else's perspective, you are open to all and any possibility as far as the best route down. In all art, in all creativity – and working an unknown river is as creative as any painting by Picasso or Dali – you have to be completely open and unhinged. When you spot that runnable side channel, when you see that seam amid the torrent, when you swerve around a rock and pull into the eddy below, you are painting a smooth line in the soft edges of a violent piece of nature. It is the most fleeting of art; it happens in the act of doing it, in the moment. Once the rapid has been run, the art is visible to no one, but stays within your soul for the rest of your life. No one else can see it, no one can buy it. It is gone but is there forever. It's also utterly original.

Tomorrow the river will be different, the water at a different level, which will make it a new river, a new canvas. A few boulders will move about, forever pushed by water, so really the river will never be the same again from one moment to the next. It's like drawing on an Etch A Sketch, which is reset with every shake, leaving a blank piece of water for the next artist to create their line down it. That's why, really, guidebooks to rivers are useless and should be thrown away. How do you make a truly accurate guidebook for an ever-changing entity? It's quite impossible.

We're camped eight kilometres away from the rapids on McDougall Lake, an easy paddle to the corner where the first drops occur. The day is sunny and still, ideal for negotiating Rock Rapids. The boulders along the edges will be dry for scouting and lining, and there'll be no big winds to throw us off of our course through the rapids. McDougall is glassy, and as we paddle across, I keep one ear turned toward the distant corner where the whitewater begins. It's eerily silent for the first few kilometres but then slowly, surely, the rumble creeps into earshot, a growing crescendo that welcomes us to a morning of engaged action.

The whole lake squeezes into a powerful corner. After a quick scout, we run the left-hand side of the broad, 100-metre-wide rapid, riding the flow to the river-left side where it splits around an island. Stepping out, I walk up to a high perch on the ridge to get a bird's eye view of the maelstrom. This is one of the best parts of river running, viewing the character of your opponent. Like surveying a chessboard, you are looking for a weakness that you can exploit, a soft point in the armour of the river where you can slip through unscathed. Portaging is always the last course of action.

From my vantage I inspect the drop to the left of the island. There's less water moving through it, but it looks like it runs through a steep boulder field around the blind corner at the bottom. The main power of the river goes right and a few hundred metres downriver spills over a beefy drop. On the far side I see that it seems quite straightforward and manageable, like we can sneak along the big drop via a slower channel to the right of it. The crux of this move is to ferry across the 100-metre breadth of the river, pointing the canoe upstream at a 45-degree angle and paddling hard to hold our position through standing waves in order to move straight across to the other side. The 45-degree angle will utilize the river's power to traverse us across, while our paddling will hold our position. The danger is that if we can't hold our line, we'll be pushed by the river down to the big ledge, or even worse flip in the middle of the crossing and be helplessly swimming into the ledge like so much flotsam and jetsam. Ryan stands alongside me as I tell him what I see. I know what a loaded canoe is capable of and he yields to my decision.

We ferry into the main current, point upstream at a 45-degree angle, and hold our line in the relative calm of three-foot haystacks a few hundred metres above the big drop. Ryan throws in hard, steady strokes up front while I follow his cadence in the stern, occasionally throwing in a correction stroke to hold our line. We execute perfectly, traversing in a plumb line across the river to the opposite shore. Once there, we work that side for the rest of Rock Rapids, negotiating all 12 km of the feature by running and lining the edge rapids without a single portage. We even manage to paddle and line a side channel around Sinclair Falls, the burliest drop in Rock Rapids – a series of large cascades that would pound any canoe to smithereens. On a broad river like the Great Fish there are options if you ferret them out, weaknesses in the armour of the river that allow for steady progress. Our backchannel seam slides us smoothly and easily around them; a satisfying move indeed.

We get through the rapids in the course of the morning, and paddle on for the rest of the day without maps, or a care in the world. Even with slower movement through the rapids, we still cover 61 kilometres, so our pace is really clipping along. The north wind hasn't really revealed itself yet, though I know it's lurking downriver for us, waiting to pounce and slap us around. This thought drives our movement, pushing us to lay down the kilometres, knowing that we may be sitting and watching the wind at any moment. I'm quite satisfied now at not having attempted the Kaleet route. We'd have missed the exhilaration of the Rock Rapids and would have been subjected to endless hours of dragging through a shallow, potentially even completely dry, river system. That evening Ryan catches a grayling and a trout. We eat the fish quietly and contentedly, basking in the afterglow of getting through the main crux of the river.

CHAPTER 51

Like its namesake stealth
It crept up and tried to bite
Wolf Rapids action

The next day, we get into the groove once more. The river has decent push now, with smooth sections interspersed with rapids. We run several sets throughout the day, riding powerful wave trains around ledge drops, boulders, and falls. The day is warm and calm. We reach a long, smooth section of water, take off our life vests and roll our wetsuits down to our waists. The river begins to narrow and I see a large boulder in the middle of the flume. There is also the unmistakable sound of either a falls or a big whitewater set. The river is moving quickly and we are in the middle of the channel. The walls steepen, with no eddy for us to get to at the side of the river. I stand up in the back of the canoe for a quick boat scout. On the left is a perfectly smooth horizon line – an indication of a ledge or falls. On the right, I can see the tips of haystacks popping up below the entry. I make a split-second decision and plop down in my seat, kneeling.

"Get your knees down! Paddle hard…we're going right!"

Ryan springs into action, digging for all he's worth. As we power the canoe to the right of the boulder, I hope I've made the correct decision. We enter a steep but smooth green tongue of water in the middle that leads us through a bouncy set of standing waves into a quiet pool below. I look back to the drop on the left side of the boulder to see what we've just avoided and it is indeed a heavy, sticky drop. It's about a ten-foot cascade into a wide hole that would have sent us for a nasty swim sans life vests. I give out a hoot of joy. A close call, but as the old saying goes, close only counts in horseshoes and hand grenades, so all is good.

I hadn't expected the rapid but then again, we don't have maps. We check Ryan's phone maps later and realize we'd just done a blind run of Wolf Rapids, which we thought was further downstream. Our fast pace throughout the day put us far past where I thought we were.

The river transitions into a large lake that takes us past the mouth of the Meadowbank River. At one point in my planning I thought this might be our route out from the Great Fish. It would lead to Baker Lake, the only interior community in Nunavut – an easier way out than trying to get to Gjoa Haven. We were in it now, though – fired up and motivated to do the whole river to the sea.

A little way north of the Meadowbank mouth we pull into shore to set up camp. A quick weather check informs us that a big northwest wind is going to blow in. We decide to have a quick dinner where we are, and then paddle another ten km or so up this wide part of the river to an east-west shoreline aspect where we'll be able to tuck into a nice lee for the night. If we stay here, we'll get nailed squarely by the wind.

We set off in the grey evening, headed toward the high hills in the north where the Great Fish makes a hard turn to the east. The water is silky, black, and calm – the canoe gliding quietly over glass. At the turn, we see our first sign of humanity since meeting Karsten. A couple of roofless plywood shacks sit up on the hillside, well past their expiry date. A tangle of old tools, building materials, and cooking implements occupies one of the spaces – a dream died, abandoned, or just simply never completed. Probably an old winter fishing and hunt camp that a long snowmobile tour from Baker Lake could access. Backed by high hills, our camp below the shacks is perfectly tucked out of the wind. The northwest won't get us here. Our kilometre tally is 81, our biggest day of the trip distance-wise. An ice check with Shannon tells me that Chantrey Inlet and Simpson Strait are now clear but Gjoa Haven is not. Until it clears there, locals won't be travelling down to the mouth of the Great Fish. It's still perhaps a week until we get to the mouth, but this big north wind is just the thing to clear out the final bit of ice in "Joe." Hopefully, that will set the people to travelling to their camps and provide an avenue for us to get to the town. But that is out of our hands, a bridge to cross when we get to it. The north wind is coming and is guaranteed to throw a wrench in the works.

CHAPTER 52

Big Northwest wind day
Speed and spray down the wave face
Surfing the canoe

The north wind makes you paddle hard. There are no breaks, no lazy strokes. The north wind is relentless and so we have to be relentless too. Paddling in cool six-degree weather we have an easy time for the first 15 kilometres, but then turn into the wind and battle for the remaining 40 kilometres of the day. The wind drives into the current, creating large standing waves, and we find ourselves surfing the waves for long sections, sometimes burying the bow in an explosion of spray. We work the lee side of the river all day, feathering the edge as we try to stay out of the brunt of the wind while still taking advantage of the current and not getting caught in the back eddies.

A surprise highlight of the day is coming upon a government water survey cabin. I've run into these before on the Kazan and Thelon Rivers. They're generally constructed of corrugated steel, built for the harsh conditions. They are also always left open as a shelter cabin – and all of them seem to have a percolator, Coleman stove, and coffee. This one was no different and we have a luxurious lunch inside, out of the cold wind...hot coffee on the stovetop percolator to wash down the peanut butter, honey, and tortilla. It timed out perfectly for lunch, but we weren't going to stay beyond that. To be out of the wind for a half hour, to get a taste of the four walls of civilization, makes you instantly comfortable in a physical sense. At the same time, I have an itching, scratching feeling that this comfort is false because we still have a way to go...this is not home. It's merely a reminder of home. And right now, after a month, my real home is on the river, moving. This place reminds me of the stagnant comfort of the city, where I can sometimes be found crawling up the proverbial walls, my mind on fire, needing to break from the velvet handcuffs of a soft bed and dry room, to instead be on the literal, pulsing river of life.

We are soon back there, on the Great Fish. The wind is ramping up steadily and our lee is deteriorating as the river angles northward, so we have to keep it moving. Sometimes that north wind feels like it will blow and blow and blow, never stopping for the rest of eternity. It pushes me, tells me to get my ass in gear. The comfort of those four walls and that warm percolated coffee clutched in my hand instantly becomes a distant memory as we engage the river, the wind, the land. Perspective is instantaneous out here.

CHAPTER 53

Into the wind's teeth
Sneaking along the lee side
Then nowhere to hide

A month into our journey, we near the river's end. Ryan proudly shows off the haul of grayling and lake trout he's pulled from the pool below the rapid where we've settled in for the bright night. I notice that he's quietly busying himself gathering small bits of dwarf willow and birch to cook over; he seems to have shed the clasps of technology and fallen into rhythm with the land.

Earlier in our journey, I feared Ryan would be lost to Kurzweil's prophecy. Listening to podcasts while canoeing and watching YouTube videos at night, separating himself from the reality of our journey, from being present in such a spectacular landscape.

Things have turned for him in recent days. He's removed his earphones and replaced them with the rush of the wind and with silence. YouTube videos have ceased to glow in the tent as he instead reads one of my books. His awareness has sharpened and he begins to spot animals onshore before I do. We are unified in the canoe, deftly running booming whitewater sections of the river like Wolf Rapids and Rock Rapids. Where once he tried to maintain a barrier between himself and the wild with technology, Ryan now seeks union with it by simply opening up all his senses to what the Arctic has to offer.

The north wind has blown for days now, those easy few weeks a distant memory. I'm glad we made distance while we could, as it seems there will be no easy days from now until Chantrey Inlet. My mindset is that the wind will never stop. If it does, the relative ease of travel will be welcome. It won't be better, just welcome. Resistance is engaging, and nothing resists your progress like the Arctic north wind.

We only did 21 kilometres today, bumping along an open windy, lake-like section of the river into a flat, hard blow. We're tucked into the lee of a rocky hill, our tent placed on a flat bed of gravel surrounded by hot pink fireweed. I walk up to the high point and stare out over the broad expanse of Franklin Lake. The large lakes on the Great Fish are obvious in that they break up the narrower flow of the main river. Even without a detailed map, Franklin is distinct as it's the last big body of water before we hit the ocean and is named on my overview territorial map of Nunavut. The surface of the lake is dappled with lines of wind and whitecaps, telling us it's futile to go any further today. The air is cool, with no insects willing to brave either the temperature or the stiff breeze that stings and chaps the parts of my face not covered in a beard. Tomorrow the wind should switch to a West and ease, allowing us to move again.

When there's nothing to do but wait, waiting is pleasurable. I wander. Ryan fishes. We drink afternoon coffee. Ryan makes a curried fish soup. We eat. Only when the wind tells me to stop and enjoy where I am do I accept the moment of peace from the incessant, addictive forward motion. The wind does this on every journey, and I appreciate its ability to put its hand out and say, "Stop! Time to chill out, Frank." And so I chill. In my own way, anyhow.

I do some vigorous Wim Hof breathing and headstand stretches at the high point above the camp, with the wind whipping off the lake and rolling up and over the hill. The dwarf willows and birches whip and rustle around me on my patch of moss. It's almost like Stonehenge up here, with black, angular, car-sized boulders arranged all around me as if some alien giant has been playing Lego with the earth. It's an unexpected, serene moment, still frozen in time in my mind. I am utterly alone, and utterly content. The contentedness comes from the realization of my smallness in the world and revelling in that obscurity. And though I'm alone, I'm not lonely. I feel part of this great wilderness we're moving through, everything intertwined within the ancient pulse of life. When you're part of something, human or otherwise, you can never be lonely.

CHAPTER 54

Icy rain outside
Hordes of bugs under the tarp
Back River luncheon

The day starts calm, with a mild northwest wind. It's cool and wet, so we gear up in our Farmer John neoprene suits and snug the tunnel of the spray deck up to our armpits. Ryan doesn't have a warm toque, and his jacket is so porous he may as well not have one on at all. I'm reminded again how he turned down my offer of a neoprene toque and full waterproof outfit before we left Vancouver.

Halfway through the day, he remarks, "Man, it's cold…maybe we should pull in early."

He's tried this several times on the trip and I'm tiring of it. If this cold weather and north wind doesn't get it in his head that we have to keep moving, what will? If for some reason we can't arrange transport and we have to paddle the 170 km of open water to get to Gjoa Haven, we may just get tight on our food rations.

Unable to help myself, I niggle him about his clothes once more. "So why didn't you bring your good rain gear again?"

"I didn't want to trash my good ski gear on this trip."

I poke some more. "And here we are, five degrees and raining, with you soaked to the bone."

"Here we are…" his voice trails off.

The rain is coming down in sheets when we pull in for lunch at a miserable, drenched spot in a field of low, slick boulders. I hastily set up the tarp so we have a dry minute to eat some fish tacos made up of the leftover trout from Ryan's haul the day before, and to have a quick smoke…a moment of relaxation before we hit the fray again.

Once the tarp is up, a horde of black flies and mosquitoes descend in a thick cloud. Amazing. Even in this miserable cold weather they're out. These lower Great Fish insects are a hardy lot indeed. The smoke from the clove cigarette fumigates them somewhat, but we're soon paddling away from that fetid little pause.

Usually there aren't rapids in the middle of a lake, but what do you know: a large 500-metre-wide set looms in front of us. There are three big, broad sets. We run a sneak line on the left of the first, then manoeuvre the second to the edge of its final ledge drop, which we line. The whole river then pinches into a curve of haystacks which we ride through to a sprawling, flat bit of tundra below a high, rocky point before what looks like another ledge drop.

"Good enough," I tell Ryan, "it's time to camp. We'll scout and deal with that final piece of business in the morning."

We are both soaked, but I'm still warm and comfortable in my neoprene toque and functioning rain gear. I watch Ryan shiver as he jerkily changes into dry clothes under the tarp. Yet again, I can only shake my head. He's such a stubborn bastard, but I have to realize that stubbornness has seen him through a lot of big trips and will see him through this one. I'm similarly stubborn, with a distinct lack of empathy for my trip partner, seeing him in that moment as a piece of trip gear not functioning to full capacity rather than as a human being. It's an admittedly sociopathic trait that rises from within me on my journeys.

The inReach forecast shows a big North coming the day after tomorrow, so hopefully we can reach Chantrey Inlet by day's end. Ryan has a friend who has a friend in Gjoa Haven who can apparently arrange a pick-up for us, but we haven't heard from him and it's been a few days. I've contacted Shannon to see if she can hunt someone down or at least assess the possibilities. She's always reliable and on point with these sorts of things. For now, Ryan and I sit quietly under the tarp.

Two corners of the tarp are connected to the canoe, which is on its side, back to the wind. The other two corners are wrapped around boulders and a paddle in the middle props the tarp up. The cold, grim rain washes across in sheets but we're dry and cozy for the first time all day, sitting on our life vests, each with a select boulder to support our lower back so we can lean back on the foam and lounge. If I were to rate the function of a life vest on trip, I would lean toward their usefulness as seats more than life savers. I definitely spend more time with my butt on one than having it wrapped around my torso. It's a truly multifunctional piece of equipment. I usually wear one on windy crossings, for shooting rapids, or if I'm photographing an action sequence for potential publication shots. Some magazines won't publish images of paddlers without life vests, thinking it irresponsible. Freedom by nature is completely irresponsible, and I'll choose freedom over responsibility any day.

CHAPTER 55

Storms rake the landscape
Cold and wet with driving wind
Time to sit and read

The wind did a 180-degree turn overnight, forcing me to reverse the whole canoe/tarp set-up in the morning so we'd be sheltered. It's about one or two degrees, just barely warm enough not to snow. Though the wind is howling, it favours our direction and I think we can move along with it and get to Chantrey. I get the water going on the stove under the tarp and throw in four heaping tablespoons of coffee. I let it boil up for a while to get it nice and strong, then cover it with a lid to let the grinds settle. After that, it's another pot of boiling water for the oatmeal – three packets of Peaches and Cream with a hand full of raisins thrown in for good measure. Ryan still hasn't stirred from the tent, so I step out from under the tarp and walk over to rouse him.

"Ryan, breakfast and coffee are on."

I hear a mumbled response from inside the tent. "What's it like out there?"

"Oh, you know...two degrees, sideways rain from the east, windy. Pretty standard stuff."

There's a pause, then Ryan says, "I need a day."

"A day? Day for what?" I'm a bit confused.

"I need a day off, man. I was freezing and soaked yesterday...I don't want to get hypothermia."

I unzip the tent door so I can see him. He's propped up, still in his sleeping bag, looking up at me.

"Just need a day, man," he reiterates.

My blood boils. This pisses me off. I trusted him, based on his experience in the mountains, to come into this prepared. I've offered him extra gear, anything he needed. "No, no, no, I'll be fine," he always said.

It doesn't help that I'm admittedly in a "Horse to the Barn" type of mode. With Chantrey Inlet only a day's paddle away, I'm champing at the bit.

A young boy swings from a pole beside the outstretched hide of a polar bear in Qikiqtarjuaq, Nunavut. April 24, 2018.

John McClelland skis along the toe of Coronation Glacier on Baffin Island, Nunavut, looking for a way onto the top of it. April 29, 2018.

John takes the lead roped up as the team begins the long haul up the Coronation Glacier to the Penny Ice Cap. April 30, 2018.

The team camps on Turner Glacier on Baffin Island, Nunavut, below the surreal spectacle of Mount Asgard. May 3, 2018.

Dave Garrow and John are dwarfed by Thor Peak on Baffin Island, Nunavut, as they make their way down the frozen Weasel River. May 5, 2018.

Bernie Kohl and I pose along the shores of Ptarmigan Lake, Northwest Territories. Notice the metal pot by Bernie's foot that is full of fish waiting to be deboned. July 10, 2018.

Ryan (bow) and I run one of the 83 whitewater rapids along the course of the Great Fish River (Back River), Nunavut. July 17, 2018.

A herd of thousands of caribou congregates just inland of the Great Fish River, an amazing gift on my birthday. July 21, 2018.

A bold wolf prowls the edges of camp, then disappears like a ghost into the vast barrens. July 24, 2018.

Ryan displays his haul of lake trout and grayling caught while windbound one afternoon just south of Franklin Lake, Nunavut. July 30, 2018.

The team serendipitously encounters the Atqittuq family of Gjoa Haven in Chantrey Inlet, Nunavut, at trip's end. From left to right: Ryan, Jacob, me, Marcus, Martha, Ellen, and Samuel (Marvin Atqittuq took the photo). August 2, 2018.

David Reid and Richard Smith work one of the sleds over an ice heave at the mouth of the North Pole River, Nunavut. March 31, 2019.

David and Richard haul their sleds over wind-blasted, frozen drifts as they make their way toward Committee Bay, Nunavut. April 3, 2019.

Richard's icy face covering reveals the cold conditions during a break on Committee Bay. April 8, 2019.

Lionel Tigvareark poses beside the Kellett River in Nunavut in his blood-spattered parka and pants his mother made for him. Lionel would later come to fetch me when I pulled out of the expedition. April 15, 2019.

My swollen, bruised feet the morning I decided to leave the expedition near Kugaaruk, Nunavut. April 16, 2019.

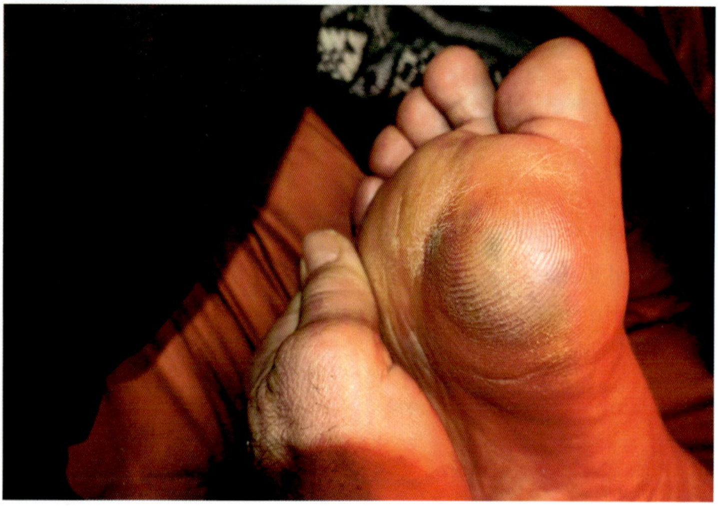

I just can't help myself – I want to power through the finish line. We have plenty of food and have made great time so far. Plus, I don't do days off…never have on these journeys. I'm so amped to move forward and see what's around the next corner, to figure out the next puzzle nature throws our way, that I can never conceive of twiddling my thumbs unless nature tells us we have to. Only the wind can make me stop, not a partner with inadequate clothing. The wind is workable today in my estimation, so I want to go.

"The wind's not terrible, we can move in this," I say bluntly.

"I need a day. I asked for that hour on Artillery Lake to fish and I'm asking for today," Ryan states more firmly.

I glare at him. "Will you finally admit you didn't bring the right gear for this trip?"

"Fine! I fucked up! Now give me my day!"

With that admission, I relent. It's petty of me, but it feels good to get this stubborn young lad to actually admit fault.

I stalk back to the tarp, open my journal and rage into it about all the perceived faults I see in Bougie…he smoked weed chronically for the first three weeks of trip until he ran out…he tried to bring toilet paper… he brought inadequate clothing…he listened to a podcast while in the canoe…he watches videos on his phone at night…he wants a day off, even though its a manageable wind…and we're only 40 km from Chantrey Inlet! I should be so thankful for Bougie, for his effort and willingness to come on this journey, but in this moment I'm not. I'm a hard taskmaster, and I know I'm being unreasonable, but everything, both good and bad, gets amplified on trip. An outsider would probably deem me insane, would say I should chill out. But I can't. I'm wired this way and inefficiencies on trip enrage me.

Shannon got in contact with an outfitter in Gjoa Haven named Charlie Cahill. According to him, it would cost about $3,000 to come pick us up by boat from Chantrey Inlet as it's about a 350-km round trip. Also, I find out that the ice has indeed cleared from around the hamlet, thanks to that big north wind that's been blowing the past few days. Theoretically, people from there will start to come down to the mouth of the Back River to fish and hunt now that the ice has released them. The outfitter mentioned something about "The Waterfall" where they often set up. I have no idea where this waterfall is, whether it's on the Back River itself, some tributary, or out in Chantrey somewhere. We don't have maps after all...the uncertainty of everything is exciting.

Ryan pipes up that he'd be willing to paddle the 170 km up Chantrey and then cross 16 km over to Gjoa Haven.

I lose it. "Are you kidding? We're sitting here now instead of paddling. It's way more exposed on Chantrey – it's open ocean, it's farther north, it's colder. If you can't handle today, how are you going to handle that? We're going with the pick-up option...paddling all the way up is a last resort."

Ryan spends most of the day in the tent, but I have to give him credit. He's reading, not listening to podcasts, at the moment working his way through *Paddlenorth*. Despite our disagreement today, he's shed some of the technological skin that he was wrapped in for the first few weeks. He's a generally good guy. I look at him as stubborn, but is he any more stubborn than me? Look at what I'm writing about, railing against the one person who's been in the canoe with me, moving forward at blazing speed through a rough landscape. His desire for a day off triggered a purely negative response in me. I get so wrapped up in the present on these journeys that I sometimes lose perspective.

I spend the day bundled up in all my clothes under the tarp, framing a couple of articles I have to write for magazines, including an article about this journey. Time, usually only bestowed upon me by an unmanageable wind and not an unwilling partner, is not something I often give myself. Focused time with my journal, without any other distractions, is a rare and treasured gift.

CHAPTER 56

35 days long
Yellowknife to Chantrey Bay
All done, no more fun

The next day is calm and we get off of our campsite early. We paddle down and portage the ledge at the corner, then carry on along the meandering course of the river. The current is still there, though lighter, and we work our way down to the Hayes River, which drains into the Great Fish right at its mouth. There's an island there with a hunting cabin, which we investigate during lunch. It's a pretty basic four walls and a roof, with scribblings from Inuit hunters, mostly about how many caribou they've taken on the various trips they'd had there. We still seem to be in the river, though it's rapidly broadening and braiding out around us.

There's no sign of this theoretical "waterfall" that people camp at so we push off and paddle past the mouth of the Hayes toward Chantrey Inlet. We run into various sandbars that appear more frequently as the tide drops and threatens to leave us on a damp bed of sand for six hours. Through a combination of dragging and paddling, we eventually find a deeper channel and keep working out to open water. On the outer edge of the outermost sandbar, I reach down and cup some water in my palm, bringing it up to my mouth to taste. The brackish water – an elixir composed of Chantrey Inlet, the Great Fish River, and the Hayes River – tells me we've reached the sea.

We pose, arm-in-arm, for a photo commemorating the moment, a backdrop of golden sand and water framing our smiling faces, the discontent I had with Ryan yesterday washed away in the achievement. There's nowhere for us to stop though, nowhere to camp here in the water-saturated sand flats. We push on out into Chantrey, away from the Great Fish. Far in the distance is a rocky ridge, the only rise of land in this flat seascape. There seems to be a white streak running through the middle of it. It's the only thing we've seen that even slightly resembles a waterfall. Maybe ten kilometres away?

We set out for it, for the first time all trip hoping for a sign of human life. I recall Aussie John's casual remark about just meeting up with Inuit at an encampment from where he'd arrange travel up to Gjoa Haven. It seemed like such an assured comment, but we've seen no one so far, no camps, nothing. Perhaps we're too early? It's quite possible as the ice literally just cleared a couple of days ago. Only the keenest, most prepared Inuit would be out here so quickly. Paddling toward that white streak, hope was high but tempered. Stay open to the moment and, hopefully, it will come to fruition.

CHAPTER 57

After a couple more hours of paddling across the breadth of the inlet, we finally approach the ridge. I take out my spotting scope and see that there is indeed a waterfall pouring through a cleft in the cliff and spilling down the rock face. Additionally, two white canvas tents are set up along a creek at the base of the flume.

It's nearing 10 p.m. and we've been paddling for almost 14 hours to this point. Ever since we left that cabin on an island in the delta, we've been in a matrix of wet, intertidal sand, with no place to settle down for the night, so we just kept on paddling. As we near the little encampment, the kilometre tally for the day racks up to 68.

Our canoe grinds to a halt on the gravel beach. I step out and walk toward the camp while Ryan remains with the canoe. No one is out in the evening swarm of mosquitoes so I knock on the wooden frame of the first tent. I hear someone speaking in Inuktitut, then the tent flap opens and an older woman's eyes go wide and she gasps the word "*Kabloona*!" (white person), before the flap is quickly closed again. I hear her exclaim "*Kabloona*!" once again to someone inside.

The entrance flips wide and out comes a stout, barrel-chested Inuk. He is grinning ear to ear and shakes my hand warmly. His wife is the one I surprised and she quickly goes about baking up some bannock and getting coffee ready. I communicate via charades with the man as both he and his wife only speak Inuktitut, until a younger man named Marvin emerges from the other tent.

Marvin is fluent in both English and Inuktitut. The older couple in the tent are his parents, Jacob and Martha Atqittuq. Marvin is here with them, his wife Ellen, his son Marcus, and his brother Samuel. They'd set up their camp just the day before and are the only people from town in the area as far as they know. Finding them was truly a stroke of luck, and they promise tomorrow to try and arrange via satellite phone to have someone from town pick us up as they're planning on staying at the mouth of the Great Fish to, naturally, catch a great number of fish.

Over the course of the evening we learn that for the first quarter century of their lives, Martha and Jacob, now 75 years young, lived nomadically in the area around the mouth of the Great Fish River in skin tents and igloos, before moving into the permanent settlement of Gjoa Haven in the 1970s.

Unlike many Inuit Elders I've met over the years, Jacob is sharp and spry, still providing his family with sustenance from the land as he has done his whole life. He feeds Ryan and me slices of raw, air-dried meat from a caribou he shot just yesterday. The flesh is so tender it melts in my mouth. Martha emerges from the tent with fresh bannock cooked on their Coleman stove, along with margarine and jam to put on it. Jacob hands us pilot biscuits as well, with peanut butter to boot. This sudden bounty is our dinner, a welcome break from our usual freeze-dried food fare. From his kit Jacob shows us a fishing lure he made from caribou bone that he's used for years to pull 80-pound lake trout from below the last rapid of the river, which is the very spot where we had our last camp. These huge lunkers are what the river is named after, a far more appropriate moniker than that of a random officer from the British Navy who bumbled his way down the river once.

As the midnight hour draws near and the mosquitoes come in ever-thicker waves, the Atqittuqs retire to their tents once more. Ryan and I are full of energy, having encountered this amazing family, and realizing the journey has actually ended. We both had to have the mentality that the 170-km paddle up to Gjoa Haven was a possibility until now, but it seems almost assured that Marvin can get someone to come get us. Armed with a full flask of whisky and a couple of clove cigarettes, we hike up through the cliffs alongside the waterfall to the top of the ridge. There's a light breeze that keeps the mosquitoes down as we plop ourselves among some boulders and light up our cloves. It doesn't take long for me to get a buzz in my head as we drain the flask…our usual five-sip ration goes out the door as we toast the completion of the Great Fish River. My miserable attitude toward Ryan yesterday has evaporated in our euphoria.

"I think we should still try to paddle to Gjoa Haven if the conditions look good tomorrow."

I laugh. Yesterday he didn't want to paddle because it was cold and wet; now he reiterates he's keen to paddle up to "Joe." This time it washes from me like water off of a duck's back. He's only half-serious, and I don't care either way. The final say is mine and I will take full advantage of the gift we've been given by meeting the Atqittuqs. I also realize that had we not had that extra day off and pushed on to this point, the Atqittuqs would not yet have been here…we would have missed them completely, and it is unlikely we would have met them in the big blue of the inlet, where we would have been a mere speck crossing over to the opposite shore. Ryan's desire to stay in camp allowed this unlikely meeting of *kabloonat* (white men) and Inuk to happen.

We stare over the vast blue of the Arctic Ocean, the other side of Chantrey Inlet just barely visible as a pencil-thin line. It's getting dusky and cool. Light dew settles on my jacket. My head swims with alcohol and nicotine coursing pleasantly through my bloodstream. I appreciate what we've done, where we are, and how Ryan is an equal part of all that. It's a good feeling.

"Well, I guess it's bedtime," I say.

With that, we amble back down through the boulders and cliff to our little orange tent, now set up beside the white canvas frame tents of the Atqittuqs.

The next morning I wake first. I see that Samuel and Jacob are already up. Jacob smiles at me and waves me to join them by his tent. Samuel is their eldest son. He was a year old when Jacob and Martha came in off the land and moved to Gjoa Haven. He is in his late 40s now but looks much older and speaks in a raspy voice. Jacob smiles and grins as he pushes some bannock and caribou on me for breakfast. Samuel translates anything I can't understand.

Everyone is soon up, including Ryan, and we sit around chatting as Martha cooks up fresh bannock in their tent. In the middle of conversation, Jacob suddenly turns his head. He's just spotted a distant caribou on the shoreline, and springs into action like a rabbit. Grabbing his ancient rifle, he stalks nimbly to our upturned canoe, where he braces the rifle and waits, peering at the spot where the caribou is. The animal is at least half a kilometre away, well out of range. Ryan follows along behind Jacob, walking in his footsteps, wanting to learn from the master. They both crouch by the canoe, side by side, looking and waiting. After half an hour of waiting, the caribou fails to draw any closer and melts slowly into the distance. But the interaction has given me a glimpse of Jacob's synchronicity with the land.

Marvin chuckles with pride as he tells us how on a snowmobile trip the previous winter his GPS broke, and his dad accurately navigated hundreds of kilometres of frozen tundra to Baker Lake purely by reading the shape and direction of snowdrifts. Jacob is a living example of an ancient Singularity – one of the last true holdovers of a time when man and nature were one.

Marvin gets in contact with a guy in Gjoa Haven who agrees to come and get us by boat. I negotiate a price of $1,000 plus my shotgun (a $300 value). It's much better than the $3,000 we were quoted by Charlie Cahill. Also, I book our flights back out. We have free vouchers from Canadian North Airways but can't get on a flight until five days from now.

I turn to Ryan. "Well, the good news is our flights are booked, but we're going to have to hang out in town for five days."

Jacob asks Marvin what we were saying. Marvin tells him and Jacob replies in Inuktitut.

"My dad wants to know where you're going to stay in town."

"Well, we can't afford $250 per night at the hotel, so we'll find a place to camp."

Marvin relays this information to Jacob, who replies with a short sentence.

"My dad says you'll stay at his house."

I'm blown away by Jacob's generosity and hospitality and think of a way to repay him somehow. My mind immediately turns to the red Esquif Prospecteur 17. The canoe is the ultimate tripping machine – made of a three-layered ABS plastic and foam combination that is relatively light yet virtually indestructible. You don't have to treat this boat with kid gloves. You can drag it over dry rocks fully loaded going upstream or run it over boulders on the downstream. It has a slippery surface that doesn't "grab" but rather glides over obstructions. Its hull design is supremely nimble in whitewater yet tracks amazingly straight on deep-water lakes and ocean. It's the best possible tool to do what I do and would last most people a lifetime. Ultimately, though, it is merely a tool, and the job it was meant for is now done. Despite the price tag of $2,500, it would cost more than that in time and money to get it back home from here. I live in a condo in North Vancouver so there's no place to store canoes there. The only home would be the cottage in Ontario where we already have two canoes hanging under the deck.

I have canoes I've given away or sold for cheap all over the North. The first Esquif I ever gave away at trip's end was to Harry Towtongie in Rankin Inlet. I remember pulling onto the sticky clay shore at 9 p.m. with my partner Taku. It was August 16, 2009, and we'd just completed the 46-day, 2000-km journey. I figured we'd get a hotel room for the night, clean up, then camp until we could get a flight out. It was low tide so I tromped 50 feet up to firmer ground, leaving Taku with the canoe.

There were three men talking by the side of the house we'd pulled in front of. It was already getting dusky, with the 24-hour daylight cycle of summer long past, so I only saw the men as shadows. The shadows stopped and looked at me as I walked up from the sea. One of them stepped forward. It was Harry. He was tall and lanky for an Inuk, with loose, curly black hair and glasses.

"Hi there," I said in a friendly tone.

"Hey, where'd you come from?"

"We just paddled here from Yellowknife…a 46-day trip."

He stopped for a thoughtful beat, then asked, "How'd you get to Rankin? You paddle down from Chesterfield Inlet?"

"Nope. We cut in at Barbour Bay and paddled the Meliadine River right to here."

Another thoughtful pause from Harry.

"Wowww. Not many people have been up in that country for years. I was in that area in the late '70s doing some survey work. I'm big into explorers...got a ton of *National Geographic* magazines. Where you staying in town?"

"I guess we'll just stay in the hotel tonight."

"You can stay at my place for as long as you want," he said.

"Wow! Thanks! Where do you live?"

He thumbed in the direction of the nearby house. "Right here."

We ended up staying with Harry and his family for three days until our plane left. I gave Harry my canoe, which he was excited to use for caribou hunting. It was a fair deal for such a generous offer of accommodation. It felt great not to be attached to it or have to deal with it, and to know it would be well used by someone who appreciated wilderness travel and would utilize it in his own way to help feed his family.

Since then I've left canoes all over the Arctic and northern regions of the boreal forest. Harry got his canoe in 2009; an Ojibway man in Peawanuck on the south shore of Hudson Bay bought my canoe for $400 in 2011 after a 1150-km canoe trip from Pakashkan Lake. A young Inuit man who'd brought us caribou stew and drove us to the airport in the town of Kangiqsualujjuaq on Ungava Bay bought my canoe for $250 after a 620-km canoe trip from Nain, Labrador. In Fort Severn in 2014 an Ojibway woman who worked in the local band office bought my canoe for $300 after we'd finished a 1350-km canoe trip from the narrows of Lake Winnipeg. In 2016 I donated our canoe to the school in Baker Lake after an 1800-km trip there from La Ronge, Saskatchewan. In 2017 I sold my canoe for $400 to the local Parks manager in the Inuit town of Umiujaq on the east shore of Hudson Bay after a 1350-km trip there from the Pekans River Bridge on Highway 389.

And here I was again, at the end of a long trip with a canoe to dispense of. This was the perfect opportunity with the perfect human being. Like Harry, with his generous offer of us staying at his place for five days, Jacob would not be paying for this canoe.

I ask Marvin, "Would your father like to have our canoe?"

Marvin smiles and then speaks to his father in Inuktitut.

Jacob beams. He always seems to be smiling, but now his smile is brighter than ever. He stands up and walks over to me and shakes my hand, speaking to me in his native tongue.

"He says, yes, he'd love it. He can use it in Gjoa Haven to check his fish nets."

Martha is also beaming and she speaks to Ryan and me, Marvin translating once more.

"My mom says she'll make you some sealskin mitts in return for the canoe."

"Wow, that would be amazing. Of course, we'd love those."

With that Martha comes up to me, has me hold my palm out to her, then puts her own outstretched palm against mine. She does the same for Ryan. Having made a mental note about our hand size, she nods and smiles. That's all she needs from us for measurement.

The Atqittuq clan pack everything up and stuff it into Jacob's boat. They're headed to the "last rapid" which we'd camped above for our last two nights before we met the Atqittuqs, when the weather was grim and I resented Ryan's unwillingness to move. That seems like eons ago now. We've got a boat coming to pick us up, we've made friends with the generous Atqittuq family, and we are snacking on fresh caribou.

Apparently, the guys who are coming to pick us up will be arriving later in the day, but time is a fairly fluid concept in the North so who knows when that will be. With a dusky light still lingering throughout the 24-hour cycle, they could arrive anytime. We just have to be ready.

Jacob, Martha, Marvin, Samuel, Ellen, and Marcus all get ready to depart. The canvas tents are down, with their things all bundled and packed up into Jacob's open 18-foot motorboat. Marvin shows me the barren ground grizzly fur that his family sleeps on. He killed the animal a few years earlier and its pelt now acts as his Therm-A-Rest. I run my fingers through it. The yellow/brown fur is shiny, lustrous, and soft.

The boat has to be pushed ten feet offshore to float up at the mouth of the creek that spills out below the cascading waterfall. Jacob, Samuel, Marvin, and Ellen have knee-high rubber boots, but Martha doesn't and she's less than overjoyed to have to wade into the chilly waters to get into the boat. I've just been canoe-tripping for 35 days. I'm wiry and strong. After a canoe trip, I'm the fittest I can possibly be. Moving all day, every day with no off-days (except for, ahem, one), I've dropped from my beer-infused city weight of 180 pounds down to a trim 165 pounds…skin painted over muscle and bone with nary an ounce of fat. Paddling, portaging, lining, and scouting my way through the landscape is better than any cross-fit gym membership. If I can throw a 90-pound canoe on my head, then I can certainly carry Martha over the water and deposit her safe and dry into the boat.

She's standing on the shore, a stout five foot two, wearing a knitted toque and worn insulated jacket. I point to my back and then to her. She looks surprised, then turns to Marvin to confirm that I do indeed want to carry her to the boat. She smiles and nods less than assuredly. I bend over and hoist her over my shoulder, her legs in front of me and her torso and head hanging over my back. She is surprisingly heavy for such a small woman…a mass of dense bone and muscle packed into her small frame. Each step is unsteady through the shin-deep water and pebbled bottom, but I focus and swear to myself that I won't drop this sweet woman into the water. Step by step I cross the chasm, more focused on this one portage than any other of the journey. I deposit her gently in the boat and she grins with both joy and relief. Everyone else has a good chuckle over it. Soon we're shaking hands vigorously with the others, and they depart.

"We'll see you in Joe!" Marvin shouts as they leave.

We watch as they slowly motor across Chantrey Inlet toward the Great Fish, eventually disappearing into the maze of islands in the delta.

CHAPTER 58

It's mid-morning and the rest of our day is spent lounging around reading, eating, and staring at the sea. We're not exactly sure when and if these guys are going to show today, so we just leave the tent up to hang out in – a spot away from the bugs. The hours tick by and it's mid-afternoon, then eventually dinnertime. We boil up water for yet another round of freeze-dried Pad Thai, losing hope by the minute that our ride will show anytime today.

We are preparing to go to bed at around 9 p.m. when a subtle, droning whisper catches my attention. The mosquitoes are beginning to muster their forces for witching hour, but this is a different tone than that made by thousands of tiny beating wings. The reverberation grows, pulling my gaze across the rippled waters of the bay. On the horizon I spot a black speck getting larger by the moment. It grows into a dot, then a blob, then into the profile of a boat.

"Ryan, looks like our ride's here. Let's take down the tent!"

We team up and take down the tent so that it's packed away by the time they arrive. The aluminum boat with red trim is 21 feet long with a deep bow and a barrier of plywood in front of the steering console in the middle. The boat touches the gravel shore by the waterfall outlet and three young Inuit men hop out. One of them, the driver, smiles and says, "Okay, you guys ready to go?" He's the son of the man I talked to on the satellite phone. The other two, John and Silas, are a couple of his friends who simply came along to keep him company.

We load up our bags and are soon ready to go. Our canoe lies upside down, tucked in the rocks on shore. Jacob and his family will pick it up on their way back from fishing and bring it back to Gjoa Haven with them.

We're on the move by 10 p.m., skipping through the bright night to Gjoa Haven. The evening is cool and I have my thermal layers and rain gear on to cut the wind. The driver Dan is about 25 years old and wears glasses. He stands at the wheel, with an older model GPS in his hand that he consults from time to time to make sure he's on track.

Jacob doesn't need a GPS, he just knows where to go, but this younger generation lets technology guide them. I wonder what they would do if the technology were to fail? Just head north and hope for the best, I guess. There's no backup either.

John and Silas sit quietly most of the time, only speaking when spoken to. Neither of them has been down this way before and they came along for the adventure, to see something new after being stuck in Joe all summer.

We break out from the lee and into the open water of Chantrey Inlet, crossing over from the east side to the west. The waves are steep and a couple of metres high. The boat rises up over each wave and then slams down in the trough with a violent thud. Spray comes over the bow and the plywood barrier, misting us in brisk sea water. I put my life vest on the cold floor of the boat to cushion my butt from the blow of each hard landing between waves, then sit down leaning against the plywood barrier to avoid the spray.

Ryan and the other two seated men absorb the spray while Dan stands stoically at the console, his glasses completely misted over by water droplets. He constantly looks back and forth from the GPS in his hand to the horizon, driving the boat forward through the turbulent seas. I'm not exactly sure how he can see anything at all through those spectacles but his generally confident air is enough to put me at ease.

In the wee hours of the morning, we're across Chantrey and skimming along the west side of the inlet, weaving through what seems like fairly shallow water, strewn with boulders. I figure Dan's a local who must know these waters pretty well to be ripping through like this. The backdrop of land is flat and brown, a moonscape with not a stick of wood to be seen. Suddenly, there's a loud "crack" and the boat comes to a drifting halt.

Dan smiles sheepishly. "Oops, I think I hit the prop on a rock." Apparently, he doesn't know these waters as well as I thought.

He tilts the engine up and inspects the prop and sees that one of the three blades has come clean off. He doesn't have a spare prop. He turns to me again. "No satellite phone?"

"Nope."

I envision camping on this muddy patch of land waiting for someone to randomly find us or hope an inReach message reaches someone who can then send someone to get us. Maybe we should have tried to canoe this stretch.

"Well, we'll just have to try it...I'll go slow. Do you guys smoke weed? I need to smoke."

Ryan, who hasn't had a puff since day 21 when he ran out, eagerly says, "Yeah, for sure."

What the hell, when in Rome. The trip is over anyways.

Dan packs a small pipe and we pass it around among the five of us. The sun is arcing upward, it's 3 a.m., and a pleasant fog drifts over my brain. I have a bit of whisky left in my flask and pass it around to contribute to the impromptu party. Everyone is quiet, glancing around at the gathering dawn.

"All right, let's see how this thing is working."

Dan starts up the boat and it lurches forward. He's much more cautious, heading straight out to sea, away from the rocky tidal flats that dinged his prop.

Though we're moving much slower, we're moving. I hope the prop doesn't fall off somewhere on Simpson Strait to set us adrift wherever the wind chooses to put us. The Strait is one of the most historic in the lore of Arctic exploration. It's a key section of the Northwest Passage on the south side of King William Island, where Roald Amundsen squeezed through on his way to being the first person to successfully navigate it. All the other explorers before him were decimated on the north and west sides of the island by relentless pack ice that would entomb and eventually sink their boats. The doomed Franklin Expedition and others like it thought that King William Island was a peninsula, and never got to know this narrows here existed.

We putt-putt across the waterway, passing by the Hovgaard Islands. Eventually Gjoa Haven comes into view. Meaning "good harbour" in Norwegian, the hamlet was named by Amundsen and was where he holed up for a couple of seasons waiting for his chance to make a move through the Strait.

The collection of rectangular buildings gets larger with each passing moment and I'm finally somewhat confident we'll make it there. At just past 6 a.m. we pull behind a long rocky breakwater and onto shore, where we unload our gear and pile it on the beach.

"I'll come find you to get the gun and the money later on…right now I'm going to bed," Dan says. "You staying at Jacob's house?"

"Indeed."

"Until when?"

"We're here until Tuesday."

"Okay, I'll see you in the next day or two."

Dan roars off on his ATV, his glasses still streaked with sea water. Seeing clearly doesn't seem to be a priority for him.

CHAPTER 59

John and Silas drive us and our gear to Jacob's house on their ATVs (or "Hondas" as they call them). They leave us in front of the house and I walk up to the door. It's open. I knock and then walk in.

A young Inuk man is yawning and scratching his tightly cropped hair, wearing a tank top and pyjama bottoms. He wears glasses and has a row of crooked, yellow teeth.

"Hi," I say to him. "I'm Frank, this is Ryan...Jacob said we could stay here."

He looks at me for a few seconds.

"Hey, I'm Dustin. Yeah, I'll show you where you're staying."

Typical of these multigenerational households, there is family all over the place. As a gracious host, Jacob booted one of his grandkids to his auntie's place so we'd each have our own room. There are four rooms in the hallway, one occupied by Dustin, the other by his still-sleeping cousin Richard. The other empty one is where Marvin, Ellen, and Marcus sleep, while Sam's room is the one I'll be staying in.

The simple house has a living room with a big-screen TV attached to a small kitchen, then a hallway off to the right. Dustin leads us down it and shows us each our rooms.

He also shows us the small kitchen. "There's food, cereal, eggs, bacon...help yourself."

Suddenly, he emerges from his torpor.

"Oh, and there's a fishing derby today! Top prize is a thousand bucks for the biggest char. They're running along the shore this time of year."

"Yeah, sure, I'm in!" Ryan responds immediately. Ever the keen fisherman, he jumps on the chance. I can take it or leave it when it comes to fishing, but the opportunity to partake in a community event in a High Arctic community is irresistible.

Within an hour, we're doubled on the back of Dustin's ATV, equipped with rods he's given us, headed out to a beach he says is a choice fishing spot. There are already about a dozen locals casting there along the spit of the beach, and we join the lineup a little farther down. Everyone is friendly and jovial, though I don't see any fish being pulled in.

We cast for about an hour, trying different spots along the shore but with no luck. To me, that's fine…it feels good to be part of a community event – so different from the all-consuming and insular act of a long-distance canoe journey. I enjoy being part of something like this that brings people together. I couldn't do this for more than a day or two, mind you, but don't mind tapping in after a long journey. The interactive contrast is refreshing for the soul.

When we get back to Jacob's house, we have lunch and a couple of local carvers come by to show their wares. I hold off on buying any of their pieces, as I'd like to see what's out there before committing further. I suspect we'll see every artist in the hamlet by the time we're done. I've already got a few Inuit creations at home. Some stone cut prints from Baker Lake, animal carvings from Pangnirtung, and so on – so I won't let art-buying fever get to me too easily. Ryan, on the other hand, is immediately enthralled and I have to tell him to hold off until he sees more.

The next day, Dustin goes to work – part of a crew disassembling an old DEW line station on the island. Ryan and I head out to fish off the breakwater and I manage to pull in a large char – at least 15 pounds. I saw it rise and threw my "five of diamonds" lure toward it and it took right away. A day too late for a derby prize but Ryan is excited to cook it up.

We walk through town back to Jacob's house. One woman we pass by nods her head at the big char I carry in my hand. "Nice fish!" she calls out.

Back at Jacob's house Ryan guts the fish, seasons it, and stuffs it with lemon slices. He wraps it in foil and puts it in the oven to bake. When the fish is done, Ryan pulls it out and we accessorize with potatoes and rice. Word of the fish seems to have gotten out as various friends and relations of the Atqittuqs drift in and help themselves. Dustin is there, as is Rosie, one of Jacob's daughters, along with numerous other family members, until about a dozen of us are sitting around Jacob's living room eating and chatting. It's the way of the Inuit. If they have something, you're welcome to it. If you have something, they'll come and partake. No formal invitations or niceties are necessary.

Richard, Dustin's 18-year-old cousin and one of Jacob's grandsons, emerges from his bedroom still half asleep. Unlike lanky Dustin, Richard is round and chubby. Dustin works, is a volunteer fireman, and generally keeps busy and active. Richard sits around, plays video games, and eats whatever people happen to be providing. He compensates for his freeloading by being a generally fun and hilarious guy – a real character. One of his life goals is to be a professional musician. He talks about it all the time.

"If you want to be a musician, don't you have to play music, or at least practise a bit?" I ask him.

"I hate practising."

"Well, then you'll never be a musician."

He thinks for a moment. "I'll become a rapper."

"Well, then you'd have to rap, and write lyrics."

"Hmm, maybe…could I borrow some money from you? I want to buy some chewing tobacco."

"No."

"Okay."

He lumbers into the narrow kitchen, grabs a plate, and piles on some fish and potatoes, then sits on the couch and eats. No acknowledgement to anyone or a word about the food. It's like he's eating a bowl of cereal. From Richard, we've come to expect nothing more, nothing less. His generally entertaining nature is all he needs to provide.

In the evening, we hang out with the teenagers. Dustin is a year older than Richard; he's a strong, wiry kid whom I soundly trounce in a couple of arm-wrestling matches. Thirty-five days of hard canoe-tripping creates an iron body that even youth can't overcome. I play an Inuit bone game with him and another cousin, Jordan – a sweet, shy kid who seems to enjoy the time with us, constantly giggling and smiling. Richard holds court on the couch with Ryan, peppering him with questions about his girlfriend and what life is like in BC. We are novelties, white guys from the South who are pretty cool and casual, so they are relaxed and having fun with us.

Between sentences with Ryan, Richard glances at his phone, looking at Facebook updates, like any teenager. He's dating a girl in town and they are constantly messaging back and forth. Though there's no cell service on King William Island, the Atqittuqs do have satellite Wi-Fi that is slow but functional. Next year, they say, they'll have cell service and things will be great. Will they? Isn't that just more distraction from real life, from the person right in front of you who should be the object of your focus?

Regardless, it's an easy hang with these kids – though we're way older than them, our attitudes are young and they feel like peers. Having never had kids or acquired debt or the myriad other things that can bog a person down, I've managed to keep in touch with the wonder and excitement about life that I've had since I was young. I'm still a kid at heart, which I think is a big part of leading a passionate, happy existence.

What is a long canoe trip but a fantastical adventure dreamt up by a child? To be wild, free, and roaming – physically and mentally – is what we lose when life gets too heavy and serious. I often relate to teenagers and kids a lot more than adults because of this. Adults look at my journeys wistfully, as if they wished at some point in their life they had done something like that, had a grand adventure they could reflect on and talk about with their grandkids. Kids, however, look at my journeys as a possibility – their dreams haven't died and been buried in a grave of responsibility. They still have a chance at these grand adventures, because everyday life is a grand adventure for them, the possibilities still endless.

Dustin is the responsible one of the three, perhaps the one who will be first to jump on the track of adult life. Richard is a dreamer, with the emphasis on dreaming and not doing. A combination of the two makes for a great adventurer. There is no adventure without dreaming, but also no adventure without the doing. It's equal parts of both. Young Jordan, at 15 years old, is quiet and unsure.

It's hard for these kids in these remote, isolated communities to look out into the broad world and see all that's going on. There's a level of FOMO, the feeling they're trapped up here while all the fun is happening elsewhere. They don't realize that every kid in every town across the planet is exactly like them. Everything is amazing on Facebook or Instagram, where life is perfect. That's all that people show. And it can be depressing, thinking you're missing out on all of that; that life is passing you by. The thing is, most posting is done out of insecurity – they feel the same way and want to join the amazingness by posting only the best of an otherwise mundane existence; to validate their lives. People who are really living life are not posting. Authentic engagement and adventure are found when you shut off the phone and delve into the real possibilities around you, engage with what lies just outside the door. Adventure is everywhere. Dustin, Richard, and Jordan live in the high North, way above tree line – a world of fantastical creatures like polar bears, grizzly bears, Arctic wolves, musk oxen, caribou, and wolverine. It's a fantasyland of otherworldly adventure and possibility. Right now there's probably a kid in New York City wishing he could be in Gjoa Haven, having FOMO about the life these kids live up here.

CHAPTER 60

Jacob, Martha, Marvin, Ellen, and Marcus arrive back from the mouth of the Great Fish River the next day. Jacob and Martha have a cabin on the water on the east side of the island and they'll be staying there. Marvin, Ellen, and Marcus occupy the corner room and I make way for Sam in his room. Jacob tells Richard to move out of his room and go stay with one of his aunties. Dustin simply passes on the message, "Grandpa wants you to give up your room for Frank." There is no question or protest. Whatever Jacob says, goes. He is the ultimate host and wants Ryan and me to have our own rooms while we're here.

Later in the day, the whole Atqittuq clan are stuffed into Jacob's living room. It's boisterous with talk and laughter as over 20 people gab and carouse. Martha walks around, pressing coffee and food on people and there is a general feeling of celebration. They've come back with several large trout and char, along with the caribou – a successful outing on the land. Jacob sits in the corner, by the table, taking in the gathering of his clan. Rosie, sitting beside him, asks him a question, and he begins to speak. Suddenly the whole room goes from raucous chatter to rapt silence. Everyone turns toward Jacob as he talks in a low Inuktitut rasp. He speaks steadily, seriously, and all in attendance seem to hang on his every word. I of course don't understand a thing he's saying, but really don't have to. This man commands respect. He is an Elder who lived in the old ways and is as strong and vivacious a human as I've ever met. He's someone to aspire to in these modern times, a man rooted in the ancients who is a lighthouse in the storm that often gathers In these isolated communities with their myriad problems. It's because of Jacob's example that the Atqittuq clan is so strong and functional. We haven't seen a drop of alcohol or drugs in and around this family in the three days we've been here.

Jacob seems delighted that we're his guests. In fact, we seem to be the primary form of entertainment. He pulls out a couple of fish and a caribou leg and begins slicing up the raw meat on his living room floor. He hands us a couple of slices of the caribou. Ryan and I happily eat it as we'd experienced the tender, uncooked flesh back at their camp and knew what to expect. Afterwards, we're fed char eyeballs, char tongue, and char belly. I choke these items down while Ryan seems to actually enjoy them. Everyone in the gathered clan watches us closely for our reactions. I try to act casual, with a feigned nod of enjoyment, and they smile, maybe thinking, "These white guys are just like us!"

Having been warmed up with raw caribou and char, Jacob decides it's time for us to step up to the next level of Inuit cuisine. He says something to Marvin, who smirks and then goes outside. He returns a minute later with a blue Rubbermaid bin. The whole assembled clan laughs with glee and nod to each other. I'd seen this bin in the shed outside when I was digging around for some duct tape but thought nothing of it. It was sitting innocently in the corner, not of any particular interest to me.

Marvin sets the bin in the middle of the living room and opens the lid. It looks like a tub of oil, with a shiny, grey, gelatinous blob floating around in it that instantly throws a stench into the air.

"What is it?" I gasp.

Everyone laughs, which can only mean we are expected to eat this mystery food.

"It's *igunaq* – baby seal," Marvin tells us. "It's been fermenting in that bin for three months. This is real Inuk food. My dad loves it."

Jacob speaks up, gesturing to us with his index finger as he talks.

"My dad says he better feed it to you if you want to try it. If you touch it with your hands, you won't get the smell off for at least a couple of weeks," Marvin interprets.

We grin. We're both keen travellers and this is an adventure like no other.

"I'm game," Ryan says, wide-eyed.

"Me too...bring it on. I've always been curious about this fermented country food I've heard so much about."

With that, Jacob sticks his finger into the gelatinous blob and scoops up a bit of grey goo. He feeds it to Ryan, putting it directly into his mouth like a bird would feed its chick. Ryan's eyes are like saucers as he processes the flavour. The whole room guffaws, with people slapping their knees and doubling over.

Finally, Ryan blinks and speaks. "Hmm...not as bad as I thought it would be."

More uproarious laughter. Tears of joy stream from Jacob's eyes. He composes himself and scoops his finger into the cesspool again, this time presenting me with my portion. I dutifully allow him to drop the goo into my mouth and brace myself for impact.

The laughter amps up again as I contemplate this strange taste in my mouth. It has the flavour of limburger cheese multiplied a hundred times over – overpoweringly strong and lingering but not terrible. As a fan of bitter, hot, and sour foods, I can actually see how this is considered a delicacy among the Inuit. I've never tasted anything like it. Not that I was about to dig in for seconds, thinking perhaps it's best for me not to tangle with the possibility of botulism.

Everyone filters out eventually and Ryan and I are hanging out in the living room when a man walks in carrying two soapstone carvings. *Great*, I think, *another guy coming to hustle his wares*. I've seen a myriad of pieces paraded in front of us by various carvers in town who heard there were a couple of *kabloonat* hanging out at Jacob's house. The ubiquitous lineup of caribou, polar bear, walrus, seal, and musk ox carvings were often quite nice but nothing really grabbed me or made me sit up and notice. They seem all too generic. I appreciate art that has its own style and flair, where an artist has a distinct vision and idea that sets him or her apart from others in the genre.

The man standing in the living room is calm, serene...perhaps 50 years old, with straw-straight salt-and-pepper hair and a thin moustache. Wayne Puqiqnaq, a third-generation carver well known in Inuit art circles and by collectors, lays down his two pieces of art in front of us and immediately has my attention.

One piece is of a man, twisted in a sort of dance, with big white eyes that have pinprick black pupils turned toward the sky. He holds a spear in one hand. It's dynamic, interesting. The other piece is even more intriguing: a black carving of Sedna, the sea goddess of Inuit mythology who is half-woman, half fish. Sedna is lying down, an *ulu* (woman's knife) made of caribou bone in one hand and her face twisted skyward from her prone position, bright eyes looking straight up while her mouth is warped into a scream. I want this piece.

"Wow, this is amazing, Wayne. How much for the Sedna?"

"Seventy dollars."

I don't argue. It's a very fair price. "I'll buy it."

Ryan buys the other piece.

"I'm working on a bigger piece right now too, if you're interested. It's kind of like the one he bought," pointing at Ryan's new purchase, "but different."

"Sure, I'd love to take a look at it."

"I'll be finished with it later today. Come by my place to have a look." And with that, Wayne leaves us to our company.

CHAPTER 61

Later that afternoon we're sitting in Jacob's living room watching a 50-year-old NFB documentary series called *Tuktu*, which filmed Inuit seal hunting, building igloos, making sealskin clothing, and playing communal games using pre-contact methods. Jacob actually knows the folks in the film, and he laughs with glee as he nods and recalls a life he once lived. We watch as a man acts like a seal, crawling patiently and slowly on his side along the sea ice, waving his hand like a flipper as he mimics the pinniped. Over the course of a half-hour he slowly but surely approaches the animal, eventually getting right up beside it, where he suddenly springs up and flashes his spear into the seal before it can escape back into the safety of the water. Jacob nods his head, recalling a time when he had to use such craft and guile to put supper on the table. A later scene shows the multigenerational life of a time long past, where smaller igloo "rooms" were connected to a large communal igloo where families would congregate, socialize, and play games. Nowadays the small igloos are rooms in this house – Marvin, Ellen, and Marcus live in one, for example – and Jacob's living room is the communal gathering place where they all come together to socialize and laugh, like when Ryan and I were trying their country food for the entertainment of all. The structure is different, but the heart of it, the feel of it, is the same as that shown in *Tuktu*.

This engaged way of living, of the Singularity with the wilderness shown in *Tuktu*, was so interesting it was deemed worthy of capturing on film. It's unlikely a series will be made of someone sitting idly as nanobots keep them alive for hundreds of years. It would be like watching paint dry. This is what Richard should aspire to – this mastery and intimate knowledge of the land, not a bathroom selfie in a fancy hotel in New York. This is life. That phone is death.

Though Kurzweil's prediction of a man/machine amalgamation may very well be prophetic, it doesn't mean it's good. His Singularity envisions a dystopia similar to that portrayed in the film *The Matrix*, where sedentary humans are irrevocably bonded with technology.

Jacob's version of Singularity – where man and wilderness are intimately intertwined – is quite the opposite.

As we hurtle ever closer to Kurzweil's prophecy, the Jacobs of the world will soon exist only in grainy NFB footage. The Singularity isn't near, it's already here, and it seems we've passed it by. Marvin, and perhaps Dustin, seem like members of the younger generation who might be able to carry on Jacob's legacy. But they never lived on the land like he did – they've grown up in the technological world and no matter how hard they try, that authentic connection to the land is forever lost. Putting a machine like a snowmobile or ATV between you and the earth creates an instant disconnect. It's practical for sure, but you can't be connected to something if you're not a part of it.

Later in the day, I drop by Wayne Puqiqnaq's place. It's a simple abode, like all the others in town: a rudimentary box with four walls and a roof to keep the elements at bay just as any house in any part of the world is designed to do. Out front is a grinder and chisels surrounded by a pile of broken stone. It's where Wayne does the initial cutting and shaping before he fine-tunes and polishes his creations. There are a few such piles of stones around town – a sure sign there's a carver in the house. I tap on the front door and Wayne appears. He lets me in and walks over to his kitchen where he's been working on the piece. He brings it out and I'm instantly taken by it. It's of an Inuk man in a parka, standing on one leg with the other raised in the air. His arms are up, with one hand holding a bolo that they once used to throw to entangle a caribou's legs, and the other holding a club used for the killing blows once the animal was down. The face is twisted upward, with the wide eyes and black pupils characteristic of Wayne's pieces. He calls the piece "Old Time Hunter."

I want it. "How much?" I ask.

He says flatly, "$120."

How about "$100?"

"Nope. $120."

He knows he has me; he sees it in my eyes. It's a great deal no matter what. I've seen his pieces in the local gallery of similar size and quality for $600.

"No problem. Done." I hand him the six 20-dollar bills and he accepts them. No smile, no thanks, just a financial transaction. He hands me a small piece of his soul and I say, "Thanks Wayne, it's beautiful." He nods glumly.

I head back to Jacob's to pack up. Our flight leaves this afternoon. I meet Ryan out in the street – he's coming back from another carver's place. He bought a green soapstone fox he had his eye on. Not my taste, but he loves it. As we amble back to Jacob's house, Richard and Jordan join us, chatting and laughing. We take a selfie of the four of us in the street acting goofy. We'll miss these kids for sure, likely never to see them again.

CHAPTER 62

It was January 5, 1984. I was 13 years old. The temperature was -30°C and I was skiing a kilometre across frozen Blind Bay with my brother, sister, mom, dad, and two black poodles. Our destination was a rustic little cabin my folks had recently purchased. After years of camping in the area, they finally decided to set down roots by buying a piece of land with a roof that was somewhat more substantial than the leaky canvas of our kitchen tent.

I had never personally seen it before. It was on a peninsula with no road access…either you got there by boat, by ski, or by walking the long way around via a shoreline trail. Unlike most of the locals, we weren't a machine-oriented type of family so a snowmobile was never a consideration. The physical journey was part of the charm of the place.

Built near the town of Parry Sound in the late '50s with boards milled from the numerous giant white pines along the shore, it hadn't been occupied for seven years. The woman we bought it from lived in Georgia. It had been her husband's fishing and hunting camp. They divorced, she got the cottage, and eventually got around to selling it.

The cabin sat on 1.5 acres of prime Canadian Shield in the 30,000 islands region of Georgian Bay, with a nice rock outcrop on one end of the shoreline, and a beach up front, only a dozen feet from a stairway that ran down from a huge deck that wrapped around the structure.

These days, the cottage, three hours north of Toronto, would fetch a princely sum on the real estate market. Back then, though, you could get these properties for a relative song. They sat around for years on the market before they ever sold, but once my dad put in an offer, our now-neighbour decided he wanted it too. So the bidding war began, upping $100 at a time, back and forth with the realtor. My dad eventually sealed the deal when he threw a whopping $200 raise on the cabin, along with sending a personal note to the owner. That did it. The neighbour balked at the price bump, the woman down south liked the fact that a family would be using it, and my parents finally signed on the dotted line and were cottage owners. Total selling price was $30,200.

The cabin slowly came into view on that cold, crisp day. We marched up onto the deck. My father handed me a shovel and I dug out the metre of snow that blocked the door. Pushing it open, we stepped inside. I was immediately hit with a smell of pine, mothballs, and dirt. It awakened something in me, something that said, "This is home."

We spent the weekend trying to stay warm, huddled in down comforters we'd hauled along with us, clustered around a small, narrow "Quebec stove" that barely pumped out enough heat to warm a bedroom, much less the high-ceilinged living room in which it was situated. Despite the rustic nature, we did have electricity. A line ran through the forest so there was a functioning stove, fridge, and lights.

The only running water was from a hand pump that sat behind the sink, but that only worked in the summertime. In winter Blind Bay freezes solid. My dad chopped a hole through the two-foot-thick ice with an axe so we could haul water up to the cabin in a bucket. Going to the bathroom meant a trip to the charming two-seater outhouse in the back. It was all so new, so engaging, so different from life in the city. We all loved it.

At nighttime, you had to walk 50 feet out back of the cottage to get to the outhouse, its yellow interior bulb the only glow in front of the seemingly impenetrable darkness behind it. You hurriedly stepped inside and latched the door behind you, then let out a little yelp as the bare skin of your ass came in contact with the ice-cold toilet seat. The chill only lasted a moment as your butt quickly went numb and you settled in. At that time, the only decorative feature of the outhouse was a sign behind the toilet paper dispenser. It read: "Handle this with special care, it seems we ain't got none to spare. If everyone is paper *hawgs*, we'll have to go back to *catalawgs*."

This was scrawled below a cartoonish, bearded man sitting on a toilet seat with a grim look on his face tearing a page from a Sears catalogue hanging on the wall. Charming kitsch that fit perfectly in the bowels of an outhouse.

Over the years, as I spent much of my youthful summers at the cottage, I became bonded to it and to the surrounding landscape of rock and windblown pines. When I moved to the west coast after university, I would still come back for about a month at the end of my annual summer journey. Canoeing the clear waters, running through the open forest, and doing the usual upkeep that an old cottage needs was the perfect airlock within which to transition from expedition mode back to regular life. It was where I got to spend quality time with my parents, and where I would reconnect with Shannon by doing a week-long canoe trip with her in nearby Temagami or Algonquin and hang out with her in the golden days of late summer. I even blended some of my summer journeys in with the cottage, paddling 3100 kilometres to there from Winnipeg in 2007 with my friend Taku, and paddling 750 km from there to Ottawa in 2015 with my buddy Peirson, who was promoting his latest album with the canoe as touring van.

My father passed away in 2014, then my brother passed away in 2015. The cottage had always been my father's place, where he did most of the maintenance and puttering around the property. Once he was gone, though, the cottage remained, and I took over the primary maintenance of the place, the responsibility bonding me with it even more. With the Toronto house sold and my mother and sister renting, the cottage became the only true family home, where we could gather with memories of people close in our lives, both present and passed. My mom and I have always been close, and we both enjoy the quality time spent with each other on the shores of Georgian Bay.

Flying back from Gjoa Haven, Ryan made his way to Vancouver while I made my way to the Wolf Den, as the cottage is affectionately known. I settled in there until mid-September, Shannon joining me for the last couple of weeks, then headed back to the west coast.

PART THREE
BITTER COLD

CHAPTER 63

Since I left MEC, I've made most of my living through regular features writing and doing talks about my journeys at corporate and other events, which generally happen in the fall and winter. When I returned to North Vancouver that year, work began on the feature article I was writing for a national magazine about our trip from Yellowknife to Chantrey Inlet. I'd also just delivered the manuscript for my first book before I left on the trip with Ryan – a collection of previously published magazine articles and some new stories as well. Back at the home office on the west coast, I set to work on the final touches of editing and discussing graphics with the publisher.

In the midst of all this, on November 4, I received an email out of the blue from a man named David Reid:

> Hello Frank,
>
> Hope this finds you well.
>
> My name is David Reid. We've never met but I think our ski tracks may have crossed somewhere on Baffin Island.
>
> Earlier today I was talking to a mutual friend of ours Dave Garrow – always a pleasure.
>
> I'll get straight to the point. I'm leading an expedition next year that will retrace the route taken by Orcadian explorer John Rae in 1854. One of the team has had to drop out and I'm currently looking for a suitable replacement. I'd be interested in having a chat to find out if this might be something you'd be interested in.
>
> Naujaat to Gjoa Haven, 650 km, starting March 25th, 35+ days, self-supported, human powered, team of four, funded and sponsored, honoring John Rae, highlighting Indigenous Knowledge, end goal is to see the restoration of the Hall of Clestrain in Orkney into an Arctic Interpretive Centre.

The note jogged a memory of Dave Garrow talking about this trip to me during our Baffin traverse. He'd been asked to do it way back then but was noncommittal at the time, expressing low interest in the project due to its length and lack of mountains. He said, "It'll just be a long grind, so I doubt I'll do it." I was curious about the journey at the time but was ambivalent as I had nothing to do with it, and Dave's description of it was not glowing. The unparalleled spectacle of the Norse Mountains around us made me think that a flat grinder over the Arctic wastes would be one of those trips where you're trying to be anywhere else but in the moment. A journey where you just want to get to the end is not where you want to be. The experience, the journey itself, should be all and everything, whereas the end is just that – the end. The end of an all-immersive and engaging exploit.

Despite my reservations, I was intrigued. I hadn't explored the particular section of the Arctic in question, and I was a fan of Rae himself. When I was part of a team attempting to row the Northwest Passage in 2013, I became familiar with Rae through Pierre Berton's book *The Arctic Grail*, an exhaustive account of the history of colonial exploration of the Northwest Passage. Compared to all the other explorers in that book – Franklin, Perry, Ross, etc. – Rae stood head and shoulders above them. Unlike his contemporaries, Rae learned from and travelled with Indigenous Peoples, using their methods to survive the often-harsh rigours of the Arctic by living in igloos, wearing traditional skin clothing, and subsisting off the land.

Rae's most notable accomplishment, and what the mission would retrace, was an out and back overland trek through the frozen landscape of early spring from Repulse Bay to the strait now named after him. Employed by the Hudson Bay Company, Rae set out in 1854 to complete the first survey of the area – and serendipitously solved two of the great mysteries of the Northwest Passage.

His first discovery was that the land mass now known as King William Island was indeed an island. By gazing across at it from where he turned around at Pointe de la Guiche, he confirmed that it was not a peninsula as was previously thought. The importance of this observation was that all previous attempts to sail through the Passage had been along the western shore of King William, and they all failed. Rae's discovery provided another avenue, which would be the one used by Roald Amundsen 50 years later to finally get a ship through the Northwest Passage.

Speaking of failures, Rae's second discovery was confirmation that the entire 129-passenger crew of the lost Franklin Expedition had indeed perished. They'd been missing for seven years and scores of explorers had tried unsuccessfully to find and rescue them. Meeting travelling Inuit along his route, Rae recorded their consistent stories of *kabloonat* they'd found dead of starvation in areas to the west, including strong evidence they'd resorted to cannibalism in their final, desperate attempts at survival. As proof, Rae acquired from the Inuit engraved items that irrefutably came from Franklin's ships, the *Erebus* and *Terror*.

In spite of his discoveries, Rae never received the recognition he deserved. Luminaries of London's high society, including Franklin's widow and even Charles Dickens, bristled at his claims that members of the Royal Navy would resort to cannibalism, and discredited Rae in the press because of it. In retracing Rae's route, Reid hoped to bring recognition to his accomplishments and to drum up support to turn Rae's birthplace, the Hall of Clestrain in the Orkney Islands, into an Arctic interpretive centre.

A week later, I had a good chat with David. He reiterated that he was looking for a fourth teammate, and we talked in detail about the journey and its outreach.

David stressed, "I'm the leader of the expedition. All final decisions are mine."

I replied, "No problem at all. I'll be a good soldier."

It would be nice to be a pack dog rather than leader, to not have to make all the decisions. Most of the time, I end up conceiving and organizing my journeys. David had initiated and bankrolled this one with a GoFundMe campaign that raised more than enough to cover our expenses. I've never taken this route to fund a trip, though it seems to be the way to go these days. There are too few grants for far too many expeditions, so people have taken the funding public. I've never done it, and probably won't, because it doesn't feel right to me. It feels like public begging – like I was asking strangers to pay for my passion in exchange for a T-shirt or other minor perk that entices them to donate. David obviously had no problem with it, and also garnered large donations from companies like Adventure Canada and the Royal Institution of Chartered Surveyors, with which he has longstanding relationships.

By the end of the conversation I said, "Sounds like a great trip, David. I'm in if you want me, but I know you're weighing other candidates."

He replied, "I think I'm good. I made up my mind. You're in."

Just like that, I was on a mission again. My role would be to photograph and write about the journey and help with navigation. David, originally from Scotland but now a Canadian resident with deep ties in the Arctic, would be our leader. Garry Tutte, a videographer from Toronto, would be along to film it, and Richard Smith, a veteran Arctic traveller who lives in Scotland, would complete our team of four.

CHAPTER 64

I'm always up for a new adventure, and I prioritize my life to take on these projects. My life is analogous to that of a trout, holding its position in the current of a stream. Most of the time, it swims in place, but is always ready for opportunity. When a fly lands on the surface, it strikes. This phone call was like a fly for me – an opportunity that contained all the elements that I look for in a journey, and so I grabbed it.

We would try to be the first to follow in Rae's footsteps. As David said to me over the phone, "It's a great story." He was right – it had a lot of layers. As a writer and photographer, I saw that there was good material in the concept. There was adventure to be had, of course there was Inuit culture to be experienced, and there was a rich historical angle. Also, I never repeat myself on my longer journeys, so from a selfish perspective this provided a fresh landscape I'd never travelled before. Finally – and this was the rarest of rare occurrences in my own experience – we would each be paid $5,000 to do the trip on top of all the expenses being covered. It would be an actual paid gig.

David had big plans for this expedition. He wanted to create a documentary film, produce a book, do live interviews from the field via BGAN and satellite phone, and use the trip to promote the conversion of Rae's birthplace into a museum. All this while also needing to cover about 20 km per day pulling 200 pounds worth of gear in temperatures that drop to -40°C. On this last point, I expressed concern about the time of year he wanted to start. He proposed going at the end of March, citing concerns over sea and river ice breaking up.

On previous trips to the Arctic, I've travelled from the end of April into the middle of May, when the ice is still rock solid everywhere. Breakup in the rivers doesn't happen until later in June; the sea ice doesn't go until July.

The time of year he wanted to start would make everything unnecessarily difficult, considering our objectives. It would be very cold, and cold snow is slow snow. It would be like trying to glide on sandpaper, so we'd be working extra hard to cover the kilometres needed. Most problematic from a documentation perspective is that batteries for the drone, video camera, still cameras, etc., are extremely difficult to keep charged at such low temperatures. In addition, pulling your hands out to handle equipment at these severe temperatures can lead to frost nip and frostbite in a matter of seconds. May is the best time to go, I told him. That month comes with warmer temperatures, faster snow, and 24 hours of daylight.

Despite my suggestion to set out at least a month later, David booked us to land in the hamlet of Naujaat for our start on March 27. I didn't think too much of it in the end. The human condition is such that the good times stay strong in your mind while the trying times fade away. I knew it had been cold, dropping down to -30°C or so when I'd crossed Baffin Island with Dave and Johnny the previous spring. The hard conditions were no longer in my head. All I could remember was the adventure, beauty, and out-of-the-box fun associated with that journey. The passage of time had put that at the forefront of my mind, with all misery erased. So another Arctic trip, a month sooner than ideal? Sure, what the hell.

A key part of Rae's experience was his encounters with Inuit who were travelling on the land, hunting and fishing for their keep. Without the knowledge he gained from them, he would not have survived the landscape, and without their evidence, he would never have discovered the truth about Franklin. Like Rae, we'd harvest what information we could from the locals.

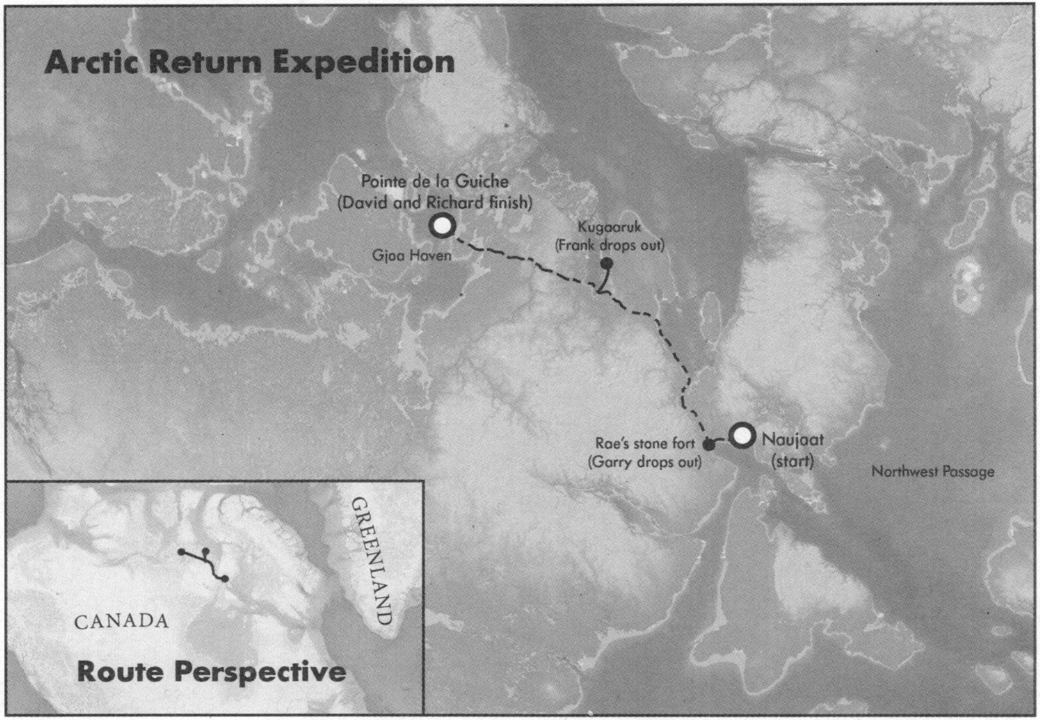

Arctic Return Expedition
Pointe de la Guiche
(David and Richard finish)
Gjoa Haven
Kugaaruk
(Frank drops out)
Rae's stone fort
(Garry drops out)
Naujaat
(start)
Northwest Passage
GREENLAND
CANADA
Route Perspective

CHAPTER 65

On March 24, I board an Air Canada flight to Ottawa, where I'll rendezvous with the other guys on the team for the first time. David and Garry are already in town while Richard and I fly in this eve. Everything links up smoothly and we convene in the baggage area, greeting each other for the first time. David is polite and serious, with a list in hand of things that need doing before we head north. Garry is easy-going, friendly – filming me going down the escalator as I arrive, and then filming Richard when he arrives an hour later. Like me, Garry and David are balding and what remaining hair we have is cut tight. Richard is easy-going and friendly too, with a quick wit. He's built strongly and stands out among the four of us with his coiffed, thick red hair.

We head back to the hotel rooms David booked for us, where we'll stay for a couple of nights as we get ourselves organized. I room with Richard, while Garry and David have the room beside us. Just like that, we're thrown together, and I'm sleeping beside a snoring man I've never met before. It's the first true test of my new custom earplugs and they work amazingly well, dropping me into a cone of silence that no snore could possibly penetrate. Our biggest task is buying food, and we purchase a ridiculous amount from Costco the next day. I can't imagine how we'll carry it all, plus the freeze-dried food already waiting for us up at our starting point in the hamlet of Naujaat.

Garry and I hit it off. It'll be fun doing this trip with him. He has the least amount of experience in this realm, and his role for the trip is as our cameraman. Looking at his mound of lenses, drone, tripods, and other assorted bric-a-brac, I wonder how he'll possibly pull it off. He'll have to be by far the strongest member of the trip if he wants to film this thing, but I'm pretty sure he's the weakest. Also, the extreme cold we'll be facing will render much of his equipment useless as the batteries won't hold a charge. We shall see, though, perhaps he'll surprise me.

Making our way up to Naujaat, we have a dozen large duffel bags and our skis to check in. David pays massive amounts of baggage overages, but we end up getting to Naujaat without a misplaced piece of luggage.

Once there, we settle into the local Inns North hotel at $250 per night and begin the sorting and repacking.

We quickly realize we have way too much stuff and end up leaving most of the freeze-dried food behind as we have enough to feed the entire Franklin Expedition. It'll be donated to the local hunters and trappers association, which will most likely never use the stuff. We rig up our hauling sleds, and with the amount of shit David wants to bring along, we'll have to tow double sleds behind us.

The first day's weather is bright and calm; the low collection of utilitarian buildings is bathed in a pink glow from the slowly setting sun. Garry and I wander around, taking photos. We watch a few kids sledding on the edge of town, catching air off of jumps with their snow racers – the ubiquitous three-skied sleds that mimic the configuration of snowmobiles. They pose for photos, arm-in-arm with each other like boys everywhere will do, grinning as they've been taught. Snow plowed from the road is piled so high along the edge that it's flush with the stop sign written in Inuit syllabics at the only intersection in town.

We settle into the hotel that night, then the next day attend a presentation about our trip at the local school. Beforehand, we meet a couple of Elders who give us some beta about the journey and the best routes to take. Laimmiki Malliki and David Mimitaqtuq show us the routes they travel by snow machine through the area and what kind of terrain we should expect, going over the maps with us and showing us the way.

David gives the presentation to the kids at the school. I'm not big on talking up a trip before it's done – it's all theory until it's completed. Anything before then is really just hot air. This is David's baby though and he's keen, driving home the point about what we're doing. The kids are polite but generally bored, as you'd expect them to be, and the teachers are just happy to have an hour off. Laimmiki gifts us a wooden sled he made in the wood shop at the school. David takes it and says we'll bring it with us.

"Are you kidding? It's useless to us – it'll be ballast," I say to him.

"It would be impolite."

"They're practical folks – they won't mind at all."

"We're taking it."

I roll my eyes. *Man, what have I gotten myself into.* I need to remind myself I'm being paid, that this is a job.

After the chat at the high school, Oscar, a young Inuk I met on the plane, and his father, Lawrence – who apparently knows the lay of the land better than anyone in Naujaat – meet us at the hotel restaurant. Laimmiki and David gave us good info on the general snowmobile route from town, which goes overland, but no one knew anything about travel along the North Pole River since it isn't the direct route out of town. Rae took the North Pole River and so we have to as well.

Thankfully, Lawrence has travelled there earlier in the season and has even dragged a small fishing hut out there. He tells us travel by snow machine was decent, so it should be fine for us. It's good to hear this... we would have gone there anyways but knowing the travel is somewhat efficient gives us confidence in the route. After looking over the maps with Lawrence, Garry interviews David about it on camera. Richard and I are whispering in the corner of the room about something when Garry suddenly scolds us like two children. "Come on guys! I'm conducting an interview here. I need silence!"

We look at each other with mock wide-open eyes, then scurry out of the room. I'm not sure why that moment has stuck in my mind, but perhaps having made expedition films myself, I know you shouldn't sweat the small stuff. If Garry manages to shoot a whole film of this, his dry interview with David will be left on the cutting room floor anyways. Plus, his curt way of dealing with us before the expedition has even started leaves a bad taste in my mouth. It doesn't show well.

That evening we pack up everything in the hotel room and load it onto our sleds. Everyone has their gear distributed on two sleds while I try to load it all into one giant sled. The amount of gear and food we have seems ridiculous...two shotguns, 40 days' worth of food, various sponsor-labelled pieces of clothing, charging equipment, camera equipment, two tents, four stoves, etc. David says he won't cover another night at the hotel as it's too pricey. He is a cheap Scot after all, his fist habitually clenched over the proverbial sporran. He should have saved money on the two-thirds of our food we're leaving behind instead.

Through the course of the afternoon, the weather has steadily deteriorated, with a driving north wind sending everyone in town inside. It's forecast to be -55°C with the wind chill overnight. In dusky light, the four of us drag our loads behind us through the empty streets of Naujaat, fully clad in our winter parkas and pants. We head out onto the sea ice and set up the two tents during the big blow. This is the first time we've worked as a team and neither Garry nor I has used these tents before so we follow Richard and David's lead. It's almost completely pitch black now and we lose one of the tent stuff sacks as the wind grabs it and sends it to Toronto, ripping south across the breadth of Hudson Bay. All we can do is watch the red sack spin into the blizzard, neither man nor machine able to run it down.

Richard and I are thrown together in one tent, David and Garry in the other. Perhaps this will be the configuration the rest of the way. We snuggle into our bags on the ice and Richard immediately breaks the zipper on his. I'd assumed these were new, sponsored bags that we'd be able to keep so didn't bring my very fine -30°C Polar Ranger bag. It turns out they're used bags from David's last expedition, with apparently very flimsy zippers. Our bags still have loft so it's not too bad tonight, but I wonder how things will be after a few days of use. The loft will dampen and compress, then we'll get cold. Richard is a good tent mate, with a positive attitude and sense of humour, a good fellow who will roll with the blows of trip, whatever they may be. I try to stay positive too. I'd voiced concerns about starting this trip so early – we should have waited a month rather than fight this bitter cold. It's true that Rae also travelled this route in April, but he wasn't filming and photographing along the way. Constant cold management will make that difficult indeed. I'll do the best I can under the circumstances, but am concerned that Garry will be pressed, to say the least.

CHAPTER 66

Relentless it is
It never sings easy songs
Naujaat north wind

The next morning, we eat breakfast at the hotel though we're no longer guests and linger there most of the day as the north wind continues to power away. The school is closed as the temperature is below -50°C, the cut-off line for this community. Richard and I go to the Parks Canada office and talk to Jen Lukacic, the park manager for Ukkusiksalik National Park, a remote and rarely visited park about 50 km south of town. We ask if they possibly have a replacement bag for Richard and she happens to have a synthetic -40°C bag. We walk over to her house and she invites us in. It is lovely and warm, and we're greeted by her two dogs, Blue and Bear – friendly pets who live a life in complete opposition to the miserable dogs chained up around our tents. Jen offers us hot chocolate and we happily accept, lingering in the warmth. Richard slips into the bag and it fits, with the two dogs licking at his face while he's in the bag, and we all have a good laugh. Richard will ship it back to her at the end of the trip. I wonder how long my zipper will last, or anyone else's for that matter. There's nothing to be done now – Richard got the last good sleeping bag in Naujaat.

CHAPTER 67

Alone on the ice
Left to wither on their chains
Naujaat sled dogs

The thermometer stays around -50°C and the wind continues to howl. We again spend most of the day at the Inns North, where the manager Karen allows us bottomless coffee and cooks us up a lunch of caribou, even though we are no longer guests and eat our freeze-dried meals in the restaurant instead of ordering the 40-dollar meals she serves up. There is internet for the other guys to use...I don't have a phone with me, only an old school iPod with a bunch of podcasts on it. It's a chunky old thing with a thumb wheel, not touchscreen, and the battery lasts forever. Perfect for the Arctic.

We sleep out yet another night in front of town. A couple of particularly miserable dogs are chained up by our tent, curled up against the elements. They are tough fucking bastards for sure. I guess they get fed every couple of days though I haven't seen anyone come around since we've been here. I used to feel sorry for these dogs but this is their lot in life, and pretty much always has been. The main difference between the current and historic role of these dogs is that they used to get to run, pulling sleds that were the transport lifeblood of the Inuit. Now they are generally constrained to a small patch of ice. Having seen this in every single Inuit town and village I've been to, I've become jaded to it. You can't impress southern values on the Inuit, as things are viewed differently up here.

The storm doesn't abate so we end up sleeping yet another night out on the ice, hoping for a break in conditions the next day. We awake to a balmy -35°C and the wind has eased so we break camp and finally hit the trail, following a snow machine track over the windblown sea ice that will take us toward the North Pole River mouth. We each head out at our own pace, figuring out our loads as we ski on the dead flat track. Garry wanted to get a shot of us leaving, but it's too cold to fly the drone – too cold to do anything with any of his equipment in fact. Not a second of footage is captured that day. He essentially carries 40 pounds of ballast in the form of a mound of equipment. Meanwhile, David immediately bolts off into the distance, leaving Garry far behind. I watch Garry as he shuffles awkwardly on his skis – he "duck walks" rather than gliding efficiently – like he's never been on skis before.

For months he posted Instagram shots of himself dragging tires through the snow in Toronto's Don Valley, but he was always hiking rather than on skis. To shoot a film like this, the cameraman has to be the strongest person on the team – able to keep up with the flow of the journey as well as document it. Garry, as is evident in the first hour of this day, is the weakest member of the team. To compound things, David continues to simply stride off on his own on every pull (we gather up every hour for a break), so the leader of this expedition is a speck in the distance the whole day.

A man of few words, David is quite mute throughout our initial foray, saying little to us on our breaks. And Garry, as the filmmaker, should definitely have words with him. A lot of time, money, and effort has been spent to get Garry up here to shoot this thing, so David should probably co-ordinate the logistics of filming with Garry. But Garry also says nothing all day as David continually tromps off on his own across the ice. It's amusing, really.

I've got a few nice still shots, which is all I'm here to do, and tonight I'll write about the day in my journal. Throughout the course of the day Garry doesn't pull out his video camera once, as it's all he can do just to keep up. David doesn't seem concerned in the least. From my perspective, if you're going to film an expedition, you should cover the first and last day extensively. Every scene shot in-between can be moved around like chess pieces.

Toward the end of the day, we work our way through jumbled ice, with David seemingly targeting a cabin on the shore. It seems unwise to veer from the main snow machine track but he's off and running and we have no choice but to follow. I told David before the journey started that I'd be a good soldier, so here I am soldiering on. At one point, one of the shotguns, which was lashed to the top of my rear sled, slipped off somewhere in the jumble. Richard notices when we convene for a chat and, unencumbered by my sled, I ski back for a few hundred metres before I find it. It felt so light and so free to not have a couple of hundred pounds attached to me, to glide and turn nimbly through the ice at triple the speed of "man-hauling." It evoked days at the cottage in February where I could go out for an hour or two, skate skiing the broad expanse of Parry Sound among the ice-locked islands, flying like a bird over the snow. But alas, I tease myself, as I'm soon again harnessed to the double sleds like a horse to the plow and plod on.

We stop at the end of the day a few kilometres short of the North Pole River, by the shelter cabin that David had targeted. We set up the two tents on a rise behind the locked cabin, pegging them into frozen, windblown tundra. I'm tenting with Richard again, and Garry is with David. One amusing thing we discover is that it's impossible to eat uncut rounds of pepperoni and blocks of cheese that have been super-frozen in -50°C temps for a few days. One of the joys of trip is figuring out how to solve problems on the fly, so I immediately resolve to fix the issue. There are a few tools in the forward shed of the locked cabin and I proceed to break the 40 days' worth of meat and cheese into edible bites with the brute force of a hammer.

Garry pulls out his camera for the first time all day to film the smashing action. You can't base an expedition film on camping and hotel footage; you have to shoot when it's hard. Garry is essentially crafting a home video from what I can see. Still, it's good fun and I manage to have bagfuls of bite-sized meat and cheese by the end of the bludgeoning session. For some reason, no one follows my lead.

CHAPTER 68

On the way to Rae
A group appears in our camp
Inuit hangout

I hear the distinct horse fly tone of a snow machine and I look up from my meat and cheese bashing. A black speck is crossing the bay below us, headed our way. I call out to no one in particular, "Looks like the boys from town are paying us a visit."

The four of us unfold from our various tasks, and we gather up to see a snowmobiler come over the rise, running his machine over the barren tundra and then over a crusted snowdrift, eventually stopping within a couple of feet of me.

He steps off and pulls down his parka hood to reveal himself. It's Laimmiki, the man who gave us the lay of the land back at the school, and who also crafted the wooden sled for us to take along on this trip. David wanted to bring it along as a courtesy but eventually prudently decided to leave it in town when it was apparent we already had way too much stuff and it was a completely superfluous thing.

Laimmiki asks, "What're you guys doing here? We were waiting for you at the North Pole River. We wanted to show you the Rae house."

"Um, we saw this cabin and decided it was a good place to camp," I reply.

"Well, it's off course a bit. The main snowmobile track's the best way to get to the river."

I shrug. There's no need for further explanation on my part. "Where's the main track?"

"If you follow my trail to here, you'll hit it. It's the easiest way to go."

A couple of minutes later four more snow machines arrive, and we're suddenly hosting guests at our site. Among them are Aubrey, a large bearded white man who's the school principal, and Jerry Kaluk, a strapping young Inuk clad in a sealskin jacket and pants his mother made for him.

Jerry glances at the cabin and sees we've made our way into the mudroom with all the tools at the front of the place. It required us to slide out a stack of two by fours put there to keep animals out.

He points to it and says matter-of-factly, "That's my dad's cabin."

I tour Jerry around our camp and he crawls into our tent to check it out, then poses for a picture lying in the vestibule.

The whole convoy, led by Laimmiki, had gone ahead earlier in the day, expecting us to be at the mouth of the North Pole River already. It's hard for them to fathom how slow we actually go since they calibrate everything by snowmobile speed. What takes them half an hour takes us an entire day. One particular landmark that's important for our journey is the remains of the stone house that John Rae built up on a hill at the mouth of the river. He constructed it on one of his early forays into the area, and then used it again as a base before he set off on his overland journey to the Northwest Passage. Laimmiki and his crew hunted down the remains – apparently not easy to find in winter – then marked it with a pole and flag.

They linger with us for a while and the temperature wanes into the -30s. We've not quite set up camp, haven't completely changed into our camp clothing, and haven't eaten. It's a delicate balance between being polite and getting warm and fed before another night in the cold tent. In half an hour they'll be back in warm houses, but in half an hour at this rate, we'll be frozen.

It's rare they get visitors up here, particularly on skis. We're a novelty I suppose, something to break up the monotony of a long, dark, isolated winter. I understand from that perspective. I've had metaphorical long, dark, isolated winters. You're in a funk, in a rut. Then something unexpected appears on your periphery and you seize upon it, engage with it and winter gloom subsides, replaced by an optimistic spring.

The group eventually assembles, gathering around their snowmobiles. Before he goes, Laimmiki draws us a map on the snow of our best route to the North Pole River and Rae's stone house. One by one they board their steeds and in minutes are gone and will be in their snug homes before we eat our dinner. We hurriedly get things going – change out of our trail clothes, get the snow melting, etc.

I pull out a small flask of whisky and offer it up to the group. I also produce a kretek cigarette to share.

"Here you go boys, something to savour our first day."

Garry happily takes a pull.

David says, "No thanks, I don't drink."

"Well, it's not really drinking…it's just a taste – and it's Highland Park, they're a sponsor," I say hopefully.

"No, I'm okay."

David is seemingly a very serious man, rarely cracking a smile. And he's a Scot…who doesn't drink whisky! Weird. Highland Park is a distillery only eight km from Rae's ancestral home, and David worked on them for support of this trip but in the end only got a few pieces of urban clothing branded with their logo, and embossed "Highland Park" flasks. The whisky we have is a bottle we bought in Ottawa. What did David think, that we were going to carry the booze as ballast the whole time? Strange.

I turn to Richard and offer him a sip. He follows David's lead, saying, "I'm okay."

"How about a smoke?"

They all decline, Richard and David somewhat incredulous that I've even brought cigarettes along. Disappointing. What is life if you can't enjoy a bit of sinful pleasure at the end of a cold day on the trail? We're all going to die anyways, might as well smoke 'em while you've got 'em. I put the smokes away…my fingers are getting cold and the lighter's not sparking. A bunch of "sticks in the mud," these guys. I'll need to work on them.

Soon the other three are in the tents, settling in for the evening. I linger in the pressing cold, looking off to where the Naujaat crew have gone, then over to where we're going. It's 9 p.m. but still bright out, the sun adding ten more minutes of light per day. It's not a warm sun though, and I feel the fingers of cold creeping in through the cracks in my clothing, which is another annoyance gear-wise. First there's the old sleeping bag loaner, and then in Ottawa David hands us our Canada Goose down jackets that are a size too big. Canada Goose is an urban, boutique brand. Heavy and bulky, it's fine for walking around on a northern lights tour of Yellowknife but is not ideal for an activity-based Arctic expedition. You'll see the brand most often in big cities like Toronto, where trendy urbanites laughably sport the gigantic fur-trimmed jackets, which are grounds for the occasional mugging due to their cost and the degree to which they're coveted. The Skreslet parkas we have retail for around $1,200 – Canada's version of haute couture.

I have a relationship with Arc'teryx, an outdoor apparel company with extremely tough and light gear. I outfitted the team with shell jackets and pants from the company and could have probably provided the insulated stuff too, but David stuck with Canada Goose. So now we're wearing two competing brands. *I have to be a good soldier*, I remind myself again. Plus, it's free gear, so I shut up and go with the flow. All the Canada Goose stuff David gave me is a size large, though I requested medium. He brushes it off, saying, "They were out of medium. You'll have to make do with the large." There was no word of this until it was too late.

I scold myself for nitpicking, and smile wryly as I look out over the frozen expanse of Hudson Bay. John Rae would kill for First World problems like mine, though I'm sure his caribou skins fit far better than this parka, that's for sure.

Inside the tent, it's spacious. These are actually four-person tents, but only if those four people were children. As it is, they seem like the perfect size for two people, with plenty of room for both Richard and me. After a few journal notes with freezing ink that transfers intermittently to the page, I fall asleep.

CHAPTER 69

A teammate injured
By the mouth of the North Pole
And then there were three

I end up being cold all night in the sleeping bag. It seems the loft is not what it's supposed to be and it probably dropped to -40°C overnight. I threw on the light down jacket as well, but to no avail – I just stayed bloody cold. Dawn and getting up was welcome as I only slept in spurts and wanted to get the blood going again. Hot coffee and freeze-dried eggs in the vestibule begins the process. Soon enough, we're on the trail and in a couple of hours of skiing we're nearly at the North Pole River mouth and the "official" start of the journey, where we actually begin to follow Rae's route.

I notice again Garry doesn't take out the camera to film, though the day is warmish at -30°C and the wind is light. He lags behind and we gather up after the second hour to have a snack. Afterwards, Richard and I head onward to the river mouth that lies between high hills only a kilometre or so away. David and Garry are in conference with each other, and before Richard and I get too far on, David shouts out to us.

"Guys, hold up!"

David skis to us with Garry coming up behind.

David says to Richard and me, "Group talk."

We gather in a loose circle and David says, "Garry's leaving the trip. His heels can't deal with his boots."

Richard and I take in the news as Garry stands sheepishly by, saying nothing, preferring David to speak for him.

Richard tries to look for a solution, asking Garry, "Is there anything we can do to help? Take some of your weight?"

Garry says, "My heel was bugging me before the trip, but I thought I'd give it a go. It's not getting better, so I think I should step off now before we get any deeper into the trip."

I wasn't going to try and talk him out of it. His heel could be sore, sure, but there was not a mention of it until this very moment. I read his face and there's something else there. Defeat and realization. This is not filming from a zodiac on a cushy trip with clients while sleeping on a comfy mothership each night. This is not a ravine in Toronto. Garry's here to film this thing, but he hasn't done a lick of it – he's unable to. He should not be here, and realized it in the first hour yesterday. The heel injury, whether real or not, is an excuse. Like Charlie Sheen stabbing his own leg to get out of Vietnam in *Platoon*, this was Garry's way out of the predicament he'd put himself in.

The sun is shining today, with little wind. It's the most comfortable day yet. We're standing on the sea ice with hilly country to our north. The four of us shuffle quietly for the last kilometre until we reach the actual mouth of the river. Large ice heaves seem to block the path up the river itself. The Inuit crew yesterday broke a trail up a wind-scoured hill to get to Rae's hut and mark it for us, but it would be near impossible to drag our heavy loads up the wind-drifted and snow-free ground. David pulls out the satellite phone and makes a call to Laimmiki in Naujaat to come pick up Garry. While he's doing this, I chat with Garry for a bit.

I lightheartedly say, "Take me with you." I do like Garry. He's easy-going and I have a good rapport with him. Now I'm stuck with the two Scots.

He smirks. "You could film this if you wanted – you could borrow some of the gear."

I laugh, thinking of the 40 pounds of cameras, lenses, drone, and other recording equipment.

"No thanks, man, that's your gig. I'm just here to take photos and write."

I tap my chest, where I keep my ultra compact Lumix ZS200. Not much bigger than a cell phone, it's something I can keep warm against my body, pull out for a few seconds, then return to its place. In these conditions, it's the only way to shoot. Dead simple.

David gets off the phone with Laimmiki and says he'll be here to pick up Garry in about an hour or so. In the meantime, we have to reorganize everything in the spur of the moment to travel as three instead of four. Months of planning for four people and we suddenly have less than an hour to switch it up. Out goes a quarter of the food, out goes one of the tents (we're going to stuff three of us into one), and away go Garry's two sleds. For some reason we keep two shotguns. I argue for one but David insists.

It feels good somehow to purge this stuff, even to purge Garry. I could see we'd be waiting for him the whole trip, and the sudden simplification into a single tent and the elimination of the filming aspect is a mental relief. I love a streamlined trip and we're getting closer to that with this surprise turn of events.

With the gear redistributed, Richard and I use the time we have to seek out Rae's stone house and scout out our best way up the river. We amble up an embankment and then to a ramshackle Inuit fishing hut that sits on a high point. From here, we see that the jumbled ice at the river's mouth extends for a few hundred metres to a blind corner in a canyon. We walk steadily uphill over a mix of hardpan snow, frozen tundra, and shattered rock to see what the canyon reveals. It's the first moment I really feel like I'm on an adventure – seeing if a theory is possible, if we can ski right up this river.

At the edge of the canyon, we can see a kilometre clear up and it's smooth glare ice. Like on the Weasel River last spring, we have the possibility of excellent travel if we wear our crampons. The glide should be resistance-free. Richard and I smile and are both buoyed by the possibility of walking straight up the river like Rae did. We meander inland, following the approximate location of Rae's stone cabin that I have marked on the GPS. Moving through shallow gullies, we climb upward until we get to a wide depression. There in the middle sits a ski pole with flagging tape attached to it. Snow machine tracks approach the spot from the other direction, from where Laimmiki and his crew marked it for us the day before. There was very little visible of the stone hut – it was almost completely covered by hardpan, windblasted snowdrifts. Had the pole not marked the spot we would have walked right past it.

Upon closer inspection, there are indeed at least three corners to the hut. Scraping away some of the snowdrift reveals walls about four feet high. It's a very crude hut indeed – good only to cut the wind, perhaps, but not much more. Only a white man would build something like that up here. Considering that Rae actually utilized igloos on his northern travels, I surmise the stone hut was built more as a permanent headquarters versus a sleeping shelter, as igloos are far superior in terms of insulation. Perhaps Rae envisioned establishing a settlement here one day.

Richard and I return via the track the Inuit had put in with their snowmobiles, which takes us down the other side of the hill and back to David and Garry. Having seen this steep, frictional tundra and breakable-snow route, we've settled in our minds that the best, and correct, route is straight up the gut of the river.

Back at the river mouth, David and Garry wait around the sleds. We don't say much beyond describing our scout of the river and the stone hut. It remains sunny and virtually windless in the protected bay.

Richard turns to Garry. "It's not far to the stone hut if you want to film it."

Garry shakes his head. "Naw, unless I keep going there's no point."

The film was now dead to Garry, and Garry was dead to the trip. At this point I just wanted Laimmiki to get here so we could get rid of Garry and be on our way.

Within a few minutes Laimmiki and Jerry roll in on their sleds. Laimmiki has a *qamatiq* rigged to the back of his sled and within a few minutes we have Garry's sleds and the extra gear loaded onto it. Laimmiki goes to the front of his sled and pops off the engine cover. His starter belt is gone so he's using an old rope to turn the engine and fire it up.

"Inuit style!" David comments. Laimmiki smiles broadly. These guys know their sleds as intimately as they know their own children and possess all the tricks they need to keep them running during their annual eight months of winter. Garry slips in behind Jerry on this sled, gives a big "oh well" shrug, and within a minute he's gone. Now it's just the three of us. We quickly harness up our sleds and head for the mounds of ice that block our route up the North Pole River. We weave our way in, around, and over the ice heaves where we can, and in areas where they're over ten feet high and more than double that across, the three of us work each of the six sleds up and over together before continuing. It's slow going but engaging. Like a maze we have to find our way through.

After an hour of pushing, pulling and dragging we clear the last ice heave and gaze across a clean, clear expanse of ice ahead of us. We lash our skis to the sleds, pull on our crampons, and begin to tromp up the aqua blue, snow-free ice. The sleds virtually fly behind us, resistance-free as they glide over the glassy surface. We make steady uphill progress, winding around thin drifts in order to stay on the ice and keep moving at a good clip. After days of delays caused by weather, logistics issues, and injury, we're all champing at the bit to make some progress.

At our first pause after we've cleared the section of heaved ice, David lets out a loud, grunting "Yaaaaaahhhhhh!" He then turns to Richard and me and exclaims, "Now we're going! We're finally doing it!" It's the first sign of exuberance I've heard from him – he seems happier than anyone to be free of the anvil of Garry and his film. Now we can just move, get on with it. Also, months of talking and prepping are finally over for him. I know the work and sacrifice that goes into planning something like this, and David did by far most of the glad-handing and schmoozing to drum up support for the trip. David also left behind a 3-year-old child and his wife, something I've never had to deal with. Anyhow, all that obligatory rigmarole must have been wearing on the guy. Now he's finally free to simply drag his sled through the snow and ice, everything else be damned. So that exuberant howl of his was one of liberation – a rare expression of emotion from a typically laconic Scot.

After all the faffing about dealing with the Garry situation and the slow travel through the ice heaves, we set up camp after covering about ten km. Our quarters are going to be much tighter now with three of us stuffing into one tent. Set-up is extremely fast with all of us working together. Once the tent is up, I pull out the flask of whisky and offer it up out of courtesy. Surprisingly, both David and Richard take sips.

After his first sip, David's eyes widen. "Wow, that's so smooth!"

Richard, perhaps not partaking yesterday because he wanted to follow David's lead, takes his sip and says, "Oh yeah, that is good!"

"That's what I like, boys – just a nip in the evening to savour the day. We'll have a nip every evening from now on. I didn't bring this bottle of whisky as dead weight."

They both seem quite agreeable to my plan. The trip feels like it's finally, properly, underway.

Somehow, I end up in the middle spot in the tent, which is kind of like the middle seat on a plane where you're crushed between two people. The advantage of the outer sleeping spots is that you have ample place to lay extra things like water bottles, books, clothes, etc., in the pockets on the tent sides and you can turn away from the person beside you to grab a modicum of privacy by facing the tent wall. In the middle, you have no space for yourself except inside your sleeping bag. I'm a light sleeper and, like with Dave and Johnny on Baffin, position my head at their feet to stay far away from potential snoring. Richard isn't bad, a fairly light snorer overall, but I hadn't experienced David yet.

There are, however, two particular advantages to sleeping in the middle. Firstly, you're sandwiched between two warm bodies so theoretically it will be in the warmest spot in the tent. Secondly, if a polar bear ever makes a foray through the side of the tent, I'm buffered by either a David or Richard burrito.

It drops into the -30s fairly quickly and we huddle around the comforting roar of our MSR XGK stoves, which are the best stoves available for melting snow, though also the loudest. We have the stoves running simultaneously, one person constantly sitting by and loading more snow into the pots for melting while the other two busy themselves with setting up their space. We're definitely on top of each other; these are tight quarters. Both Richard and David eat double meals while I stick with one. I've always been fine with just one bag of freeze-dried food for dinner. I've eaten literally thousands of these meals over the years and even on the most challenging trips a single meal has always done the trick. I also don't want to have to get up in the middle of the night and go take a shit outside in -40°C temps.

We all slide into our bags and settle in for the evening. We also make a satellite phone call to a friend of David's. We leave a message there which he will then transcribe to a daily blog on the expedition website. Richard's spiel is an excellent, witty take on the day. I have no interest in saying anything as I have little to say really, while David's stoic blow-by-blow description of the day sounds like a weather report. After his summation I say to Richard, "You just became our daily blogger – congratulations."

Within about 30 seconds of the satellite phone being hung up, David zips himself into his bag, lies on his back, and is snoring like a sputtering chainsaw. I wrinkle my forehead and look over at Richard, who smiles knowingly, having been David's tent mate since Naujaat.

"Wow, that was quick," I say.

"Yeah, he goes down like that every night…and he snores. Get used to it."

I stay up for another half hour, writing in my journal until my fingers lose all feeling to the creeping cold outside the opening of my bag. I then escape for half a chapter to the warm, breezy climes of Peru as I read about Thor Heyerdahl's preparation for his famous balsa raft adventure in the classic book *Kon-Tiki*.

CHAPTER 70

Chunks of shattered ice
Flash frozen one fine cold day
Gleaming Christie Lake

We wake for the first time as three in a tent. David is up first and gets the stoves going to melt the snow for breakfast and the day's water. I sit up and begin to get myself organized. Being in the middle made for a warmer night and I pull out my clothes for the day that I'd laid around my body inside the bag.

"Mmmmmmmoooooooohhhh." I hear a strange sound – like that of a wounded cow – emanate from the lump to my left. The large red caterpillar suddenly sits up. Two slitted eyes appear from within the opening of the bag, which is encircled by an explosion of hoar frost.

"Morning, Richard!" I exclaim.

"It was a bit cold last night wasn't it?" he quips in his dry, understated way.

"I didn't think it was as bad as the night before, but you guys double-spooned me here in the middle so I had a few extra degrees on you."

We're eventually all up and out of our bags. David is manning the stoves but instead of sitting down beside them he stands over them with his ass to us in the main body of the tent. When Richard and I are at the helm, we sit down to the side of the stoves on a padded bag of mine, still able to load snow into the pots while conversing and eating with each other. I suppose I should have said something but it seems like an obvious way to enjoy the morning with some banter as we ease into the day.

Eventually, David goes out to take a shit and I slide into the padded seat where I have my first coffee of the day – a double hit of Starbucks instant coffee with a hearty helping of Coffee Mate, the "cream of the North." Ideally, I have two cups per day – first the good stuff, then the sub-par but deliciously sweet Nescafé all-in-one coffee/cream/sugar combo packet. Like wine at a wedding, you always bring out the best first.

We break camp fairly quickly, eager to get our first full day of unimpeded travel under our belts. The North Pole River is narrow, about 40 metres across and blown clear of snow, save for the occasional ribbon of white stuck to the aquamarine ice. I decide to put crampons on right out of the gate, pulling them over my cross-country boots. I knew it would be cold on this journey so I wear size 45 boots instead of size 43 to accommodate an Intuition Liner. The liner is closed cell foam that traps heat, which is ideal for a trip such as ours. Richard had purchased a $1,000 arctic boot with the same liner, but I'd balked at the price so instead purchased $200 boots that I can stick a liner into. They felt good when I'd skied them a bunch of times on the west coast and they've felt fine to this point so I figure my gamble has worked. David has a pair of Alpina Alaska boots, essentially an insulated hiking boot with a sole that can click into a ski binding. Today, though, he wears a pair of leather mukluks with a rubber sole and pulls the crampons on over those.

Pulling the 200 pounds of double-sled over the ice is amazingly resistance-free. It's like night and day compared to dragging over the cold, Styrofoam snow. I get a little ahead of Richard and David through the narrows of the North Pole River in the first hour of the day as I want to get a few shots from the high bank of them coming up the river. I unhitch from my sled alongside the ten-metre-high sloping bank and scramble to the top. The surrounding landscape is an endless wind-blown plain of rolling hills. A distinct inukshuk catches my eye as I set up the shot, and then I see that they're lined up every 20 metres or so along the upper edge of the bank. I've read about this use of inukshuks by ancient Inuit to funnel caribou into a natural terrain trap but have never seen it. This section of the river is particularly narrow, so caribou travelling down the river would be spooked by the rock figures on the bank and stay low, where hunters hidden atop the bank could ambush and spear the assembled herd from land or in kayaks.

Earlier in the day we spotted a pair of older caribou tracks, but today only the plodding figures of Richard and David appear before the ancient stone sentries. These inukshuks would very likely have been around at the time of Rae, who passed by this very spot. I take a few shots of them as they amble by, then pause to watch them, though my mind is somewhere else. I find I'm struck at times by moments on these journeys that come out of the blue. I'm looking at my teammates and their sleds but I'm not seeing them. I'm lost in a cosmic thought. It tumbles over me like a collapsing wave, the fact that life is ephemeral and fleeting, all of us passing through it, moving by inanimate watchers like these, who will see other travellers pass through here long after the three of us are merely scattered dust in the wind. It reminds me that I have to make the most of my limited time on this planet. Whether freezing my ass off in this desolate land qualifies as a good use of time is perhaps questionable, but at the very least it's an interesting diversion from routine.

In the second half of our day, we break out onto North Pole Lake, the first of several big lakes we'll pass over on our way to Committee Bay. The surface is blown mostly clear, with white cracks running endlessly in all directions through the turquoise ice. As Lawrence mentioned, we should find a small hut he dragged out here in September. We spot it soon after hitting the lake, sitting by itself in the middle, drifted-in and lonely-looking. There isn't much to it – just four walls, a roof, and a bench inside, perhaps six by eight feet. It's a spot where two people could typically sleep or sit, but the door has been open a crack so it's filled with snow. We dig out the area around the bench and sit inside out of the wind to have a bite to eat. It's -25°C in the breeze so the reprieve inside these four walls is welcome. Lawrence said he hasn't been out here since October and wouldn't come out here again until sometime this month when things aren't quite so gripped in cold. We have to keep going, and the drifted-in shelter is no great comfort anyways. Once you stop moving, the icy fingers of Malina, the Inuit moon goddess, soon take hold of you.

A narrows after North Pole Lake leads to Christie Lake, which is remarkable in that the entire lake is composed of pans of white ice connected by crystal clear blue ice, as if the pans were just drifting about and then instantly froze in place like Lot's wife, who turned to a pillar of salt when she glanced back at the sinful city of Sodom. These pans of ice weren't victims of a vengeful god but rather of the dispassionate and ever-punishing north wind.

That evening we set up on the ice along shore in the shadow of a high bluff, the sun veiled behind wispy clouds. My feet are sore from the tromping on hard ice with crampons in cross-country boots all day. We covered 28 km, a big day considering the terrain and the loads we are carrying. I don't think much of the soreness, figuring it's just my feet breaking into the rhythm of the trip. I've never had significant foot problems over the years, so I think nothing of it. My boots for camp are a pair of cozy, clunky Baffin -100°C boots, and my feet nestle into them like angels on a fluffy cloud.

I pull my sleeping bag from its stuff sack and notice it has frozen patches of ice all over it. It is also flat and crackled when I spread it out. Running the stoves in the tent creates a lot of moisture and it's affected the bag already, which has no hydrophobic qualities whatsoever. On Arctic trips to Bylot and Baffin Island the previous two seasons in the pleasant travelling season of May, we'd always cooked outside in order to keep moisture and fumes out of the tent. The bitter cold and date of April 1 emphasizes the foolish time we'd chosen to travel. We huddle around our stoves like they're fireplaces, basking out of the wind in the relatively warm vestibule. The irony, of course, is that while we're warm in the tent, the down of my sleeping bag is wetting out and losing its loft evening by evening, making for colder nights as the trip draws on.

As I'm getting into my frozen bag that evening, the very fine zipper breaks. I should have known from Richard's ordeal in Naujaat that this would happen. He was lucky his zipper broke first and he got the only other decent sleeping bag in town. Not only does it have a robust zipper and is rated to -40°C, it's also a synthetic bag that won't be affected like the spongy down bags David and I have. I watch with envy as Richard happily zips into his cozy cocoon that night, while I bring my down pants, big down jacket, and pretty much all of my clothes in with me to create some sort of warmth in the coffin-like bag that is now vented by a broken zipper.

CHAPTER 71

No glare ice cruising
Grinding through haphazard drifts
Head down and forward

Looking out over Christie Lake, with the cold morning sun glinting off its windblown, frozen visage, I can foresee another day in the crampons. I decide to walk in my Baffin boots since my feet are sore from tromping in the ski boots with my crampons the day before. We head off hoping for another big day of easy "man-hauling," but within a few hundred metres the ice becomes drifted in – a patchwork of grabby snow and glare that never quite lets us get into a groove of smooth pulling – a herky-jerky, stop-and-go day that is pure grind. Each of us takes our own route over the broad lake, hoping to find that magical line of clear ice that we can follow the rest of the day. But none of us find it. Hope springs eternal, and sometimes that hope is all that keeps you moving…those small victories in a long day. Four or five strides over smooth ice buoy the spirits, only to be crushed by the next line of drifts that you stomp and grind through in order to haul the godforsaken loads. Each of us struggles in our own purgatory, always in sight of the others, yet utterly alone.

The patches of ice tease us all along, so none of us ever switch to skis. We spend the whole day on Christie Lake in low cloud and typically cold conditions. There isn't much to see, just what's directly in front of me, so my head is down and moving requires little attention. All I have to do is plod along, so I put in the ear buds and listen to *Desert Island Discs* episodes where the soothing, light Scottish accent of host Kirsty Young transports me away from my situation. It amazes me that she and David are from the same country, since their accents are so jarringly different.

It's rare that I listen to anything other than the wind on my journeys. I certainly would never bring any kind of listening device on a canoe trip or mountain-based ski trip. The only other trips I have used this crutch for have been when my buddy Todd and I rode and walked through the dusty roads of northern Alberta following the route of the proposed Northern Gateway Pipeline, and when rowing the Northwest Passage, where my only view was the galley door of our pig of a rowboat. These other two trips were for a greater purpose so we had to cross through these dull sections in order to tell greater stories about climate change and oil pipelines.

This trip was different – there was no pressing environmental issue to speak of, just a historical retracing. John Rae was long dead, so bringing light to his achievements seemed more and more like a falsely noble effort to shine light on ourselves. Rae, now just dust buried somewhere in the Orkneys, is certainly in no position to give a damn about anything three white dudes are doing. Hell, if Rae were alive today, he most certainly would be using a snowmobile, not dragging two sleds behind him like some sort of madman. Rae learned from the Inuit, used their methods (which in this day and age is the snowmobile), so what were we doing dragging sleds behind us? I can't imagine he'd approve. Pure hubris drives us along. This realization is why I shrink away from the lusty daily satellite phone reports Richard provides, and why I close into my own shell to focus on writing, photography, and putting one foot in front of the other. This is a job, I'm being paid to do it, and I'll do my damnedest to find a way through. And that's why I listen to British comedian Alan Carr share his favourite songs and life stories, why I chuckle at Ricky Gervais's story of taking the piss out of the vicar at his mother's funeral. Their tales are much more interesting to me this afternoon than the monotonous, flat, and windblown sheet of ice I find myself walking over today. I understand now why people in a gym, on a treadmill, listen to podcasts. It makes me feel shameful, weak. I'm unable to embrace my present reality, so I numb myself with entertainment that takes me away from this place.

I also understand Ryan better now. When he resorted to similar distraction on our summer canoe trip, I got pissed. But the reason he did it was because he was trying to cope with boredom; I just didn't see it like he did at the time because I was in a completely different headspace. One man's joy is another's misery.

I slog along in this self-contained, imaginary world. Wearing goggles and a face mask that's caked in the ice formed by my own breath, my view is the circle of my coyote fur-trimmed hood. Inside this bubble of comfort, Christine McVie talks about what she did in her 15-year hiatus from Fleetwood Mac. David stops at the end of our hour-long pull and Richard sidles up behind him. They position their sleds sideways to the wind, put on their big parkas and huddle in the lee to have a bite to eat and a hot sip of tea. Through my hood, inside my artificial world of entertainment, they don't seem real, like they're part of a dramatic survival TV show. When I sidle up beside them, I see Richard look up at me and mouth something that I don't hear. I give him a wave that seems to satisfy him as a response, then position my sled sideways and pull out the ear buds. With that motion I'm suddenly thrust back into reality. Kirsty Young's dulcet voice is replaced by the howling, biting wind, which quickly chills me once I stop moving. I unclip my sleds from my pack, quickly dig out my parka and bag of snacks, then huddle in the lee of my load. I rip off my face mask in order to eat, allowing wind-driven ice crystals to penetrate and sting my face like tiny needles.

We sit there, quietly enjoying being off of our feet, savouring frozen snickers bars, chunks of cheese, and hot chocolate. Nothing needs saying, and there's another hour of walking to get to the end of our day. I enjoy the break but also can't wait to get moving so I can hear Kirsty's voice again.

CHAPTER 72

A fine bluebird day
Down frozen lakes and rivers
Then the pain comes on

My feet have been a little sore every evening once the boots come off, but they're worse than usual after my day in the Baffin boots. Today, it's sunny with only a very light breeze, though the forecast promises a high of only -25°C. Our mission today is to tackle a chain of small lakes and a river that will lead us over a divide to Miles Lake. The North Pole River system drains south to Hudson Bay while Miles Lake is the start of the drainage that spills north into Committee Bay and the Arctic Ocean proper. A good portion of the day promises to be overland sections between the lakes, so we're back on the skis after two full days of walking in our micro spikes.

My feet are a bit delicate but nothing seems too visibly wrong with them, though my ski boots feel a bit tighter than normal when I put them on in the morning. It was cold in my sodden bag last night, and I needed to layer all my clothes inside again to get warm enough to fall asleep. Even so, I still remained cool all night, waking every hour with light dreams of palm trees and beaches spurred on by my nightly reading of Thor Heyerdahl's incredible journey on the *Kon-Tiki*. It always takes a moment to figure out that the cold cave I'm in is a tent on the ice and not a thatched roof cabin aboard a balsa raft.

It is a morning in which I need to be present, as we climb the bank out of the north end of Christie Lake and work our way over the wind-carved sastrugi and around rocky open areas to a chain of small, unnamed lakes. We don't know exactly what to expect going up and over the rises between the lakes, but it always seems to be just gradual enough that we can drag the sleds over with our skis on, making for relatively efficient travel. It's interesting and dynamic terrain, so no need for *Desert Island Discs*, as each section between lakes requires finding the most efficient way through – you can't just put your head down and look at your feet all day. The hills around us are much higher too. I would almost say they are mountains, but not quite, with rock walls rising up from the small lakes for hundreds of feet. I lead the way most of the day, enjoying the route finding and varying terrain.

After the lakes, we access a steep, frozen river in a small canyon. It stretches due north through a mix of aquamarine ice and flattened drifts, seeming to end in a small mountain range. Somewhere ahead will be a frozen waterfall (according to the tight topographical lines on our map) that will lead us to Miles Lake, our goal for the day. After that it looks like easy travel to Committee Bay. At this point, in the mid-afternoon of a beautiful bluebird day, I notice my feet are hurting like hell.

Coming to a sharp left through a small canyon, a steep slope leads through a notch to the wide-open expanse of Miles Lake. I have the most downhill skiing experience of our group and zigzag down the slope with my double sleds, luckily avoiding any kind of complete yard sale. For the really steep bits, I swing the sleds in front of me so I can control their weighted descent and stop them from running me down from behind.

David and Richard eventually make their way down too, looking like newborn caribou learning to walk after being dropped from the womb. We all make it unscathed (no one, including myself, winning any style points) and set up camp on the broad lake. I pull off my boots and my feet throb. I can't put pressure on either forefoot; they just fucking hurt like nothing else. It isn't obvious what happened to them, perhaps a deep bone bruise from the two days on the crampons. The boots seemed so comfortable the first few days, but now my feet feel like broken glass. Something must have triggered them somewhere along the way. We're only a few days in, with a long way to go, so this is definitely a problem.

The Baffin boots feel better than the ski boots, but definitely tighter than they used to be and I hobble around camp doing the usual duties of tent set-up and snow-melting. Once we're settled into the vestibule for dinner, I tear out the whole liner of my ski boot to make more room for my swelling feet. David and Richard are amused at my boot deconstruction, but I downplay the level of pain, hoping it will settle out overnight and be better with the bit of extra room I've created. Before I go to bed, I pop a couple of Ibuprofen to help things along.

Reflecting on the day, it has probably been my favourite, with a variety of terrain keeping it interesting all the way. Thinking back to my feet, I decide I will do a Groucho Marx–like shuffle tomorrow that will hopefully take pressure off of them.

The next day is warm and windless so I lay my sodden bag over my sled in hopes of drying it out somewhat. The pathetic clump of frozen feathers can't be much better than a zero-degree bag at this point. My feet seem okay in the morning but by afternoon they hurt once again. This time the right much more than the left.

Richard decides to play a prank on our always-too-serious leader David. Just as David is about to depart, he places a large stone on his rear sled. David immediately begins dragging the sled with his robotic gait and Richard and I gleefully laugh at his expense. After a couple of hundred metres he stops to glance back and notices us bent over with laughter.

We ski up to him. He looks at us, still unaware of the stone, so we point it out.

"Oh, you fuckers." He then breaks into a big grin. I take a shot of him pointing at the stone on the sled, taking the prank in stride. It's good to see this humorous side of David for the first time.

At one point during the day, we pass by an open creek between small lakes where we refill our water bottles, hopefully saving some snowmelt time at the end of the day. In that moment we all pause in the sunshine. There isn't a puff of wind and we are down to our base layers. I've been downright comfortable most of the day, recalling Bylot Island from a couple of years earlier, where the temperature for the first week hovered windless and just below zero.

The small lakes lead into a tributary of the Curtis River, which is ribboned with sastrugi that slow our afternoon progress significantly as we haul up and over the two-foot mounds for a couple of hours. For this final section, Nile Rogers entertains me with tales of an incredible life in music that spanned decades and genres, managing to put my throbbing feet into the background for at least a little while.

A small cabin just before the confluence with the Curtis River comes into view, and we make for it. We're suddenly energized and everyone picks up the pace, hoping it will be a soft landing for us at the end of a long day. Thankfully, the cabin is open, clean, and tidy. Often these structures will have been ransacked by a wolverine or bear (either grizzly or polar bear), or just be generally strewn with junk. This cabin is pristine, with a broad sleeping platform that will easily accommodate the three of us. No tent set-up tonight, easy in and out, and a much roomier space to hang out in.

I set to work right away on my boots. I pull out my Leatherman multitool and cut out holes on the outside of the forefoot of each boot, each about five cm by two cm, that I hope will allow my feet to spread out and accommodate the swelling and give them some measure of relief. I have an Intuition inner liner so I figure I'll still have insulation despite the open holes to the outer boot. David and Richard laugh at what I'm doing to my boots, unaware of the degree of my foot pain. Not that I would ever tell them, because what difference would it make? We all have to move forward, every day; there is no choice. Complaining or whining about my predicament in no way helps the objective of the mission. It only adds an element of unease to the team dynamic, which would be detrimental.

There's probably nothing I hate more than being treated like an invalid, where someone is constantly asking me how I am, how they can help, etc. Being on a journey like this requires all the team members to be self-sufficient, to pitch in equally. When you can no longer do that, and you negatively affect the objective, that's when it's time to go. The best I can do is try everything in my power to manage my feet, to keep pace with the team, and hope the discomfort stabilizes so I could finish this journey. I have to deal with what is in front of me and take it day by day.

Richard gleefully mentions that Frank was "cutting apart his boots with a Leatherman" on the satellite report that night. Great, always good to get people worrying about shit they can't control. If it were me, I'd keep that within the team. It's not like we're being followed by anyone who didn't know us, so what's the point of broadcasting worrying news? This expectation of constant communication is one of the more distasteful things about modern expeditions.

As I hack away at my boots, I notice my wrists are quite sore and stiff. When I inspect them, I notice they are both swollen. It quickly dawns on me that pounding away on the ice with my poles for all these days has aggravated them. Not a deal-breaker by any means as I've had tendonitis in my wrists before, but another indication of my body breaking down or breaking in. Adjusting the straps on the poles should hopefully sort things out. Despite the physical setbacks, it is still a fine evening. Having been cramped in the middle for the past few nights it is nice to be able to stretch out and not be confined in the damp tent. Also, after a day in actual warmish-feeling sunshine, my sleeping bag seems to have regained at least a bit of its loft. There are still some frozen clumps of feather in there as the temp didn't rise much above -20°C, but there is improvement.

David and Richard bed down while I step outside of the cabin for one last piss before bed. It's 10 p.m., still light out, and the sun slowly dips in the west. Off to the east, the Curtis River curves through low hills toward the Arctic Ocean at Committee Bay. Tomorrow we'll hopefully get there and begin the next phase of our journey, leaving behind the lakes and rivers to travel on the sea ice of the Northwest Passage.

CHAPTER 73

Broken ice abounds
A broad expanse of whiteness
Committee Bay view

It's a bird's nest, a complete mess. We're out among the broken ice at the south end of Committee Bay and trying to untangle a nightmare of string for our bear fence. It's impossible to untangle the string with gloves on so I'm barehanded in -25°C temps, trying to delicately unravel a seemingly impossible riddle. This, to me, is unacceptable. A year of prep seemingly focused on extraneous things like filming, press, and other activities unrelated to the actual journey, and taking the time to actually set up the polar bear fence in advance to make sure it can easily be deployed was never done. Neither of us talks; the silence says it all. Richard wisely stays in the tent, tending to snow-melting duties by the stove. We have to cut the string in a couple of spots, and a few of the wooden stakes that hold the corner posts break when being pounded into the ice.

Having used Dave Garrow's customized and diligently prepared bear fence in Baffin, the difference is night and day. This fence seems flimsy and low, something a bear could easily step over, but it's something… at least a mental fence if nothing else. I can't feel my fingertips after the ordeal and decide I will take over while we are on Committee Bay to streamline the process. David says nothing about this folly at all, like it's perfectly normal to be fucking around on the sea ice for an hour untangling string. No point in arguing, it is what it is. Too late to complain now. *Be a good soldier*, I remind myself.

Halfway through the day we emerge from the Curtis River onto Committee Bay. We'd come through the labyrinth of inland lakes and rivers to complete the first phase of the journey. We'd seen fresh wolverine tracks just before hitting the bay, and also spotted some older polar bear tracks when we first reached the Committee Bay Ice. About 30 km away, on the other side of the bay, there's a broad area with lots of broken ice where a healthy population of bears hunt ringed seals. We'll be travelling up the west side, but there's still a high probability of running into a bear as they tend to wander and travel about quite a bit. We're in proper polar bear country now.

By the end of the day, I am pleasantly surprised that my feet don't hurt. My surgery on the boots seems to have worked, so I am hopeful that they will stabilize and maybe even get better from this point onward. Once the debacle of the bear fence is done, spirits are generally high in the tent that evening as we drink hot chocolate and sip Highland Park whisky to celebrate our arrival on the sea ice.

At 1 a.m., pitch black in the tent, I suddenly wake up, drawn out of a dream where I'm walking on coals somewhere in the South Pacific, my feet burning. The air inside the tent is icy cold as usual and David and Richard throw snores back and forth over the foot of my sodden sleeping bag. What woke me was my right foot, pounding with excruciating pain in the forefoot area. I'd packed away my own first aid kit thinking that my foot problem was licked, so I can't access my Ibuprofen. I know Richard has some heavy-duty codeine/Ibuprofen combo pills in the pocket on his side of the tent so I manage to dig around and find those, popping a couple of them, and then take a piss in my pee bottle while I'm up, sticking the warm vessel in the corner of the tent by Richard's feet. The pain meds kick in and I eventually drift off to sleep.

The next morning the foot is still quite sore, somewhat swollen and puffy, and I can't feel the toes, though the skin looks healthy so I know it's not frostbite. My fingertips are also still numb from the bear fence epic the night before. As I change into my day clothes inside my bag, I look to my left on the tent floor and notice that there is ice all around my pee bottle. It apparently tipped over in the night, was not properly sealed, and leaked all over the floor. Cleanup isn't too bad though, as the piss is frozen solid and it's a mere matter of me picking it up and tossing the salty shards out the back door. I decide I'll dump my night piss out the door immediately after urinating from that point on rather than risk further spillage.

CHAPTER 74

Broken Glass all round
Haphazard alabaster
An endless sculpture

In the morning I further modify the boots by cutting holes in the inside of both boots where the balls of my feet line up, and also cut out the part of my boot over the crease of my foot to relieve any downward pressure. My boot is down to an exoskeleton that merely holds the liner, a shell of a shell.

"The modifications continue," Richard observes.

"You've got to make sure you keep those when the trip is done. Those are some legendary boots you've created," David chimes in.

"Yup, the deconstruction continues," I reply.

Meanwhile, I'm thinking, *If I get to the finish*. I can only keep hoping that my feet will stabilize enough to get me through. I won't talk about that other possibility until it becomes an unequivocal reality.

I squeeze my swollen feet into my boots, and after a few minutes the pain seems to numb out as I pound my barking dogs into submission. The day is interesting travel as we work our way through the broken, upheaved ice at the southern end of Committee Bay. It spreads out before us like a seemingly endless scattering of giant puzzle pieces, and we meander through jagged shards of ice sticking straight up and in piles. It seems like ideal polar bear country, a place with plenty of air holes for seals to pop up and get their heads knocked off by a giant, pan-sized paw. We stay closer together as a result, David in the front with a gun, Richard in the middle with a "cracker gun" (essentially a starter's pistol that shoots blanks and flares) and me in the back with the other gun. We're well armed, prepared for a whole platoon of polar bears if need be. We have to be bundled up on this day, wearing our shell tops and bottoms, goggles, and facemasks as a steady north wind cools the sunny day into the -30s.

Near the end of the day, we're following in behind David when his rear sled suddenly detaches after bumping over an angled pan of ice. He keeps right on marching, completely unaware that he was suddenly dragging a hundred pounds less behind him. Richard turns to me and grins. "Let's see how far he goes before he notices."

However, he doesn't notice, and keeps right on marching.

We have a good laugh, and keep on laughing out on the ice, the wind in our faces freezing ridiculous joyous tears that squeeze from the corners of our eyes and solidify instantly. Two men buckled over, and another head down on a mission for Rae. I am half laughing at the detached sled and David's obliviousness to it, and half at the absurdness of what we were doing. What would an objective observer think of three men out on this vast, forlorn sheet of ice, arbitrarily dragging double-loads of sleds? They would think we're lunatics. We didn't need to be here; it's all just a bloody lark, isn't it? We volunteered to be here, to somehow attach ourselves to a simpler time when people were actually exploring, actually seeking the unknown, a time before Google maps, snowmobiles, and permanent towns meant you didn't need to be out here. We're out here because we're creating our own unknown, our own adventure, one that's about personal discovery but does little to expand knowledge beyond ourselves.

This all flits by as a feeling, in mere moments, and then I return to where I am again. Richard and I have had our laugh and now shout at David through the wind, but to no avail. He has his hood on and the wind in his ears – and his hearing isn't great at the best of times.

Our laughter subsides when we realize one of us may have to take on dragging a third sled.

"Shit, I don't think he's going to stop," I muse.

At that moment, we see David pause suddenly to glance back. We both wave our ski poles in the air to get his attention and it finally dawns on him that he's short a load. He spreads his arms in acknowledgement and turns around, heading back our way.

When he skis up to us and our shit-eating grins, he smiles wryly and quips, "I was wondering why I felt suddenly so damn energetic at the end of the day."

CHAPTER 75

Three mere little specks
In a sea of endless white
Skiing a treadmill

In the course of the day we clear the broken ice, skiing mostly on snow, with only the occasional ice heave to manoeuvre. There's a steady, cold breeze from the north and a constant, low fog that limits our visibility to a couple of hundred metres. Without much interesting ground to negotiate, it becomes a head-down-and-grind kind of day. With the aerated, Swiss cheese boots, my feet get quite cold despite the intact liner I still have around them. Snow keeps getting into the holes I've created, which doesn't help either, and I spend much of my time skiing thinking how I can seal the holes while still maintaining the extra room I've created by removing the area around both sides of my forefoot. It's a good way to occupy my mind as the brain-numbing terrain slips by.

We have a snack bag of trail mix, chocolate bars, and energy bars to see us through every day. Our biggest calorie source is from the rolls of salami and blocks of cheese that have been frozen rock solid and have been inedible since day one. I'd broken apart my cheese and salami ration at the end of our first day out of Naujaat and had been happily munching on these calorie- and fat-rich snacks every day. Richard got in on the game at the Curtis Lake cabin, putting his meat and cheese in his sleeping bag overnight and hacking them up into bits with a saw he found there. David had done nothing, however, leaving his meat and cheese uncut and impossible to eat – mere ballast. On this day, however, he had a full-on "bonk" and ran out of food and energy by 3 p.m., so had to dig into his next day's rations.

Once at camp, he is lost to us. After setting up camp, Richard takes on snow-melting duties, I set up the bear fence, and David desperately hacks at his meat and cheese with a knife, manically trying to break up at least a few days' worth of slow-burning sustenance. As usual, he says nothing. He just forges ahead and does it. Neither Richard nor I communicate anything to him; we just carry on setting up camp and let him do what he thinks needs doing. His quiet, grim focus on that block of cheese tells us all we need to know. An odd little fellow, this David. Generally serious but with an occasional dry sense of humour. A funny quirk of his is how he answers you if he can't quite hear you, only a few feet away.

In our little hovel inside the vestibule this evening, Richard asks David to pass him his thermos so he can fill it with hot water. David literally shouts, "HEY?!" Richard repeats the request, and David hands over the thermos. It's a quirk we eventually get used to – this shouted "HEY?!" when he can't quite make out what you're asking but realizes the words have been directed at him. He's like an old man with a hearing horn. You get to know guys better than their wives know them on trips like this. All of our eccentricities are laid bare. I'm sure the others notice my own quirks. We humans are a funny lot.

CHAPTER 76

Rambling over snow
Ball of muscle, teeth, and fur
Wolverine sighting

David sees it out on the ice during a break, a small brown dot moving swiftly, coming from the middle of Committee Bay, headed toward land. We aren't sure what it is at first, as it seems so out of place in the pure white of the landscape. I pull out my spotting scope and see that it's none other than the elusive, mythical wolverine. Thick, dark brown fur with streaks of rusty yellow run down the length of its body – this looks like a robust, healthy creature. It's a few hundred metres north of us and there's a light south wind pushing our scent toward it. As I watch, it seems to have picked up our presence, darting quickly across open sections to small ice heaves where it pauses, glances toward us and then quickly scurries to the next sheltered spot, inexorably moving back to land, where it most likely has a den. We continue skiing toward it but it has long crossed our path, disappearing into the ether where the dark line of distant land blends in with the sporadically broken ice.

Wolverines travel long distances on their scavenging forays. I'm guessing this one was probably coming back from scoping out polar bear country on the other side of the bay, 30 km away, where it might chance upon the remains of a seal carcass. Often bears will just eat the rich outer blubber of a seal and leave the muscle and organs behind. Looking around this vast, seemingly barren landscape, I can't imagine where else the wolverine would get its meal. I try to pick up its track line as we pass where I approximate it crossed, but don't see a trace of anything. We all saw it though, so it wasn't a ghost.

Today has been the warmest we've yet experienced, which is not surprising with the shift in wind from north to south. According to the inReach the high will be -11°C, so quite comfortable all things considered. A half-hour before we spotted the wolverine, another black dot appeared on our horizon, moving quite quickly toward us. It was a lone Inuk on a snowmobile, travelling from Kugaaruk to Naujaat. He was the first person we'd seen since Laimmiki had come to pick up Garry. It seems like eons ago but has been less than a week. I haven't really thought about Garry at all since then. We picked up the snowmobile trail earlier in the day and were generally following it where it made sense. It should be the most efficient way for us to get overland, though we've found that snowmobile routes aren't the best for us, as their uphill, overland lines aren't ideally suited to a human dragging 200 pounds behind them. On the mindless, flat grind of Committee Bay, though, it makes for easy navigation.

The man on the snowmobile is wiry and wears a hood lined with wolverine fur and sunglasses he never takes off. He doesn't have too much to say and seems unsurprised to see three white men dragging sleds over the ice.

"How's the trail from here to Kugaaruk?" I ask.

"Pretty good," he responds.

His face is dark from windburn and his lower teeth have rotted down to black, sharp knife points.

The three of us stand around him and he sits there silently. For us it's awkward; for him quite normal. We feel the need to fill the quiet with mindless conversation. He seems content to fill the conversation with silence. Soon enough, he whirs off. He'll be back in Naujaat in a few hours.

The route is flat and white for the rest of the day, putting me in a monotonous trance. Nothing to do but put my head down and move. I play all four Beatles albums I have loaded on the iPod, which I appreciate as much as when I first discovered them when I was 16 and just getting into music. As a youth I wasn't into the latest songs of 1986. Instead I went for the best of the best. On this day *Sgt. Pepper's Lonely Hearts Club Band*, *Revolver*, *Let It Be*, and *Abbey Road* sparkle in my ears like the surrounding snow. I listen to the tunes and drift off in thought...thinking about writing, of this very book you hold in your hands. It will be, as I write in my journal that evening, "about the past year of trips, but also the searching and drudgery of existing between the trips – a look into existential purpose and the drift and discontent I feel in society as compared to on trip." Dramatic, perhaps, but a seed from which to grow a book if nothing else.

In camp that night, Richard inspects our shotguns. One of them doesn't work, jamming every time, and the other sticks a bit too. If a bear came into camp, we'd have no reliable way to fend it off. We do have the little starter pistol to set off a bang to scare it from a distance but that is about all. Richard has spent several years in the British military and he is familiar with the mechanics of firearms so he spends the evening taking the gimpy gun apart, oiling it, and putting it back together. It takes a couple of hours but he figures it out and we have an operational shotgun once more.

CHAPTER 77

Always from the Side
Blasting brown snow from the land
Pinning west-southwest

The next day remains relatively warm at -10°C, with mostly whiteout conditions as a west-southwest wind huffs in and out with powerful gusts from the mainland. It hits us from the side so we have to lean to the west all day to maintain balance and momentum. The wind-driven snow is mixed with sand, giving the snow on Committee Bay a beige hue. I drag a bit behind most of the day, and David and Richard slowly but surely get ahead of me. It's as much boredom with the monotonous landscape as anything physical. I pause for a piss and then put on a lively dance mix featuring Lady Gaga, Katy Perry, Kesha, and others that ups my stride tempo and motivation. Pumping along to the band Tik Tok, I quickly close the gap on the fellas and stride right on by. This sort of thing shouldn't be necessary on trip – the motivation should all come from within. But some days it doesn't, and you turn to Gaga for help.

In camp that evening, we set up in the lee of an ice heave. David arbitrarily says, "We don't need the bear fence tonight." I don't argue. I'd be the one setting it up anyways as the duty had fallen to me. We'd seen not a sign or track of a polar bear since we'd hit the bay anyways. Tired at the end of a long day, being eaten by a bear seemed a better prospect than setting up measures against it with a dysfunctional alarm system. David's the captain of this ship.

CHAPTER 78

Two creatures darting
Not just a pair of buntings
Wolverine and Fox

The next day we continue along the coast for ten km until we approach a cabin, located on a rise above the shoreline. We see our second wolverine of the trip in that stretch too. It again comes over the ice from the east, darting from shard to shard. I scope it with my monocular and it seems to be as healthy and robust as the other one we'd seen a couple of days earlier. Was this the same one, 50 km further up the bay, or a different one? I can't be sure as they are such prolific wanderers.

At the cabin, a concentration of snowmobile tracks all around indicates this is a main hub for anyone travelling between Naujaat and Kugaaruk. Out on the sea ice, we would pick up random tracks but they weren't always going in the direction we wanted...though I'm sure that ultimately they all led here. Both Laimmiki and Lawrence had said the trail over to Kugaaruk turned off at a cabin, though on the map they seemed to have marked one further up the coast. Richard and I inspect the cabin, which is open. It has a bare bed platform and a Coleman stove but little else. A decent little shelter to hang out from the wind but that's about it. I hear the distinct chirping of birds and spot two snow buntings frolicking over a windblown, open patch of sand at the top of the bank close to the cabin. An early sign of spring? Unlikely, but wonderful to hear a burst of birdsong shatter the frigid silence of the Arctic.

It's only halfway through the day so we push on from the cabin. David stays down on the ice while Richard and I come to check out the cabin on a different line. The main tracks inland look like they go up and over brown hills mostly blown clear of snow – like the initial tracks from Hudson Bay along the North Pole River, they're not the ideal surface to drag our sleds over. We decide to push on to a river that drains due east into Committee Bay that we hope will gradually lead us overland and across the divide into the Kellett River system that drains into Pelly Bay.

We're unlikely to hit snowmobile tracks there, but we're following Rae anyhow, and this is where he sensibly cut overland, so we need to be here too. As with any road or trail, it's always easy to follow something that's established – to somehow justify the easier path, expedition objectives be damned. You can be lazy, put your head down and amble along mindlessly. Let the snowmobile trail do the work for you. There's no anxiety related to navigating this way. No blank landscape, no checking your compass and GPS, or finding the best terrain to move over. But it's also far less engaging – and isn't that what we're all here for in the first place?

The ice in the mouth of the unnamed river where it meets the ocean is jumbled and cuts deeply into the surrounding hills. It's best for us to go overland, through the brown, grassy tundra with just enough snow to make the skiing work – and still far less steep than the snowmobile track from the cabin. We plod along westward, quickly leaving Committee Bay behind; we're now moving over a vast, frozen plain. My feet are murdering me this afternoon, the right forefoot pounding like someone's hitting it with a hammer. The mornings are always okay as I break the feet in initially for the day, but by the time afternoon comes around the pain crescendos. I drag a bit behind, waiting for the merciful end to the day, and also to take a few pictures of David and Richard, two small dots moving over the broad expanse of the tundra. A lone creature darts away to the north – an Arctic fox scouring the tundra for game. I envy its feet, unencumbered by bludgeoning boots, free to pad over land they were designed for. It takes my mind off my feet for a moment, and for this I'm thankful.

We camp on the grassy tundra, 50 metres or so above the river valley we're following. It feels like a different world, camped on the earth for the first time since the trip started, no longer on a frozen lake, river, or sea. I hobble around in my liners, helping with the usual tent set-up and snow gathering before I can take the weight off of my feet for the evening and night. I further modify the boots, cutting out the area at the top of the arch to relieve downward pressure and installing laces to seal the zipper runner I'd accidentally cut in an earlier surgery. The trial and error with the boots is enthralling at least, always pushing me to try new things in order to keep on going. After all, necessity is the mother of invention.

CHAPTER 79

Encrusted in snow
Caribou skull and antlers
Remnant of the past

After we spend a morning on the edge of the river valley, it flattens out into a broad plain, with the river twisting through the landscape. I lead most of the way on the river through the morning as it's easy travel and heading in our direction. Various glimpses of wildlife grab my attention through the day. I spot three ravens passing overhead, another Arctic fox scurries across our track, and the bleached bones of long-dead caribou stick up through the snow from time to time. In the late afternoon Richard insists on bee-lining overland as it seems to have flattened out everywhere and we won't be crossing down into and then out of steep valleys as we were earlier. David is ambivalent, just saying, "Let's just keep moving steadily along."

Richard is frustrated with our distance, as the meandering up the valley is not as efficient. I'm fine with his straight-line plan as it does indeed seem to be a broad flat plain, a plateau from which the rivers all drain gradually.

Richard decides to take the lead and push on for a long day, to make up the distance he feels we should do every day. We want 20 km per day, which we did easily on the flat surface of Committee, but not on the rolling terrain here inland. Once someone gets ahead on a trip like this, you have to at least get to where they are, as everyone's camping in the same tent. Richard doesn't inform us of his plan; he just decides to go on for two straight hours, all the way until 6 p.m. instead of our usual 5 p.m. finish. My feet are in agony. The longer we keep going, the worse they get. I curse Richard as I hobble along. It's like every man for himself on this trip, it seems, or at least Richard and David versus me.

They natter on about John Rae and what they're going to do after the trip in the name of his and their glory, topics that just don't interest me really. I'm in the here and the now, not the "if and when." I'm becoming delusional from pain and frustration, and to keep me focused I calculate the weight in each of our sleds. I am convinced Richard has the least – David and I each carry a heavy shotgun after all. I also reflect on having given Richard my snug, athletic boxer briefs. I'd lent them to him a few days earlier as he was experiencing bad chafing with the loose pair of underwear he was using, his "boys" rubbing the insides of his legs raw. I'd done something similar in 2006, marching with a group of Australian soldiers who were retracing something called the Sandakan Death March in Borneo. One of the officers, a nice quiet man, had been marching "commando" in the muggy conditions just like the rest of the troop, and the insides of his thighs were literally open wounds. I gave him my extra pair of boxer briefs at the time and it worked like a charm.

On this occasion I give my boxer briefs up again to keep the trip going smoothly, and Richard's complaints soon end as the snug lululemon underwear keep the jangling in check. They're my extra set, and he now has them. His chafing is gone, my feet are disintegrating, and he keeps marching on, the thankless bastard. No mention of it since – how about some bloody acknowledgement?! My misery really is making me irrational. It's petty anger on my part, projecting my pain on others. Thankfully, my inner voice doesn't become my outer voice and I march on in silence. No one likes a complainer, and David and Richard can do nothing for my feet, so there's no point in whinging, as the Scots would say. I can hear the spirit of John Rae scolding my shameful disposition.

CHAPTER 80

The snow machine hares
The sled dragging tortoises
Who wins in the end?

The next morning we continue over the broad plateau to a low north–south running valley that cuts through rolling hills, which we follow gradually downward. Another fox scopes us out and scampers away, just 30 metres from us, its button eyes inspecting us through an explosion of white fur, before evaporating into the surrounding hills. It's a foggy, relatively warm day, approaching -10°C – easy travelling temperatures. The cloud base is low, which limits visibility, the nearby hills appearing and disappearing through the mist. We spread out a bit going down the hill, with me in the lead. It looks like the valley will take us to the Avalikuarjuk River on the other side of the divide, which eventually flows into the Kellett River, which drains into Pelly Bay. At the end of a flat section, a couple of objects appear in the distance that aren't natural – not rocks, not animals, but rather something man-made. You can always tell. These are things that haven't been moulded, blended, and assimilated by millions of years of evolution that make everything in nature fit together somehow.

I ski up to the objects and a couple of abandoned snowmobiles materialize. Not ancient models, mind you, but new ones, left sometime in the past couple of weeks. They are already partially drifted in, and also mark our intersection with the Inuit snowmobile tracks that must lead from that last cabin we inspected on Committee Bay. I look at the partially blown-in track and doubt it would have been any better than the route we took. When Richard catches up, he does some hilarious headstand poses on the snowmobiles for the camera, and then we carry on. Someone might come for these machines sometime, but who knows. I've seen all sorts of abandoned machines strewn about the Arctic over the years and these two may just end up being another couple of relics blighting the tundra landscape.

We follow the partially blown-out trail through a saddle in the hills and then descend to a lake, where the trail is no longer visible. The heavy west-southwest wind from a few days ago disguised everything quite nicely and no one has travelled through here since. As we aren't sure which way the trail will go, we bee-line it west to the Avalikuarjuk, slowly breaking trail for two kilometres through suddenly deeper snow. It's hard work, each of us taking turns, eager to get to the river, which we hope will provide decent travel, perhaps even blown clear of snow like the North Pole River – down to bare ice for easy sled dragging. My feet won't appreciate crampons, though, and speaking of the feet, they've felt inexplicably good today, not too much pain at all, even in the afternoon. Can I dare hope that they're stabilizing, or have they simply numbed right out?

We roll over a low embankment and into the river, which curves further west. It's certainly not free of snow, being well covered with intermittent soft and firm sections, with no sign of snowmobile tracks anywhere. We camp on the river, glad to be through the overland section though we only covered 16 km today, just like yesterday – our daily progress slowing. We check the forecast on the inReach and it looks like it's dropping to -30°C overnight, which immediately jolts me back to the reality of another cool night in my sodden, broken sleeping bag. I'll be wearing all my clothes in there again tonight.

My freeze-dried mac and cheese tastes especially good. I chop in a pepperoni stick and add a scoop of butter. The finest meal I've had in a while. I slip into my frozen bag of feathers feeling content and hopeful that perhaps my feet are getting better. However, within a few minutes they begin their nightly pounding as they decompress from the day. I reach down and give them a rub. The toes on both feet have lost feeling, like disembodied stumps at the end of my swollen feet. The skin on my little piggies looks healthy, so at least it's not frostbite. The nerves in them must be gone. I pop a couple of Ibuprofens, read about the intrepid men of the *Kon-Tiki* being circled by sharks, then fall fast asleep.

CHAPTER 81

It should go downhill,
Yet we are always grinding
Magical River

There's definitely a lot more snow on this side of the divide between Committee Bay and Pelly Bay. It snowed an additional few centimetres overnight on top of an existing couple of feet. Our dream of easy travel over ice on this river seems to be just that – a dream. We ski through low fog and powdery snow in the morning. With white on the ground and white all around, it's like moving inside a Ping-Pong ball.

By mid-morning the fog lifts, revealing a lovely valley of high hills and cliffs. We ski through canyons that must rage with whitewater in the spring melt but are muzzled to absolute silence by the thick layer of ice and snow. By mid-afternoon we reach the Kellett River, the main watercourse to Pelly Bay. Strangely, though we are skiing downstream the river seems to climb steadily. It makes absolutely no sense – to the point where I think this river must be a saltwater river flowing inland from the sea. No such river exists on Earth and yet for three straight hours we drag our sleds uphill through deep snow while travelling down a river.

Not far from where we intersect with the Kellett there's a nice cabin in good shape, but the fever to keep moving overwhelms the desire for a place to put up our feet (at least for David). In spite of my feet, David and I have been taking turns breaking trail all day long, with Richard lagging back.

He skis up from behind on one of our breaks, leans on his ski poles, looks up at me, and says, "My sled feels like lead today."

I smirk. He and I had reshuffled our gear as I thought his sled that morning was far lighter than ours. I gave him the shotgun in exchange for the tent body. Perhaps it's mental, or perhaps it's the deep snow, but I'd never seen Richard drag so far behind. As long as I don't have to carry that superfluous gun, he can keep my underwear. It's a childish game I'm playing, blaming my physical issues on the perceived weight discrepancies between teammates. I'm at fault for my troubles, no one else. Everyone works through challenges on a journey – it's why we're out here – but in the moment it's difficult to step back and get some perspective. I'm hoping I don't do any sort of permanent damage to my feet, but I don't want any sort of special treatment. The last thing I want is a pity party, to have them coddle me along. It's best for me to suffer in silence, as everyone is dealing with something unsaid on this journey – it's the way it always is. There's no time or place for a therapy session out here.

CHAPTER 82

Our sleds inch along
No flow, just a grinding tug
Anchors dragged through sand

It was another cold night last night. I was fully wrapped in all my layers of down within my sleeping bag, and the forecast is for a continued drop into the mid -30s tonight. Yesterday, my feet seemed okay but today they are the worst of all. Skiing through deep snow in the first couple of hours along the Kellett River this morning I couldn't feel my feet at all, like I was skiing on two stumps. I think it's just that the nerves are dead, but with the cold and my cut-up boots it could also be that my feet are just too damn cold.

Today I'm the one trailing off the back, with Richard having caught a nice stride again. It's now my sled that feels like lead. I give a detailed search of my sleds at our first break to make sure Richard hasn't slipped a rock or two in there, as he's tried before. Cheeky bastard. There are no rocks, though, just a mental menhir caused by my feet.

For the first time since we met the lone man on a snowmobile back in Committee Bay we encounter people – lots of people. Not long after we ski off from camp, we see frozen-over holes in the river, with nets set down into them. These were probably only set up a day or two earlier.

We carry on "down" the Kellett River, though it continuously trends uphill. The Arctic can be a trickster at times. Sometimes right is wrong, left is right – and rivers flow uphill. I conclude that prevailing winds coming off Pelly Bay must continuously stack wind-drifted snow on the river to create this phenomenon.

A convoy of snowmobiles appears on the horizon of the Kellett River an hour later. We hear the whine of the machines before we see them gliding toward us like a pack of wolves. The group of eight Inuit, a mix of men and women, are from the hamlet of Kugaaruk. They stop to chat with we three odd fellows on skis, all of them dismounting to gather around us.

One of the men, Mark – a young, squat man in his 20s with a rifle slung across his chest – has just built himself a cabin: a 12' by 12' plywood structure he's towing on a *qamatiq* behind his machine.

"I just built this…pulling it down to that spot on the river – real good fishing there."

That spot, I discover, is the one we just passed, with the nets set in the frozen-over fishing holes. They're going there to retrieve netted char, as well as install the new cabin.

I ask Mark, "Why does this river always go continuously uphill even though we're going downstream?"

He doesn't challenge my premise. He simply says, "I dunno."

It's like he agrees with me but accepts the physical impossibility of it. From my interactions with Inuit all over Nunavut, they have a consistent acceptance and adaptability to whatever the land throws at them. It's a kind of "It is what it is" attitude that allows them to roll with whatever punches Mother Nature throws at them. Or perhaps it just doesn't matter because they're on gas-powered snowmobiles that render flat any terrain they encounter.

An older man named Sheldon, his face dark and creased from a life outside, sidles up to me with a puzzled look on his face.

"Why are you guys skiing on this river? Why not take a snowmobile? It'd be much easier."

I explain the story of John Rae, but to no avail. Following in the footsteps of long-dead *kabloonat* doesn't seem to be a valid reason to be doing what we're doing. He shakes his head, with a look somewhere between disgust and resignation.

"You should be down south where you came from, where it's warmer. No sense being out in the cold if you aren't hunting or fishing."

I imagine the Inuit of Rae's time saw explorers then in much the same light as Sheldon sees us now. Rae was out surveying the land for the Hudson's Bay Company, not out there simply to live and survive because there was no other choice – though I imagine they had more respect for him as he was definitely hunting for his keep. In Sheldon's eyes, we probably fall more into the category of Franklin and his crew – people who don't need to be where they are, putting themselves into difficulty when it isn't necessary.

The wise old Inuk is definitely the surliest of the group, and the others happily give us info on what lies ahead on the trail. Sheldon finally warms to us when I ask him if he'll stop on his way back to show us his char catch. He happily agrees, and the group soon departs to install Mark's cabin and to check on their nets.

On his return a couple of hours later, Sheldon proudly pulls back the caribou blanket on his *qamatiq* to reveal a stack of a dozen large char, their silver gleam muted by a skim of frost on their frozen bodies. Sheldon looks at me with a smile, as if to say, "This is why we're out here, what's your excuse?"

It puts things in perspective for me for sure, and I feel a bit ridiculous, hobbling and dragging two sleds behind me like Christ hauling his cross on the road to Calvary. The futile, arbitrary nature of what we're doing compared to these people still literally living off the land rolls over me like a tidal wave. We're following the route of merely another white traveller from another time. The Inuit John Rae encountered were probably quite confused as to what his ambitions were, particularly as they had no concept whatsoever of Rae's exploration dreams. Sheldon and his crew from Kugaaruk at least live in heated houses and have a Northern Store and Co-op store to access all the modern conveniences now available in any city anywhere in the world. The Inuit of Rae's time would have had an intimate and masterful connection with the land, so Rae and his crew must have seemed like aliens from another planet.

On the plain face of it, Sheldon is right. What *are* we doing here? It's an existential question for anyone, but particularly, obviously, one I should be asking myself right now. I'm like an ox at the cart, a beast of burden. And yet I carry on because there's nothing else to do at this point. No matter how ridiculous, there's nothing else for me to do but move forward in my misery. Or is there?

An hour further down the trail, we run into a couple more men, Germaine and Fred. They tell us that about a mile onward on there's a good cabin we can stay in up on the right riverbank. This buoys our spirits and we plod onward, happy not to have to set up a tent that evening. If it's only a mile, we should roll in around 5 p.m. and can settle in for the evening. However, the snow this afternoon seems deeper and slower than ever. Sheldon's crew told us it snowed a foot a few days earlier, turning a firm, fast snowpack into a deep quagmire. I should also have known better, that when the Inuit say "a mile," it could be anywhere up to ten km as they're estimating by snowmobile and the few minutes it takes to cover ten km probably does indeed seem like "a mile." Tricksters.

It's complete drudgery as we carry on for a couple more hours. Richard and David get ahead of me so I can't communicate that perhaps we should just camp, that this cabin could be a long way away. But they probably feel fine, and don't know the extent of my pain, which is my fault because I won't tell them.

When the cabin finally comes into view, it's almost 6:30 and my feet are murdering me like never before. I'm not sure how they got to this stage, not sure how it started, as it has never happened before. Like the river flowing upstream, all I can say to anyone who asks what happened to my feet is, "I dunno." Like Mark, I simply have to accept the inexplicable. It is what it is.

David and Richard are like horses to the barn, completely committed to the cabin accommodation once they heard about it, and have gotten a few hundred metres ahead. They approach the cabin, high up on a snowy knoll looking down on the river. At this moment, it may as well have been perched at the summit of Everest.

Looking at the deep snow and realizing I have to drag these two anchors behind me up there, I pause. Every one of my heartbeats shoots a fiery pain through the inner part of my feet, while at the same time I can't feel my toes. It's a bit of a trick, convincing myself it's just that the nerves are dead and not being panicked into thinking the -30°C temps have frozen my toes solid. I take a deep breath, preparing for a final bludgeoning approach to the cabin. Up there is rest, unwinding, food. Down here is cold, pain, and misery. I have to pass through this one last gauntlet to earn my respite.

I see that the other two are trying to take what looks like the most gradual route up the hill. They stall out and turn around to detach one of their sleds, deciding to do two trips to get to the cabin. I cut straight for it, switchbacking my way up the hill with both sleds, inch by inch, using the last of my energy and focus to get to the top. David and Richard are still getting their sleds up the hill, while I unclip from mine and enter the cabin. It's neat and clean, with a functional two-burner Coleman stove on a coffee table in the middle, and a couple of Coleman Lanterns too. There are three bed platforms for us to sleep on. The cabin, though, is an icebox. It has an oil heater in the corner but it's out of fuel. Without the heater, this place is only four cold walls, but at least it's out of the wind and we can spread out. We settle in for the evening, wearing all of our insulated gear, our breath expressed in thick frosty billows of steam. One thing about the tent is, it may be cramped, but it does actually get warm with two stoves running and three bodies in its confined space. This airy box holds no heat.

I desperately set to work on my boots once again, punching yet another hole in them and also fashioning toe warmers out of my spare socks that cover the outside of my boots and that I hope will somehow help with getting feeling back in my toes. All I can do is keep trying to crack the painful puzzle of the feet.

It seems like the coldest night yet, and for the first time I can't get the ink in my pen to warm up enough with my body heat to write, so I resort to a pencil, scrawling my notes like a kindergarten child in the seventies. It seems like it's getting colder rather than warmer. David snores like a chainsaw in the corner bed and I curse his planning for starting the journey so early. He seems to be managing okay, though we've already diverged from his original plan to go all the way to Gjoa Haven, now looking to arrange a pick-up by snowmobile at Pointe de la Guiche, where Rae turned around. It still achieves the goal of retracing Rae's route but will save us the extra 80 km, and four days' travel to cross over the Northwest Passage to Gjoa Haven on King William Island. I send an email to Marvin Atqittuq to see if he and Jacob can come get us when the time comes. We shall see.

My sleeping platform is in the corner, and I place my custom earplugs in to eradicate David's echoing snore. My head is inside the hood of my frozen bag of feathers and my down jackets and pants are wrapped around me inside. The wall, just inches from my face, is frosted white. My feet pound. I pop a couple of Ibuprofen and fall into a fitful sleep.

CHAPTER 83

The next morning I walk on the sides of my feet, unable to put pressure on the balls. Things seem to be getting worse, not better. We slowly melt snow for the day and get ourselves going. Everything I do is deliberate. With Kugaaruk so close by, I sincerely contemplate stepping off the trip for the first time. There are many Inuit from town travelling around and I could easily catch a ride. I've stuffed my feet into my boots and begin the daily process of numbing them out – basically walking off the pounding in my feet until I feel nothing at all.

We're out of the cabin and loading our sleds when four snowmobiles come into view down on the river. One of them turns from the group and comes up the hill to us while the others wait at the bottom. He zooms up to the cabin door and cheerfully says, "Hi there."

I reply, "Hi!" and we exchange pleasantries.

His name is Lionel Tigvareark, and he's showing a group of friends from Naujaat which fork among the many tracks to take to get back home. His outfit immediately catches my eye: there's a rifle slung over his chest and he wears a white parka and pants, spattered with the blood of animals he's butchered.

"My mom made me this parka and pants. Custom!" He grins.

"There's a lot of blood on your clothes," I remark.

"Yup, that's what I do. I hunt. Polar bear, seal, caribou, musk ox. I hunt for myself, my family, for the community."

He wears sunglasses the entire time, completing his air of cool. I like him immediately, and strangely feel more of a kinship with him at that moment than I do with David or Richard. I contemplate asking him, in the spur of the moment, if he'll take me to town when he gets back from leading his friends. It would be easy, he's here, my feet are shot, and there's nothing worse I can think of but being a liability. But I don't. Something keeps me from asking – I just can't bring myself to do it. I want to keep going and see, just to see. One more day will only get us closer to the town. I'll give myself another day.

I take a picture of Lionel in his well-worn outfit and show it to him. He likes it and smiles to himself. It is a pretty damn cool shot.

"Could you send that to me on Facebook?" That's one thing I've realized over the past couple of years travelling in the Arctic – *all* the Inuit are on Facebook. Even Lionel, an adept hunter and traveller who spends his days out on the land, is on Facebook. Not Instagram, Twitter, Snapchat, or other social media entities. It's all about Facebook. They love it. Every actual social network seems to be anchored to a virtual social network these days. So I get his full name and write it down, saying I'll find him and message him the images, which I will. In the back of my mind, though, I feel I might see him again in the flesh.

The day is sunny and calm, shaking off the shackles of a cold, clear night. After a couple of hours, we come to a distinct fork in the snowmobile trail. The main traffic seems to be going south, while Kugaaruk is north. The town is a good 25 km away still and pretty much all traffic should be headed up there. I assumed all roads would lead to town. But we're not going to town; we're going across Pelly Bay on Rae's route. There was no Kugaaruk in 1854, only nomadic Inuit. We stop to discuss our options. There's a big bend in the river, and it looks like the trail going south may just cut the corner. When you're dragging 200 pounds behind you and there's a foot of snow all around you, it's exceedingly tempting to stick to the beaten path. You don't have to navigate or think too much. Richard is insistent on the shortcut over the bank. I'd prefer sticking to the river. David is ambivalent. It is the path that seems most beaten so we figure it will get back on the river and out to Pelly Bay before veering north to town. It seemed like that was where the Inuit we'd chatted to said the trail went. We decide to take the route south, and painstakingly take one sled at a time up the steep embankment. On top of the embankment is a large flat plain, and the trail seems to go straight across it rather than following the river. We figure it'll turn onto the river eventually and trudge on down the trail.

My "toe warmer" socks are a failure, but I quickly adapt a new system, putting Ziploc bags over my boots to keep them warmer, and it seems to work as I don't think my feet are as cold. Could be the sun, could be the placebo effect of the Ziplocs. I feel good everywhere but my feet and power off down the plain. A great *Desert Island Discs* episode with John McEnroe pops on. He is brash, funny, and insightful – colouring the bright white world around me with a dose of unique humanity. The interview detaches me from the land and experience around me, distracting me from the obvious.

A lone Inuk on a snow machine comes toward us on the trail in the late afternoon. We are all skiing fairly close together and gather around him when he stops.

"Where you guys going?" he asks.

"Out to Pelly Bay, then over to Gjoa Haven."

"You're going the wrong way."

"Where does this trail go…it must go to town, no?"

"Nope, just a hunting trail. People come down this way from town to hunt musk ox and caribou."

Looking at the map, and finally double-checking the GPS, we see we've been moving due south instead of due east. I figure we've gone several hours in the wrong direction now. All the obvious signs of nature – the sun, the river – and our own GPS and compass (which we never checked) were overcome by the mindless, easy rhythm of the track. We are idiots.

"You can cut through that valley over there." He points a mittened hand due east to a gap in the hills.

"And continue through to Pelly, then cut across the Bay. I don't think there's a sled trail; you'll be breaking your own. All the other sled trails go to Kugaaruk, then across Pelly from there."

It's somewhat deflating to realize we've lost half a day, but what can you do? It's not like any one of us bothered to check our co-ordinates very closely, to see what was right in front of us. The lone snowmobiler continues north to Kugaaruk and the three of us are left on the track. With the sun slowly dropping across the sky to the west, we break a trail through fresh snow toward the gap in the high hills. We want to trudge along at least to the edge of Pelly Bay, to gaze upon this next phase of the journey.

The light is lovely, filtered through high wispy clouds, casting a pink glow over the porcelain landscape. It's slow going through the snow. We've followed snowmobile tracks the last couple of days, which were soft and punchy and didn't improve our pace much. At least in fresh snow you feel like you're doing something unique, carving a new line in the ephemeral snow.

At around 6:30 we settle into a site in the broad end of a small valley that looks out over the southern end of Pelly Bay. I take off my boots and lurch around in the liners, unable to put pressure on the balls of my feet. I feel like an invalid, always a beat behind when we set up tent this evening, extra slow when gathering snow. I go to take a shit and it's easier for me to crawl across the snow than walk on it. The feet just aren't working and are getting markedly worse by the day. Richard and David don't seem to notice my plight, and I don't showcase it to them either. Everyone gets so focused on the myriad tasks associated with setting up camp that details about the state of others on the team are rarely noticed. I know, though, that unless there's some sort of miraculous overnight improvement in my feet, I'll most likely be pulling the plug on the whole thing tomorrow. We've covered 350 km to this point and still have 200 km to go if we were to stop at Rae Strait – 280 km if we go to Gjoa Haven. I'm crawling around camp – a liability to the team and my health. I have no other choice.

In the vestibule, I kick back, drinking tea and eating Mountain House Rice and Chicken. As with every night the past couple of weeks, I still hold faint hope that the feet will magically heal by the next day, though they're now so swollen they barely fit inside my once-comfy Baffin boots, feeling instead like they're painfully bound in a tourniquet. So instead, I just lounge in the liners. David and Richard talk of the next leg, and of what they will do post-trip to promote the journey. They're buoyant and Richard calls in another funny post from the field to the website no one is following. I offer nothing to their dreaming or the post, already feeling a separation from the trip and from my teammates.

My feet pound as I go to bed this evening, having uncoiled from the day's walk. I pop a couple of Ibuprofen and fall asleep, accepting whatever the next day will bring.

CHAPTER 84

I awake the next morning, my feet still pounding. I unzip my bag and take a good, hard look at my swollen feet. The ball of my right foot is very tender to the touch and swollen purple, my left is a little better but similar. I can't feel the toes of either foot. David and Richard get the water going and throw on their down jackets as per usual. I stay in my bag, looking at my feet. David glances over, raises his eyebrows when he sees my feet, and says, "Oh, those look pretty bad! You've been suffering in silence."

"Well, I've been cutting my boots apart for the past couple weeks trying to manage this, but it keeps getting worse."

David says nothing, seemingly knowing what I'm about to say next.

"I think I'm going to pull out here."

He responds, "Why don't you give it another day? It won't be that much farther from Kugaaruk 20 km from now."

"I've given it another day for a good week now. We're not far from Kugaaruk, it's an easy step off. I don't have another couple weeks in these puppies, so that's it for me. The farther I get, the more of a hassle it will be for the team. I don't want to be a liability to you guys, and don't want to do permanent damage to my feet."

Richard suggests I call a doctor on the satellite phone, and perhaps they could advise me. I laugh. "Unless a doctor can magically reach out and heal my feet, I don't see the point. It would be a waste of time. They would tell me to rest."

They see my point and accept my decision. Once it's been made, it's been made. I use the satellite phone to call the hamlet office. I explain where we are and make a request for Lionel to come get me. I know him and he seems to know the area up here like no other.

"Are you hurt? Do you need to go to the medical clinic?" the person asks.

"No, I'm not hurt like that. I just need time to heal. A doctor or nurse can do nothing for me. This isn't an emergency; I just need a ride to town."

"OK, sounds good. I'll send Lionel," he replies.

When Garry left the team, I half-joked that he was dead to us, as he no longer had any relevance on the journey. Now I say to David and Richard, "Well, boys, looks like I'm the one who's dead to you now." Richard smirks at my remark.

The next hour is spent reorganizing the gear. They keep both shotguns, but dump a bunch of the useless charging equipment, extra fuel they won't need, the bear fence, and other items no longer deemed necessary, onto me. My two sleds are now heavier than ever, but hopefully I won't be dragging them for too long before Lionel comes.

Our plan is to ski together for a couple of kilometres out to Pelly Bay. I'll continue up the coast to Kugaaruk while they'll cut diagonally northwest across the bay and then continue inland toward Rae Strait. I stuff my feet in my boots for what I hope will be the last time and we all set out for the wide-open plain of Pelly Bay, visible between two islands at the end of the valley we camp in. The day is bright, sunny, and calm – a mere -20°C or so.

We ski out past the islands and then pause to congregate on the ice. I snap a couple of close-up portraits of each of them. The only camera they have between the two of them is a small Nikon Coolpix unit that seems to add a tinge of orange to every shot, so I figure I might as well squeeze off a couple more. Richard didn't have a camera to start so David dug this one up from what must have been the corner of a junk drawer and lent it to him. David himself bought a new camera but the screen in it fried in the cold snap early in the trip, so he was quickly rendered camera-less. Garry's 40 pounds of camera equipment were whisked back with him when he pulled the chute on day two. Considering they rarely thought to ever pull out a camera anyways, I wasn't about to loan them my own and send it to an early death, but at least I could get them a couple of portraits for posterity before I jumped ship. From the heady days of having this trip turned into a feature documentary covered by flying drones and long-lens cameras it's now been reduced to a single, shitty Nikon Coolpix – the documentation had essentially come to a crashing halt. All that's left is for them to get to Pointe de la Guiche, to complete Rae's line. An act of hubris perhaps, but necessary when you've trumpeted to the world in advance about what you're doing – though looking at the number of people following the journey, that world barely extends beyond friends and family.

I give each of them a quick hug, say "good luck boys," and that's pretty much it. They begin breaking trail across Pelly Bay, and I ski due north toward Kugaaruk. After a few minutes, I glance to the west and see the silhouettes of Richard and David, one behind the other, heads down, bent to their task. I take one last shot. It's probably the last time I'll ever see those guys, and it somehow doesn't bother me in the least. They are decent, respectable fellows, but we never really clicked on this journey – never truly connected. They probably think the same of me, and perhaps less of me now that I've dropped out.

I turn north, slowly pulling my load through deep snow and humps of ice. I don't have a gun or any other bear deterrent and would be exceedingly easy prey for a roaming bear right now. I also don't have any form of communication with me – no satellite phone, no inReach. Like Rae, if something were to go sideways with me, I would quickly be absorbed into the wilderness. My epitaph would read, "He was a somewhat notable person who wrote some things and made a few strange and mediocre films about esoteric outdoor subjects." This at least might inspire curiosity, though I wonder why anyone would care what people think of them once they're dead. They're dead after all, and with them goes all consciousness and realization. Epitaphs aren't for the dead, they're for those left behind.

My mother fretted to me a couple of years ago that she didn't want my father and brother to be forgotten. Not that they care – they're long gone – it's just that forgetting about someone so integral to much of your life somehow diminishes it. What was the point of it all if they aren't fondly and strongly remembered? Unavoidably, time pushes the dead away from the living – deeper into the realm of ghosts, of figments of the imagination.

My feet snap me back from my existential musings. It's been almost two hours since I parted ways with David and Richard. There are no signs of any sort of snowmobile trail out here on the ice as I continue to break a track through a foot of light snow, over ice heaves and hummocks. I didn't expect to be putting in this much hard labour today after speaking with the fellow at the hamlet office this morning. I did tell him it was not an emergency though, so fair enough.

Yesterday we'd gone about seven kilometres south past the mouth of the Kellett River and it now comes into view, cutting out through the hills. I begin to contemplate a contingency plan. What if Lionel doesn't come out today? What if he doesn't find me? I could probably find a cabin someplace around the mouth of the Kellett as it seems a logical place to have one, but without a stove I wouldn't be able to melt snow for water. I had a couple of litres with me and would have to keep them from freezing. I had enough junk food and snacks to keep me going anyhow. No tent either, so a cabin would be nicer than sleeping out in the open. Another option would be to ditch the sleds and just move light and fast to town for the last 25 km and come back for them with someone and their snowmobile. Fuck, it would have been easier to have hopped on with Lionel yesterday morning, that's for sure. But I wanted to give myself one last chance, to take any doubt out of the decision to leave. Ultimately, I have nothing to prove and don't really care what anyone else thinks. I had to make it right with me, in my mind. Still, as I drag these anchors toward a sandy bank that extends out from the Kellett, this perspective doesn't help me much in the moment. I'm off the trip so just want it to be over with.

I manage to pull the sleds up the ten-foot embankment. There's virtually no snow up top, the surface a scoured mix of hard drifts, gravel, and sand. I can see where the bank curves all the way to the hills where the Kellett's mouth is. I figure I'll cut toward the mouth and decide there whether to ferret out a cabin or ditch the sleds and make for town.

CHAPTER 85

As I ski along the top of the bank, I pick up a light buzzing sound. I look behind me and see the black outline of two snowmobilers, flying over the sea ice like a pair of flies over a bowl of molten vanilla ice cream. I'm relieved – no more need to consider hunkering in a cabin or making a slow grind toward town. The pair comes in fast, gliding up and over the bank, *qamatiqs* in tow. I give them a wave and they drive across the scoured surface until they come to a stop beside me.

One of the men is indeed Lionel, in his signature white, blood-spattered outfit. Alongside him is a grinning man dressed all in black.

Lionel steps off the sled. "Hey Frank."

"Hey Lionel, thanks for coming to get me, appreciate it."

"Yeah, we came out to get you but saw the other two guys first. They said you'd be following the shore."

The other man's name is Clayton, Lionel's friend.

"You need anything? Want coffee?

"I won't say no to coffee."

Clayton pours out three cups of black coffee into some tin mugs and we quietly sip the hot beverage. We stand looking out over the white expanse. Thinking of those two poor bastards out there on the sea ice-breaking trail, I feel strangely good. I'm not a solo traveller, but it's always a relief when you can strike out freely, away from the regimen that gets built into a team, where you're either waiting or trying to keep up. The push and pull of that can be more tiresome than the expedition itself, particularly when you're grouped together with a pair like Richard and David, where your rapport with them isn't fully in sync.

They are decent fellows for sure, but in a group of three, they had a lot more in common to talk about with each other, and I was the third wheel. I like to expound on a wide variety of subjects but they were hyper-focused on chatting about what they were going to do with the journey after it had been completed. I would never step away from a trip over inconsequential personal differences, but now that my feet have taken me away from it, I am quite content.

"I'm just gonna smoke a bit. I like to smoke. How about you?" Lionel asks.

Lionel pulls out a pipe and a bag of weed and packs a hearty amount of green bud into the bowl. Clayton watches him, then looks at me.

"I'll tap into that for sure," I reply.

Both of them smile.

Lionel lights it up and passes it to me. He coughs loudly after inhaling.

"Easy there, Lionel," I say.

I take it deep into my lungs and am washed over with a relaxing wave of THC. The snow seems suddenly brighter, the sun warmer. It's still around -25°C, and my fingertips are numb, but my soul is toasty. It's like I just woke from a dream, and David and Richard, still out there dragging through the snow, never really existed. Did I just spend 18 days with them? Did it really happen? Right now I'm not so sure.

Clayton takes a haul, and his big smile broadens even more. "Where you from?" he asks me.

"Vancouver."

"Oh, I hear you have good bud down there. My cousin went to Vancouver once."

"Yeah, it's pretty good bud down there for sure."

I talk like I'm a chronic smoker, but I usually only partake if it's coming around in a social or party situation. Kind of like right now, with Lionel and Clayton.

All three of us stand there, having a moment on top of that windswept plain, staring out at the endless horizon, the sun due south, making the noontime turn to the west. None of us says anything – no one's in any rush. Once the journey ends, the movement stops and there's no reason to be anywhere in particular.

The mission can go as planned, or it can come to a slow-moving crash that, in this case, halts right here. Either way, it ends and you have peace. No more rushing in the morning to get the snow melting, no grinding, working, moving forward – always forward – dragging those goddamned sleds through a frozen landscape, managing body and mind, looking for ways to keep on going, to hold the mission together. Once you've run into every conceivable wall – both physical and mental – and realize you're in a box, it's time to pop off the lid and crawl out. Once you're out, there's a window of contentment, a feeling of deep satisfaction with having done…something. Something different, interesting, and challenging that will stay with you for the rest of your life. Ultimately, it's about that peace. The journey, no matter the outcome, is simply a construct, a fabrication, to trick you into that peace. Right now, standing here with Lionel and Clayton, I have that peace. It will stay with me for a few days but will gradually wane. This is the apex of it all, the reason for doing it. Once it wears off, I'll start to get the itch again, a plan will formulate, and I'll be on a journey again. Maybe somewhere warmer next time, somewhere with temperate water you can paddle across instead of frozen ice to ski on. Perhaps one or two saunas along the way to really get a sweat on – to get you so hot you want to be back here stoned out of your mind on frigid, frozen Pelly Bay with my new best friends Lionel and Clayton.

Lionel turns to me. "You need to get to town quick? Need to go to the clinic?"

"Naw, I'm good man. I'm good."

He smiles a crooked smile, revealing a few stained teeth.

"Good."

He then packs another bowl, takes a deep haul, coughs his lungs out again, and passes it to me. The ritual repeats itself a couple more times until we all decide it's time to finally go. We pull my sleds onto Clayton's *qamatiq* and I hop into the seat behind Lionel. The machine lurches to a start and we zip along over the snow to the gap where the Kellett River meets the ocean, the scenery whipping by faster than I've seen in weeks. We amble through the mouth of the Kellett, go up it for a few hundred metres, then hang a left and head overland toward Kugaaruk. There is indeed no trail on the sea ice – it only goes inland. Ah, Richard and David, those poor fuckers, I don't envy them at all. They'll be breaking trail all the way across Pelly Bay.

Lionel acts as a bit of a tour guide as we ride along. He points to a high peak atop some cliffs and says, "That's where the ravens live." Then we go by a low valley. "I got a caribou in there last week."

We cut back out to the ocean and follow the shoreline for a few hundred metres. Kugaaruk comes into view, a cluster of low, blocky buildings, built purely for their utility, typical of pretty much any town in Nunavut. We enter the middle, cruise up one street, then another until we arrive in front of the Inns North. We unload the sleds and I immediately begin the process of purging excess equipment.

"You guys want these sleds?" I have four sleds with me. David in his overplanning had us each dragging sleds-within-sleds in case one wore through, and then we'd simply swap them out.

"Sure," Clayton grins. I pull the giant custom duffle bags off the sleds and Clayton pops the empty, orange Expedition sleds back onto his *qamatiq*.

"You want some white gas?"

"Sure," Lionel muses. I dig around in my bag and pull out two four-litre cans of white gas, hand them to him, and he tucks them in back of his sled.

We all stand there for a beat, saying nothing, comfortable in the long silent pauses that make up the majority of conversations with Inuit folks.

"You wanna come over to my place later? Gonna smoke a couple bowls and watch the hockey game."

I pause, thinking of all the shit I've gotta do to get out of here. Rebook flights, purge, and repack so I can actually get to the flight, eat, rest, etc.

"Maybe, but I've got a bunch of stuff to organize, and I need some rest. But maybe."

"Okay, I'm in the green house at the end of the street. Got a blue truck in front of it. Come by around 7."

"Okay, I'll try to make it – thanks Lionel. And thanks for coming to get me, I really appreciate it."

I shake their hands. Lionel nods. Clayton grins. Then they hop on their sleds and zoom off.

I manage to drag the two supersized duffels up the metal stairs and through the steel door, one by one. My feet are absolutely killing me by now and I hobble over to the young girl in the office.

"You have a room available?"

She looks at me – in my down, my windburned face, fronting a couple of giant duffle bags, as if people like me come in here everyday. Completely unfazed, on the very precipice of boredom, she says, "Yup."

"How much?" As if I'm in any position to bargain, as if there's another hotel in town.

"Two hundred and seventy-five."

"Sounds good, I'll take it."

"Okay."

"And can I use your phone? I have to book some flights."

"Sure…you want dinner? We serve it up at 6."

"Sure, why not."

The clock is ticking as far as changing my flight plans from Gjoa Haven to Kugaaruk, but I get through to Canadian North and they get me on a flight the next day. Theoretically, David has raised contingency money to cover all this…he'll be changing flight dates and staying in a hotel on his end too. But he is Scottish and would have a hard time swallowing a second night or more for me at $275 a pop. I'd have a hard time too; I just want to get things sorted and move on out of here ASAP. The new routing brings me through Yellowknife before continuing to Edmonton the next day. After that, I switch up my connecting Air Canada flight from Edmonton to Vancouver. So one night here, one night in Yellowknife and one in Edmonton before I get back to Vancouver to heal up.

A call to a cheap $69 hotel in Edmonton secures my night there. After an hour of sorting out these logistics – still sitting in the office of the hotel in my grimy clothes – it's time to mentally dislodge from this journey, to deconstruct the person I've built over the past three weeks.

I drag my bags one by one down the hallway to the room, enter, and then ease myself onto the edge of the bed and pull off my tortuous boots. Freed of their oppressors for the final time, my feet throb in joyful unison. For posterity's sake I take pictures of the purple, swollen appendages, then strip off all my clothes and walk on the outsides of my feet into the bathroom. Looking at my naked self in the mirror I see I've lost at least 15 pounds or so, my body lean and taut without a stitch of fat. It's pretty typical of the finish of any trip – you get your body to the hunted look it was meant to have, exfoliated of the layer of physical softness that civilized life bestows on pretty much everyone privileged enough to live in the First World. I take a picture of myself. It's what I do the first time I hit a mirror post-trip. I take that image of a skinny me, marked by the journey. A reminder to the soft me sometime before the next expedition that there will be trials along the way.

The hot shower feels good, and I linger there for a minute, which is a long shower for me. I eventually get down to business and clear out the residual dingleberries in my asshole, getting it clean as a whistle. Shards of snow do a decent job of wiping, but don't quite get everything, it seems. There's an accumulation that needs a good flushing out.

Afterwards, as I can't put even a bit of pressure on the balls of my feet, I walk around the room on my heels and dig up my cleanest dirty clothes so as to be somewhat presentable and minimally pungent at dinner. I walk gingerly down the hall in my socked feet, using the walls as support. I take a seat in the sparse, cafeteria-like décor of the hotel restaurant. Only two other people seem to be staying in rooms here. They're a couple of guys in their early thirties, doing a renovation on a section of the building. Like all contractors in these parts, they're from the South. Hailing from small towns in Quebec and Ontario, they get paid a whack of dough to work up here and are put up in the hotel with all food and expenses paid.

Tonight's simple dinner of lasagna, garlic bread, and salad costs me $52. It must cost $500 per day just to have these contractors here, on top of flying them up, then further compounded with their hefty salaries. We exchange pleasantries but don't get into much of a conversation. They go back to passing their phones back and forth to each other, sharing videos, pictures from home, etc. This seems to be the common form of communication nowadays, replacing the art of conversation. A picture is worth a thousand words, I guess.

After dinner, I hobble back to my room. I can't believe I was walking on these feet for the past week or so as they deteriorated. The body and mind have a way of dealing with extreme discomfort when the situation demands it. Now, my body seems to have relaxed and the feet have completely shut down on me. I stay up late and there doesn't seem to be anyone around but me. The kitchen area is open and I dispose of the three weeks' worth of trash bestowed upon me by Richard and David, along with my miserable, cut-apart ski boots, and anything else I no longer need. I'm trying to get my gear down to whatever fits in the ski bag and two smaller duffels, which I achieve by midnight. I also book an Airbnb in Yellowknife as I'll be coming in late and leaving the next afternoon. I don't bother Eric and Kate for a space in their garage... besides, I'm pretty sure they're on a year-long sailing trip with their new child now. At this point I don't feel much like rehashing the whole journey to anyone anyways.

CHAPTER 86

The next day, the woman at the office has her boyfriend drive me to the airport, where I go about checking my stuff. I'm pretty sure they've never had a skier come through before, as at one point I have about ten of the counter and luggage people surrounding my skis and discussing whether they'll fit on the plane. I try to resolve it with the guy who seems to be in charge of baggage.

"I've flown all over the place with skis, it's never been a problem."

"Don't think so, I've never seen anything this long go on the plane."

"Could you check with HQ? I'm sure there's an allowance for skis."

"I dunno. I think it's way too long." The other assembled workers nod their heads in agreement.

Eventually, he calls the head office and is told that skis are acceptable.

"They say it's okay, but I think it'll be tough to fit in the baggage area. This is a really long bag."

Eventually, the bag makes it on just fine.

"Thanks for getting that on," I tell him.

He smiles proudly. "It was tough, but we did it."

I'm sure the stories from "the day the ski bag got on the plane" will be told for years to come in Kugaaruk.

I stand by the exit, about to get off the plane in Edmonton. I feel weak and exposed as I stare down the jetway, like I'm teetering on the edge of a cliff. The impatient inertia of the passengers behind me forces me forward so I hug the wall of the gangway and hobble forth, with pride alone preventing me from requesting a push in one of the wheelchairs lined up by the door.

An 80-year-old grandmother with a walker pushes by me. Close on her heels is a man who must be 400 pounds, seeming to race by as if he's Usain Bolt. Soon thereafter, a 2-year-old meanders past like I'm standing still. All three of them merge with the stream of disembarking passengers, leaving me behind like flotsam on the shore.

I lurch along pigeon-toed, trying to stay off the blood blisters that cover the balls of my feet. I traded in my size nine Baffin boots at the

Salvation Army Thrift Store on the previous stopover in Yellowknife for a pair of size 13 sneakers to accommodate my swollen feet. Strong and fit three weeks ago, I'm now an impediment, a pylon, a speed bump blocking the way of anyone breathing and walking on two legs. I might have a chance in a race against a crawling infant. Maybe.

I'm almost home though. One more hotel stay, and then a flight to Vancouver tomorrow. Back to Shannon to lick my wounds, rest, and recover.

EPILOGUE

I sit glowing and glistening from repeated blasts of *löyly* conjured up by a gregarious old fellow named Terri in the Tykkimäen public sauna. With my ears and nostrils stinging from the steam, I brace for the next wave as Terri doles ladle upon ladle of water on the rocks, coolly stating that this is "the best sauna in all of Finland."

My friend Todd and I pulled our canoe up on the shores of Kyrlämpi Lake just an hour earlier, in the midst of an 800-km trip through Finland. Our journey began in the village of Nurmes and will conclude in the capital of Helsinki.

It took my feet a couple of months to heal and regain feeling after the John Rae trip, after which I decided on a more refined mission this summer where I would explore the sauna culture of Finland in the context of an extended canoe trip. Ample time immersed in the luxuriant heat of saunas was sure to expunge the deep cold of that Arctic excursion, to balance that darkness with something light.

Twelve days after I dropped out, Richard and David successfully reached Rae's terminus at Pointe de la Guiche. The expedition was a success and I was happy for those guys. Despite the circumstances, that journey didn't linger with me, quickly fading into the recesses of my subconscious. Once I stopped moving at Kugaaruk, my focus shifted to summer in Saunaland.

Like moths to the light, Todd and I were drawn in from a grey, cool day of paddling by a towering, 50-foot sauna sign we spotted from across the water. Arto, a man I've been chatting with about Finnish players in the NHL, follows up on Terri's remark by turning to me on our shared pine bench and stating, “For us Finns, the sauna is our church.”

I can relate. Like canoeing or skiing in the wilderness, the sauna ritual is similarly meditative and cleansing. A sauna session is like a microcosm of an expedition, wherein you endure the rigours of the experience to emerge renewed.

As Terri lashes another splash on the stove, the bitter chill of Arctic spring doesn’t seem real to me anymore, and Rae’s route is now a long-gone vapour trail. The same goes for the Baffin ski traverse, and the canoe trip across Nunavut with Ryan. These journeys were sharp and clear as broken glass when they were happening, but like the steam that rises ghost-like from the rocks in front of me, they’ve dissipated into nothingness. Nothing exists but the present – and right now I’m here in this sauna, in the midst of a canoe trip through Finland. There’s nowhere else to be.

ABOUT THE AUTHOR

Frank Wolf has been called One of Canada's 90 Greatest Explorers of all Time by the Royal Canadian Geographical Society and has crafted a life out of adventure, undertaking thousands of kilometres of self-propelled wilderness travel in pursuit of his passion. As "Canada's most diverse adventurer" (*Canoe & Kayak* magazine), he boasts an impressive list of accomplishments, including the first single-season crossing of Canada by canoe, rowing the Northwest Passage, skiing across Baffin Island, and completing the triple crown of British Columbia sea kayaking. He is a regular feature writer and blogger for *Explore* magazine and has published dozens of features for *Mountain Life* magazine, *Paddling Magazine*, *Coast Mountain Culture* magazine, and *Canadian Geographic*, among others. His first book, *Lines on a Map: Unparalleled Adventures in Modern Exploration*, was also published by RMB. He lives in North Vancouver, British Columbia.

TERRITORIAL ACKNOWLEDGEMENT

We would like to take this opportunity to acknowledge the Traditional Territories upon which we live and work. In Calgary, Alberta, we acknowledge the Niitsítapi (Blackfoot) and the people of the Treaty 7 region in Southern Alberta, which includes the Siksika, the Piikuni, the Kainai, the Tsuut'ina, and the Stoney Nakoda First Nations, including Chiniki, Bearpaw, and Wesley First Nations. The City of Calgary is also home to Métis Nation of Alberta, Region III. In Victoria, British Columbia, we acknowlẹdge the Traditional Territories of the Lkwungen (Esquimalt and Songhees), Malahat, Pacheedaht, Scia'new, T'Sou-ke, and W̱SÁNEĆ (Pauquachin, Tsartlip, Tsawout, Tseycum) peoples.

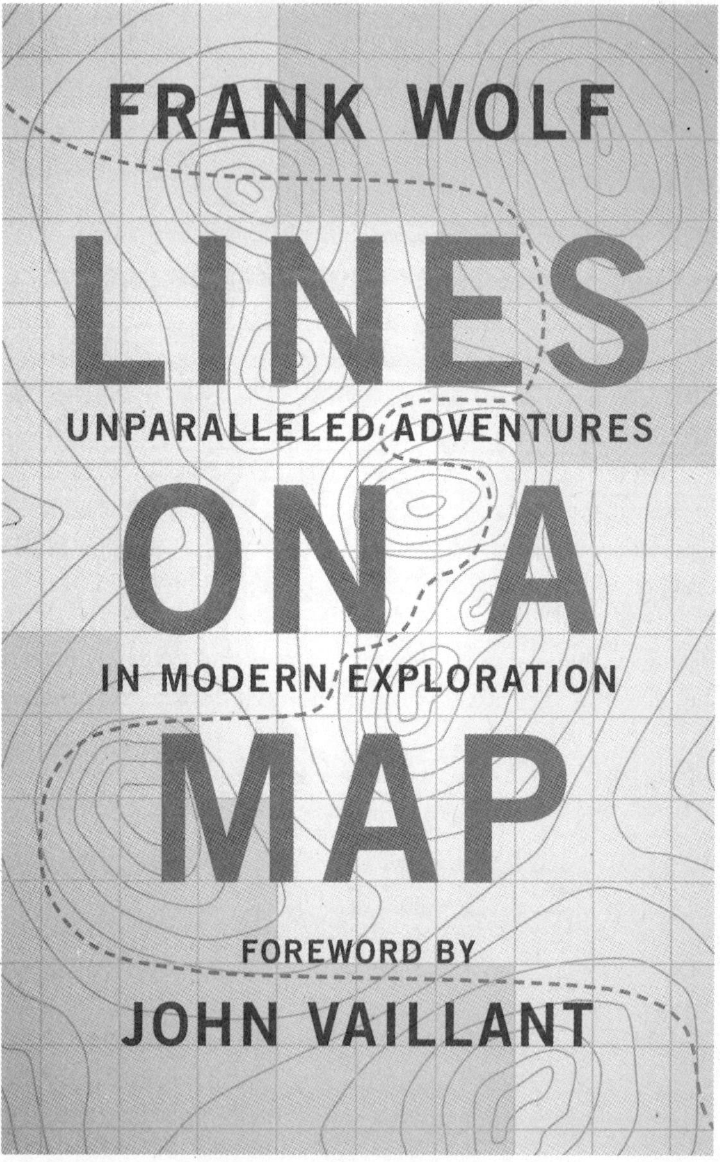

ISBN 9781771602891 (softcover) $25.00

Two decades of adventure writing are captured in this entertaining and inspiring collection of travel journalism by renowned adventurer, writer, filmmaker, and environmentalist Frank Wolf.

Lines on a Map is a compilation of Frank Wolf's best work from the past two decades. Some of the adventures include two friends on a cycling and volcano-climbing odyssey across Java, the world's most populous island, in the world's most populous Muslim country, Indonesia, in the wake of 9/11; a surreal private lunch with former Prime Minister Pierre Trudeau during an 8000-km canoe journey across Canada; discovering the past and present on a 900-km hiking and kayaking journey from Skagway, Alaska, to Dawson City, Yukon; negotiating the cultural divide during a whitewater paddling expedition in Laos and Cambodia with Russian extreme kayakers; exploring the nature and politics of a multi-billion-dollar pipeline in northern BC by hiking, biking, and kayaking the GPS track of the proposed project route from the oil sands to the British Columbia coast; conducting a mammal tracking survey in the course of a 120-km ski traverse of Banff National Park; discovering the truth about the existence of Sasquatch in northern Ontario; and retracing Viking history during a canoe trip across Scandinavia.

Complete with dozens of colour photographs, Wolf's book weaves together humour, drama, and local knowledge to transport readers to some of the outermost corners of the globe in an epic quest to celebrate the freedom to move, explore, and be wild.

PRAISE FOR *LINES ON A MAP*

"As you make your way through these pages, and into Wolf's wild hinterland, you may feel justifiably glad it's not you in the boat, but I guarantee there will also be moments when you'll wish to hell you could have been there."

– **John Vaillant**, author of *Fire Weather*, *The Golden Spruce*, *The Tiger*, and *The Jaguar's Children*

"Frank is a master at weaving together his love of the land, people, culture, and the importance to protect it. That's what really sets him apart from other extreme adventurers."

– ***Explore***

"Wolf is at his best when he's exploring his personal definition of adventure, inspiring readers to cut loose, accept the challenge, and live their most audacious dream."

– ***Canoe & Kayak***

"Wolf has survived countless worldwide explorations, and the magic of this book is reading about how he did it. *Lines on a Map* is written with self-aware humour, high-stakes survivalist drama, and a frank awareness of our fragile, beautiful planet."

– **Grant Lawrence**, author of *Adventures in Solitude* and *Return to Solitude*

"[Frank Wolf] weaves humour, drama, and local knowledge to transport readers around the globe in a quest to celebrate exploration and the wild."

– ***Paddling Magazine***

"Wilderness adventurer, documentarian, and writer. He was the first to canoe across Canada in one season, and has completed a diversity of other expeditions, including skiing Arctic islands and canoeing, ocean kayaking, cycling, and trekking incredible distances."

– ***Canadian Geographic***

"A collection of stellar travel journalism."

– ***Outside***